London Taxis

A Full History

By the Same Author

Taxi Jubilee - Fifty Years of the Austin FX4 London Taxi
Earlswood Press, 2009

The London Taxi (with Nick Georgano)
Shire Books, 2008

A Century of London Taxis
Crowood Press, 2005
(out of print)

Carbodies - the Complete Story
Crowood Press, 1998
(out of print)

London Taxis

A Full History

Bill Munro

EP
Earlswood Press

First published in 2011 by Earlswood Press, 10 Chaldon Close, Redhill, Surrey
RH1 6SX
United Kingdom

www.earlswoodpress.co.uk

British Library Cataloguing-in-Publication Data
A catalogue record for this book is available from the British Library.

ISBN 978-0-9562308-2-9

Typset by Earlswood Press in Sabon, 10pt / 12pt

Printed and bound in Great Britain by
MPG Biddles Limited
24 Rollesby Road
Hardwick Industrial Estate
King's Lynn
Norfolk
PE30 4LS
UK
www.biddles.co.uk

Contents

Acknowledgements

All historians owe a debt to those who researched their chosen subject before them and the author is no exception. Following on from Anthony Armstrong's 'Taxi', published in 1930, two authoritative books on the subject of London taxicabs were Nick Georgano's 'A History of the London Taxicab' (David & Charles, 1972) and Philip Warren and Malcolm Linskey's 'Taxicabs: a Photographic History'. (Almark, 1976) These latter works set benchmarks in the historians' knowledge of the subject. Philip Warren's 'The History of the London Cab Trade' (Taxi Trade Promotions Ltd., 1995) is a book on the politics of the trade rather than its vehicles but has proved a valuable volume in respect of this book, as has his later, 'The History of the Knowledge of London' (London Publishing Company, 2003). Malcolm Bobbitt's 'Taxi, the Story of the 'London' cab', (Veloce, 1998) provided useful information on Citroën cabs, whilst '75 Years: The History of the London General Cab Company', (London Cab Company, 1975) provided valuable information about that organisation and the trade in general. John R. Hume and Michael S. Moss's 'Beardmore- A History of a Scottish Industrial Giant,' (Heinemann, 1976) and Ken Hurst's 'William Beardmore: "Transport is the Thing"' (National Museums of Scotland, 2004) have both given a fascinating insight into the background of the Beardmore story. All these books provided an invaluable starting point for my research. Many documents stored in the National Archive (formerly the Public Records Office) have become available since the publication of the aforementioned books. Also there are many individuals who have made contributions, large and small to the content of this book, and the author is extremely grateful for their help. They are:

From the car clubs:

Robin Barraclough, Tony Beadle, Malcolm Jeal, Bryan K. Goodman and Perry Zavitz of the Society of Automotive Historians; Philip Hall of the Rolls-Royce Enthusiasts Club; Clive Loveless, Mal Smith, James Strugnell, Graham Waite, Keith White and Eddie Zetlein of the London Vintage Taxi Association; John Gray of the Sunbeam-Talbot-Darracq Register and Irving Lomon of the Asquith Association.

The independent enthusiasts:

Alan Broughton; Graham Hill; Melvyn Hiscock; Peter Kimberley; Ian MacLean; Norman Painting; Chris Pearce; Derek Pearce; Nic Portway; Mike Reid; Owen Woodliffe and R. J Wyatt.

From the cab trade and industry:

Peter Birch; Peter Bentley of the Public Carriage Office; Peter Da Costa of KPM (UK) Plc; Geoff Chater and Bob Parsons of CMAK (UK) Ltd. Roy Ellis, former Principal of the Public Carriage Office; Steven Ferris of Metrocab (UK) Ltd; David Day and Stephen Tillyer, formerly of Metro Sales and Service; Roy Perkins and the late Ken Jaeger of Beardmore Motors; Mal Smith, founder of Vintage Taxi Spares; Roger Ward and the late Geoff Trotter, MBE from the London General Cab Company; Jamie Borwick, Matthew Cheyne, Terry Fryer, Maria Holmes, Peter James, Grant Lockhart, the late Bill Lucas, Ed Osmond, Andrew Overton, Updesh Ramnath, Peter Shillcock, Jevon Thorpe, Barry Widdowson and the late Peter Wildgoose, variously from LTI, MBH Plc, Mann and Overton and Carbodies.

And last, but by no means least, to my wife, Karen, for just about everything, from her practical help to her patience and understanding and, above all, her total support.

Photographic Credits

The author wishes to thank the following people for their efforts and their generosity in supplying the illustrations in this book:

Peter Birch: 41, 51, 61, (top) 68 (lower), 74, (lower), 96 (both), 105, 106 (both), 115, 117

Malcolm Bobbitt: 54

Worshipful Company of Hackney Carriage Drivers: 19, 24 (both), 27 (top), 35, 37, 64 (top) 81 (top), 88, 92, 93, 110, 134, 135 (both): 138

Geoff Chater and Bob Parsons of CMAK (UK) Ltd.: 156 (lower, 157 (both)

Nick Chennell: 15

Bryan Goodman: 33 (both), 66

Chris Hodge Commercials Ltd.: 20, 27, 36 (top), 52

Bryn Elliott: 21

Andrew Hall: 53, 57, 67, 74 (top), 111

Peter James: 139, 144, 145 (lower), 147, 151, 153

London Transport Museum: 72, 86;

London Vintage Taxi Association: 26, 36 (lower), 38, 64 (centre) 70, 84, 125, 127, 146, 148;

The London Taxi Company: 169 (right), 176 (both), 180, 181 (lower), 182 (both), 191 (lower), 195 (both)

© The London Taxi Company is a trading name of LTI Limited. LTI Limited reproduced with permission. Fairway and TX shape is a registered design. Fairway™, TX™, The London Taxi Company logo are all trademarks of LTI Limited.

The National Motor Museum: 56

Norman Painting: 79, 89 (top)

Roy Perkins: 89 (lower), 95

Stuart Pessok: Taxi Newspaper, 58, 78 (upper), 81 (lower), 140, 145 (top), 154, 163, 166 (lower, both), 167, 168, 169 (left), 171, 172, 173 (both), 174, 175, 177, 178, 179, 181 (upper), 184, 188, 191 (upper), 192, 202, 204, 206

The Public Carriage Office: 18, 101 (lower)

Stanley Roth: 116, 120, 173 (upper), 199

Barney Sharratt: 145, 148

Mal Smith: 10, 17, 52, 58, 64 (lower), 65, 68 (upper) 70 (lower), 78 (lower), 94, 113, 123, 128, 129, 130, 136, 137, 141, 207, 212 (right)

Taxi Media Ltd.: 166 (upper)

Stephen Tillyer: 158, 160 (both), 161 164

Keith White: 126, 156 (upper)

Eddie Zetlein: 101 (both), 102, 103

All other images are from the author's collection.

Foreword

Published in 2005, 'A Century of London Taxis' was presented as 'the most comprehensive and analytical study of the topic yet published'. Six years on, there have been three significant events in the story of the London taxi and the capital's cab trade in general that have made a new edition desirable. The first event was the result of the appeal over the Conditions of Fitness, released too late for 'Century's' deadline. The second was the arrival of a new cab, the Mercedes-Benz Vito. Based on a van body, this has broken the mould of the traditional look of the London cab. For three periods over the last sixty years, Mann and Overton had the London market to themselves and had begun to make major inroads into provincial markets they could once never feasibly consider entering. When faced with challenges in those provincial markets by van-based cabs they promoted their vehicles' instant recognisability as a major selling point.

Now, in London the Vito is actively challenging that, and it has proved highly successful in the short time it has been on the market, with stories reported of passengers actively seeking Vito cabs over LTI ones.

The third event is the decision by London Taxis International to build a factory in Shanghai, China, in order to produce taxis at a far lower price for the world market than could be achieved in Coventry. This manifested itself in late 2010 with the introduction of two models of the TXII, assembled in the Coventry factory that were significantly cheaper than could be made entirely from UK-made components.

As well as bringing the story up to date, and adding some new material and photographs, this new book goes further back in time than 'Century', covering London's first horseless cab, the electric Bersey. It also includes some newly discovered material and photographs and puts right some errors and omissions, some of which only came to light some time after the original was published.

Bill Munro,

Surrey, 2011

Introduction

The London taxicab is famous the world over, and it is unique. No other city lays down such specific rules for its taxicabs, nor controls them so stringently. For over a hundred years, motor cabs have worked the streets of London and for three and a half centuries before their introduction, their horse-drawn predecessors carried out the same job.

Astonishingly, there have been over one hundred different makes of cab licensed for London, but now there are just two., and this situation was not a recent one, for within a few short years of the introduction of the rules, the Conditions of Fitness, the motor industry boomed, leaving the rules way behind and making the London taxi market a very specialist one. So specialised, that on three occasions in the history of the London cab trade, there was just one make available to be bought new, and on two occasions, none at all.

The story of the London taxi has been dominated by two groups; dynasties if you will. By far the most successful has been Mann and Overton. They were eventually subsumed by the amalgam of its suppliers, Carbodies Ltd. of Coventry who had acquired the rights to the Austin cab that they had made for decades and who became London Taxis International.

The second group was more diverse, and less successful, but nevertheless managed to make its mark. It started around 1909 when Francis M. Luther, the concessionaire for Austro-Daimler cars in Britain assisted with the financing of W & G du Cros' fleet of Napier cabs. When supplies of the Napier dried up, Luther persuaded his friend William Beardmore to make taxicabs for him.

In the 1960s, when Beardmore Motors finally ceased trading, the cause was taken up by transport manufacturing giant Metro-Cammell-Weymann, who had built the last Beardmore cabs and went on to design their own, the Metrocab. Alongside all of these, many other makers came and went, with varying degrees of success.

This story comes right up to date, with the latest Mercedes-Benz Vito, a model that, whilst complying with all the rules, has signalled a major change in how we perceive the London taxi in the future.

The Term 'Black Cab'

Nowhere in this book will you see the term 'black cab' used to describe the London taxi. 'Why should this be,' you might ask, 'when everybody calls them that?' Firstly, it is not what the licensing authority, Transport for London calls them and it was not what TfL's predecessor, the Public Carriage Office called them. And a good many of London's taxis are NOT black!

The name originated some time around 1980, or perhaps before, in the minicab business. Known in law as as private hire, the minicab business had usurped the term 'cab' to describe their vehicles, despite it becoming an offence to advertise themselves as such, and public didn't particularly care that it was. Those minicab drivers who who wanted to 'legitimise' themselves by undergoing The Knowledge of London to become licensed taxi drivers and could pass the criminal record and health checks (by no means all of them!) demanded by the Public Carriage Office, called this 'doing their black cab'. As they moved across, they brought the term with them. Unfortunately, it stuck.

Chapter 1

The Bersey

On August 13, 1897 an inspecting officer at the Public Carriage Office in New Scotland Yard stencilled a mark on the back of a bright yellow and black brougham-type cab. The stencil bore the initials of the Commissioner of Police for the Metropolis and the number of persons that the cab was licensed to carry. But this cab was different from the 'growlers', the slow, four-wheeled horse cabs that served the railway stations and carried old ladies at a dignified pace. It was very different, too from the hansom cabs, the 'gondolas of London' that these inspectors had been licensing for the past half-century. There was no horse between the shafts: in fact, there were no shafts for a horse at all, because it was powered by electricity.

It was the first of an initial number - reports vary from 12 to 18 - that the London Electric Cab Company Ltd. put on the streets of London. They were named Berseys, after the company's general manager and the cab's designer, the electrical engineer Walter C. Bersey. Cabs like the Bersey, or indeed any mechanically propelled vehicles available for public or private hire might have appeared on London's streets earlier than 1897. There was the technology: in Germany, Gottleib Daimler was granted patents for a lightweight petrol engine, suitable for use in a carriage or a boat as far back as 1883, and in 1886 placed such an engine in a four-wheeled carriage. In 1896 his Daimler Taximeter cabs were plying for hire in Stuttgart, a

The Hansom cab was the smart way to get around town in the Victorian era. Many were privately owned.
Prime Minister Benjamin Disraeli described them as 'The Gondolas of London'

petrol-powered Benz *automobildroschke* operated in Berlin and electric cabs were operating in Paris and Chicago. What had prevented the progress of the motor cab in Britain was the same thing that was stifling the development of the road-going horseless carriage in general, and that was the Locomotives Act of 1865, the so-called 'Red Flag Act'. This reduced the maximum speed of a mechanically propelled carriage to two miles per hour and demanded that it be preceded by a man on foot, carrying a red flag to warn of its approach. Such an Act, brought about by powerful vested interests in the railways was an absurdity to a number of men, who knew that the Act's repeal would allow the launch of the horseless carriage in Britain.

The British rights to the Daimler patents were acquired in 1890 by Frederick Simms, who built engines to Daimler's design. He first put them to use in boats, mostly on the River Thames, but in 1893 he formed the Daimler Motor Syndicate out of his small engineering firm with the intention of building motorised carriages like Daimler's. Simms' company was acquired in by Harry Lawson, an entrepreneur whose reputation had led to his contemporaries questioning whether he was a charlatan or a visionary. Whatever he was, his intention was to make money out of an industry that was barely in its infancy. In early 1896, as soon as he had acquired Simms' company, Lawson formed the Daimler Motor Company Ltd. and he bought a former cotton mill in Coventry, which he renamed the Motor Mills. He also acquired rights to other patents, granted to the French companies of De Dion-Bouton and Léon Bollée.

In 1896 the Locomotive Act of 1865 was repealed, and from November 14 1896 motor cars, (and that expression had yet to come into popular usage; they were more often referred to as 'autocars') could be driven on public roads without the encumbrance of a man with the red flag. Members of the Royal Automobile Club celebrated the event by organising a drive from London to Brighton. This event is still commemorated annually by the Emancipation Run, held on the first Sunday in November.

For all the freedom the repeal of the Red Flag Act gave to motor car users, the machines were very expensive and unreliable and the public at large were extremely

A Bersey electric cab, posed for the photograph in a quiet residential street. Note the bulk of the accumulator pack, slung below the cab)

sceptical of, if not downright hostile to them. Victorian Britain depended overwhelmingly on the horse for road transport and there was a huge infrastructure supporting it: breeders, dealers, carriage makers, farriers, and many more who believed their livelihoods would vanish if the motor car were to be a success. Fear of the unreliability of these pioneer machines was well-founded, and the high cost of them was prohibitive, But there was one way of proving the motor vehicle's worth, of testing it and improving its reliability and in time reducing the cost by ensuring a return on the investment needed in building them, and that was to put it to work. And there was one sure way of giving the public a chance to experience travelling in a motor car and have them pay for the privilege into the bargain, and that was to use them as cabs.

A group of the most influential supporters of the the 'autocar' then put together a proposal for the Public Carriage Office that they should operate a petrol-powered cab, similar to the Benz and the Daimler cabs. The group included H. R. Paterson of the carriers Carter Paterson, the Honourable Reginald Brougham, after whose immediate forbear the brougham style of carriage was named, J. H. Mace, a director of Harry Lawson's British Daimler Company, the coachbuilder H. J. Mulliner and the Honourable Evelyn Ellis, one of the men prominent in securing the repeal of the 'red flag act'. They wanted to use a Daimler internal combustion engine in the new cab, which they hoped would greatly enhance the reputation of The Motor Mills, the Daimler name in Britain and the cause of the autocar in general.

But the Public Carriage Office had other ideas. They, as a branch of the Metropolitan Police had taken responsibility for the licensing of London's cabs in 1843

and, in response to continued public complaints about the conduct of cabmen they had introduced driver licensing in the same year, but 1896 they introduced a driving test for cabmen. Doubtless they felt it right that a driver of a horseless cab should not be exempt from such a test, but they were honest enough to point out that they had no expertise in assessing whether a man was capable of driving a motor car. Indeed, they had no idea of how the machines worked or of their capabilities, or otherwise on the road. However, they felt that an electric vehicle was far simpler to drive. It only needed a driver to throw a switch and the cab was in motion as promptly as if the cabman had picked up the reins and given a command to his horse, and it could be brought to a stop simply by switching off the power and applying the brake. Everything else – the judgement of pace, distance, vehicle width and general traffic sense would be the same as if the cabman were driving a horse, so an electric cab it would be. The London Electric Cab Company naturally provided training for the drivers in 'the management of the switches', which they reckoned would take an intelligent man just two days to master, and sent him off the Scotland Yard for a driving test. Needless to say, the man would have already held a cab driver's licence, so there would have been no need for him to undergo the topographical test, The Knowledge of London, or have any other checks on his character.

The cabs' designer, Walter C. Bersey had experimented with electric traction and in 1894 built an electric van and run it in the City of London. He entered an electric carriage of his own design in the Emancipation Run, but its limited, 60-mile range meant that it had to be transported to Brighton by train. Bersey was well aware of the limitations of battery vehicles, and felt that they were best used in reasonably close proximity to their charging station. Thus Bersey was the right man with the right experience to head up the new company.

The cabs were built by The Great Horseless Carriage Company and were powered by 3½hp Lundell-type motors, which are constructed in a similar way to modern car alternators. The coachwork was of the brougham type, built by H. J. Mulliner. The massive batteries gave enough power for a top speed of 9mph, which is the equivalent of a good trot. There was also sufficient capacity to light up the interior of the cab at all times, a feature that would not always be appreciated by the passengers.

The company's premises were located in Juxon Street, Lambeth, just off Lambeth Road, and the equipping of the garage involved some considerable investment. The charging apparatus for the batteries was installed on a charging gallery above the main shop floor. When a cab had finished its shift, the battery assembly was removed from the base of the vehicle, hoisted up to the gallery by a lift and a fully charged battery pack lowered, ready for a quick installation. So as long as the batteries had been fully charged, the cabman could expect a reliable cab to drive.

The first Berseys went into service on August 19 1897 and by the end of 1898 the company was running twenty-five, with some reserved for the profitable carriage trade. The public's initial reaction appeared to be good. They were much reported in the press, and were christened 'humming birds', because of the noise of the motors and their bright yellow and black paint. There were reports of them being taken from the ranks in preference to horse cabs, to the annoyance of the horse cabmen who had been waiting for some time for a fare. Some cabmen were keen to drive them and their union supported their arrival but other cabmen feared them, thinking that the motors were 'explosive'. However, two early incidents tarnished their reputation. The first occurred on September 10 1897, just three weeks after their introduction. A cabman, George Smith was charged with drunken driving in Bond Street while in charge of a Bersey. He was fined £1. The next, tragic incident occurred just three weeks later, when a small boy, nine-year old Stephen Kempton was cadging a ride by standing on the back springs of a Bersey when his coat was caught in the driving chain and he was crushed. He became the first child in Britain to be killed by a motor vehicle.

The cabs were not as economical or as reliable as the company hoped. The range was suspect, and if the batteries were to run out of charge, recovering the cabs was a difficult business. The batteries proved too heavy for the vehicle and wore out the tyres, the motors began to vibrate badly and the battery box was insecurely fitted and slid about when the cab was in motion. The low ground clearance afforded by the battery boxes was considered a hazard: if a pedestrian were to be run over by a Bersey, the argument went then he might be saved from further harm if the ground clearance was sufficient for the cab to continue over him.

The drivers, who at first were happy to pay the company six shillings (30p) per day to hire the cabs soon left when that rate was put up to twelve shillings and tuppence-farthing, (around 66p) the same as that for a hansom. The public soon tired of the novelty of them too, and despite there being some keen adherents, hirings became fewer.

The original vehicles were withdrawn

in early 1899, and the company temporarily laid off their cabmen. A few weeks later, Bersey himself wrote to 'The Autocar', announcing that no less than 50 of a second type, built by the Gloucester Carriage and Wagon Company were scheduled to reappear on May 28, 1899, alongside the original 25. These had improved batteries and would be painted in new colours. Bersey denied the rumour that they would be fitted with 'taxameters', as taximeters were then known, and also announced that several of the new vehicles would be 'specially fitted and reserved for private hire'.

On Wednesday, May 24 the cabs were paraded around the streets of the capital to announce their return to service. However, Bersey was dismayed by unconfirmed reports that several cabs had been involved in accidents in the Fleet Street and Far-ringdon areas, and wrote to 'The Autocar' magazine about these reports. Apart from explaining that one cab encountered problems with a tyre, he denied that any the so-called dangerous events ever happened and announced that he had put the matter into the hands of his solicitors.

The end was signalled when a Bersey ran out of control and crashed outside Hyde Park Gate. Some elements of the press remained actively hostile, and continued to criticise the Berseys, reducing public confidence. They were removed from service in 1899 and the company ceased to trade, with some of the cabs sold to independent proprietors. Electric cabs in Paris and in New York were also, eventually a failure. The London cab trade would have to wait for technology to catch up with ambition and for four years the horse cabmen had the work to themselves.

Chapter 2

The First Motors

At the beginning of the twentieth century, Britain was on the brink of social and political upheaval. The nation suffered the double blow of the death of Queen Victoria and losing the Boer War. The new King, Edward VII had revolutionised high society by befriending industrialists, men in trade and actresses as well as, and sometimes in preference to the nobility favoured by his parents. The moral tone of the country, more staid members of society would declare, was declining rapidly. Britain's industry led the world, but was rapidly being overtaken by Germany and the USA, but Germany was also threatening Britain's empire and dominance of the open seas by building up a very modern navy. However, the prevailing attitude in the country was still that the Empire was unassailable and all that was foreign was inferior. In the new century, Britain would reap the harvest, both bitter and sweet, sown in the Old Queen's rein.

It was into this world of impending change that Henry Vernon Remnant, the managing director of The London Express Motor Service Ltd., placed the first petrol-powered motor cab on the streets of London, beginning an inevitable revolution, the effects of which have lasted to this day. The London Express Motor Service Ltd. was formed in January 1902. In Britain, where the motor car had been viewed by many as a foreign novelty and often ridiculed, public opinion was beginning to change, and alongside the French and Ger-

The Prunel, London's first petrol-driven cab was a compact, chain-driven vehicle. An Edwardian lady would have had rather more difficulty climbing into it than she would have done with a horse-drawn hansom

man cars that could be bought in Britain there were a number of British manufacturers, including Daimler, Humber and Lanchester, in business before the old century had passed and all selling their products with some degree of success.

The cab trade in Europe had already recognised the motor car. One of the world's first petrol-powered motor cabs was a Daimler, which ran in Stuttgart. A Benz ran in Berlin and electric cabs were running in Paris at the same time as the Bersey was humming its way along the streets of London. But as the French had accepted the motor car far more readily than the British, and the French motor industry was better established, London Express turned to France for a vehicle of a suitable size, small enough to be economical but of a sufficient power to carry a hansom body. They found it in the Prunel, a Paris-built vehicle with a proprietary 2-cylinder Aster engine. By the end of 1903 Express submitted a Prunel fitted with a hansom body by Henry Whitlock & Co., of Holland Gate, West London, to the Public Carriage Office (PCO) at New Scotland Yard for inspection. The PCO were not prepared to license it immediately, as they surely had reservations about public safety after the problems, real and perceived that had been encountered with the Bersey. But motor cars were now being seen in small but growing numbers on London streets and apart from the attention they drew, were causing little or no problems to traffic, so under pressure placed on Edward Henry, the Metropolitan Police Commissioner by the prominent men on Express's board, the Prunel was put on test.

The choice of the body fitted to the Prunel was limited by the Conditions of Fitness, the regulations that governed the design and construction of London's horse cabs, to either a hansom or a brougham or landaulette type, the 'growler'. As the chassis was light and the engine small by comparison to that of the Benz *automobildroschken* that had run in Berlin, the Prunel would be a two-seat hansom. London cab riders were well used to hansoms, which outnumbered the four-wheeled growler by almost two to one and had been a popular choice for the past seventy years. What was different with the Prunel was that the driver sat in front of the passengers, instead of above and behind. It was the genius of John Chapman, the man who designed the vehicle we call a hansom cab to this day, to build his cab front-heavy and use the cabman's weight to counterbalance it, whilst placing the passengers directly over the axle where they would not affect the cab's balance. The Prunel, having four wheels did not require this literal balancing act, and so the cabman sat in front of the passengers.

The Inspecting Officers of Public Carriage Office were all serving, uniformed policemen who had been transferred to this highly specialised branch of the Metropolitan Police. They were trained in the welfare of horses, they understood carriage construction and were well versed in the Conditions of Fitness and London's Cab Acts, but in 1903, besides not understanding what was required of a good motor driver, they had had neither experience with motor cars, nor any need of formal qualifications in motor engineering. However, once the Prunel had completed its tests, they formally licensed it and a second example in May 1904. In the opinion of Express's connections these two, a third hansom and another with a landaulette body ran well, giving, 'the greatest satisfaction to both the public and the Vendor Company' in both cab and private hire work. It is not known if these last two

Rational cabs, ranked up in The Strand. Its distinctive style of body earned it the nickname of 'the pillar box cab'. As a stunt for a motoring magazine, one of these cabs, registration number C360 took a passenger from Northumberland Avenue, off Trafalgar Square to Brighton, reaching the seaside town in a time of three and one half hours

were licensed as cabs or retained for private hire, as Metropolitan Police records show that only two motor cabs were licensed in 1904. But by October 1904 Express had withdrawn its Prunels and for a short time, horse cabmen had the work to themselves once more.

Chief Inspector Arthur Bassom, the officer in charge of the PCO fully understood that there was much for him to learn about motor cars. Already many would-be cab makers were following Express's example and offering their designs to him for approval and he had to take appropriate steps to understand what he and his staff were being asked to examine. In February 1905 wrote a memo to Commissioner Henry, his new chief at Scotland Yard requesting that he and Sub-divisional Inspector Beckley be trained in motor mechanics and driving to cope with 'the great increase in motor vehicles being presented.' He did not want to be 'at the mercy of every person who professes

knowledge.' Commissioner Henry approved the request and that spring, Bassom and Beckley attended a twelve-week evening course at one of the polytechnics that were offering tuition. On completion of it they passed on their knowledge to their staff. Now they felt they were ready for what they knew would be a major change in the cab trade.

The Rational

If Vernon Remnant intended to run the first company operating a fleet of motor cabs on a commercial basis, he was beaten to it. That honour went to London Motor Cab Company of Manor Street, Chelsea who put six Rational cabs to work in May 1905. The Rational also had the privilege of being the first British-built petrol-powered cab to be licensed. It was designed and made by Heatly-Gresham Engineering at Bassingbourne, Cambridgeshire. The firm's owners, Harry Heatly and Frank Gresham were members of the Automobile Club, with Heatly a founder member.

The Rational was powered by a water-cooled twin-cylinder engine slung horizontally under the driver's seat, driving through a two-speed epicyclic transmission and a single chain. Its fully enclosed body was built by a Hertfordshire coachbuilder and was similar to a design fitted as early as 1903 on a 6hp Wolseley chassis. An improvement over the open-fronted hansom, it had the look of a proper modern motor carriage, not a hybrid. David Hamdorff's book, "Seventeen Taxis?" tells the Rational story. A study of the vehicles illustrated in this book might suggest that, rather than seventeen, no more than six were licensed as London cabs as the other chassis were fitted with private coachwork. Some had a wheelbase too long or too short for cab work, but as the chassis rails were of wood, it was a simple matter to cut timbers to a length required by a customer. Heatly-Gresham Engineering soon moved to larger premises in Letchworth, Hertfordshire but it is understood that motor vehicle production was not continued at the new factory.

The Metropolitan Motor Cab and Carriage Company

Despite being beaten to the punch by Heatly and Gresham, Remnant and company continued, undaunted. The economics of running the Prunels had been carefully assessed by Chartered Accountants William E. Pearse and the venture promised to be viable. Under the chairmanship of the Earl of Ranfurly, a former Governor of New Zealand, the Metropolitan Motor Cab and Carriage Company was formed to take over the assets of the Express, with Remnant as the managing director.

The share prospectus of May 1905 carried a picture of a Prunel, with the caption 'London's New Hansom Cab', and stated that Metropolitan's aim was to put sixty motor cabs on the streets within six months. But instead of Prunels, Metropolitan ordered Manchester-built Heralds from S. R. Bailey and Lambert, Herald's London representatives and were a licence-built version of the French Hérald. Twenty were promised at first, with the rest to be delivered within three months of the date the company began trading.

The cabman, James Howe of Hammersmith, West London is understood to be the first man to drive a motor cab, a Prunel, although here, he is actually seated in a Herald of the Metropolitan Cab and Carriage Company.
The picture was taken at Scotland Yard, and the policeman in the peaked cap is Chief Inspector Arthur Bassom

The Vauxhall Hansom- Metropolitan's Folly

The new Heralds were not delivered when Metropolitan had anticipated. One can only speculate as to why, but a possible reason was that Metropolitan were unable to raise enough capital. Even at this time, the threat of war was in the air and investors on the Stock Exchange were looking for safe, quick returns, not for untried, medium term investments such as motor cab companies. However, in August 1905 Metropolitan ordered five 12/14hp Vauxhalls, reportedly at the instigation of Lord Ranfurly. The 12/14 car, fitted with a 2400cc three-cylinder sidevalve engine and a 3-speed gearbox mounted in a flitch-plated wooden chassis, was produced from 1904 at Vauxhall's original South London factory but had been deleted from the catalogue by the end of 1905. Vauxhall were moving to new premises in Luton, Bedfordshire, and the 12/14s may well have been unsold stock. Certainly the price suggests this. They were originally offered, with a 2-seat body, for £375. Vauxhall invoiced Metropolitan for £339 per vehicle, each to be fitted with a hansom cab body by Forder of Long Acre, one of the most popular and respected of hansom cab makers, with roof racks for luggage at £2/10s extra.

Metropolitan took delivery of their Vauxhalls, after one had been displayed at the Olympia Motor Exhibition, in November of 1905. They were a failure. It was not the fault of the base vehicle but of the placing of the driver above and behind the passengers, which, probably was done not through some whim or tradition but of necessity. The wheelbase was short, and placing the cabman in front of the passengers would make access for the passengers difficult.

It was reported at the time that the Vauxhall was popular with cabmen, but this is extremely doubtful. Because of the position of the driver's seat, every control had to be remotely operated, giving a very vague feel. The seating arrangement was reported to have also unnerved the passengers. The hirer of a horse-drawn hansom knew that the horse would have more sense than to run into any danger, and he could at least see the effect of the cabman taking up the reins to negotiate a hazard. With the Vauxhall, he could see no signs and word would have quickly spread of such an unpleasant experience. A potential cab passenger has to this day the right to choose any cab from a rank that he or she takes a fancy to, and if riding in a Vauxhall was now considered a very unpleasant experience, then the Vauxhall driver might well have found himself passed over.

Surviving records suggest that only three Vauxhalls were delivered: three engine numbers were recorded against the five chassis numbers. A second version with the driver seated over the engine was

The Vauxhall hansom, a design already antiquated in 1905. It is plain that the only place where the driver could be placed was above and behind the body

19

built but it is understood that it was retained at Luton for use as a factory runabout. It is also possible that cabmen began refusing to drive the cabs, as the public no longer took them. The company withdrew them by March 1906 as fifteen of the promised Heralds, fitted with hansom bodies had been delivered. Further Heralds would have landaulette bodies.

Other Pioneers

During 1905 Bassom's team did indeed have to examine many more motor cabs put forward by aspiring proprietors. These included a 14/16hp Straker and Mac-Connell, a German Dixi hansom and the Lloyd and Plaister hansom, which had a 2-cylinder under-floor engine and a roof that extended over the driver. This cab, built by Lewis Lloyd in partnership with W. E. Plaister was renamed the Simplex, and, possibly acquired at the same time by another firm, but it was short-lived. The company experienced trouble gaining PCO approval for this already obsolete vehicle but when finally licensed at the end of 1905 the cabs were put to work by the Motor Hansom Company. Some, if not all were re-bodied as landaulettes.

Enter Ford

Henry Ford founded the Ford Motor Company in the USA in 1903. UK sales were handled by Percival Perry's Central Motor Car Company Ltd., in London's Covent Garden. In his 'Brief History of Ford in Britain', Perry, who began his career in the motor trade with Harry Lawson cites that Ford's first model, the Model A was subject to a popular prejudice that regarded American cars as cheap and crude. Ford's second model, the 4-cylinder, 20hp Model B was exhibited at the Agricultural Hall in Islington in March 1905. Perry had faith in the quality of Ford cars and in Henry Ford's ability to deliver the merchandise. He felt that the Model B would prove reliable in cab work and that would convince the sceptical British public that Ford cars were worth buying. By October the Automobile Cab Company of Chester Gate, NW1 had announced its intention to put a fleet of Model Bs onto London's streets. The Ford had a two-speed epicyclic gearbox, and, according to Perry its ease of use would attract a considerable number of horse cabmen over to motors, as it would be far easier to drive than a cab with a manual gearbox. Initially three chassis were ordered, fitted

A Simplex, fitted with a landaulette body, which is raised to the cabman and a colleague to examine the engine. Behind it is another, later Simplex, which has a small canopy for the driver.

with landaulette bodies and put to work by the end of the year. So that the public would easily recognise them as cabs as distinct from the growing number of privately owned landaulettes, the Automobile Cab Company claimed that they would paint the cabs white, but surviving photographs do not show any finished like this.

The Automobile Cab Company then announced that they had ordered two hundred Fords at £360 each. In the event, Ford delivered less than twenty. At a shareholders' meeting in February 1906 the Automobile Cab Company's chairman, Sir James T. Ritchie, said that the company had received less than one quarter of its subscription target of £100,000. Sir James also said that Ford were changing their production methods and were unwilling to complete the order. Ford was about to build a new factory, the Piquette Avenue plant in Detroit where they planned to increase in production. New regulations, the Conditions of Fitness were about to be announced by the PCO and the Fords would not comply with them, so Ford's may well have refused to build a specially adapted Model B for what would be, in comparison to their potential market in the USA, an insignificant order. The Automobile Cab Company considered legal action but when they threatened Henry Ford, his reply was, "Fire away!"

As it was, Ford made just 500 Model B cars before moving on to a new model, so modifying the chassis to suit the Conditions of Fitness might have enabled him to capture a significant slice of the market and more than double his production, but it was not to be. Percival Perry would play the pivotal role in establishing Ford as a major manufacturer in the UK but in over one hundred years of Ford's history, the Model B was the only Ford that was ever licensed as a cab in London.

The Conditions of Fitness

Regulations governing the design and construction of London's horse cabs had been in place since the middle of the seventeenth century, but for the first three years of the motor cab's existence, no specific rules were in place for them. Armed with some knowledge of vehicle mechanics, Chief Inspector Bassom was moved to change this. Already in existence was the Motor Car Act of 1903, which had introduced vehicle and driver licensing. Following this in 1904 was the Motor Cars (Use and Construction) Act. For the first time, brakes, lights, tyres and steering as well as the behaviour of drivers were regulated. Bassom felt that with regard to using motor cars to convey the general public for commercial gain, and in safety, the new laws did not go far enough.

On the recommendation of Lord Montagu of Beaulieu, (who, the previous year

Arthur Bassom, the Metropolitan Police officer in charge of the Public Carriage Office at the time of the introduction of motor cabs. Said to be obsessed with transport, he was perhaps the most influential man to work at the PCO

as John Scott-Montagu MP had inherited the title from his father) engaged the services of W. Worby Beaumont who, in 1900 had written a book entitled, 'Motor Vehicles and Motors: Their Design Construction and Working by Steam, Oil and Electricity'. Worby Beaumont framed the 'Metropolitan Police Regulations for the Construction and Licensing of Hackney (Motor) Carriages, 1906', subtitled, 'Notice to Proprietors as to the conditions for obtaining a Certificate of Fitness for Motor Hackney Carriages'. In these new 'Conditions of Fitness', as they became known it was accepted, quite properly, that first and foremost any motor cab had to comply with existing laws, i. e. the aforementioned 1903 and 1904 Acts, plus the Light Locomotive Acts of 1896 and 1898 and the orders of the local government board. (In this case, the London County Council). Over and above these, the rules would demand that when the car (this expression had by now come into use for all sizes and types of motor vehicle, regardless of size or type) be presented for inspection it should have had no alteration made to it since it was last inspected. And if any were made, then the PCO would, if necessary, employ an expert, namely Worby Beaumont to advise on them.

The regulations placed safety and passenger comfort above all. They demanded that liquid fuel tanks be made of a suitable material of sufficient strength, and sited so that there should be no overflow onto woodwork where it might catch fire. Electrical wiring was to be sufficiently insulated. Neither of these points were addressed in the 1904 Use and Construction Act.

Two types of body were permitted: a hansom or, alternatively, a landaulette or brougham. Dimensions for the interior were quite specific, requiring for instance a distance between the seat cushion and the roof of forty inches. Thus a gentleman could maintain the propriety of wearing his top hat whilst riding in a cab. This is still possible in London cabs today.

The front road springs were to be fixed not less than 32 inches apart from outside to outside and the minimum wheel track was to be four feet four inches. There would also be a maximum length of fourteen feet, a maximum width of five feet, nine inches and a rule that called for a minimum ground clearance of ten inches, as far back as the lowest point of the back axle. This was to ensure that if anyone was unfortunate enough to be hit by a motor cab they would not be further harmed if the vehicle drove over them before coming to a stop. Viewed from today's perspective, this sounds bizarre, but in fact part of the opposition to the Bersey had been the very low ground clearance afforded by the battery boxes.

The turning circle was to be just twenty-five feet. There was a reason for it, although not an obvious one to modern minds and it was to do with public health. Until the middle of the nineteenth century, London's overcrowded slums and hopelessly inadequate sewerage system had caused frequent outbreaks of cholera and been responsible for the general bad health of its poorest citizens. The Metropolitan Board of Works had been created in 1855, in part to oversee the cleaning up of the capital and by the turn of the century London's streets were beginning to be covered in tarmac and the pedestrian crossings were regularly swept clean of horse manure. To prevent a build-up up manure in the gutters, the Metropolitan Board of Works' successor, the London County Council insisted that cab ranks were to be sited in the middle of the road. A horse-drawn vehicle, either two- or four-wheeled can turn in its own length, so that when a cab was hailed from the kerbside, it could turn around to pick up a passenger with a minimum of disruption. It might be argued that the waste products of motor cabs would not be deposited in piles in the road, so that motor cabs might be permitted to rank by the kerbside, but when the Conditions of Fitness for motor cabs were being framed, horse cabs were still very much in the majority. A further consideration for making the rule for a tight turning circle was that traffic congestion in London had always been bad, so anything that might cause a delay was to be avoided. If a motor cab were to be hired in the same way and the road insufficiently wide to allow a U-turn, a three-point turn, with the primitive steering and transmissions of the day would have taken far too long. Self-starters then were non-existent and if the driver stalled the motor, restarting by hand would have held the traffic up for several minutes. If a cab were capable of a U-turn then such incidents might be avoided. To illustrate how strongly the authorities felt about the possible disruption caused by three-point turns, a move to ban them within a three-mile radius of Charing Cross would be put forward, although not followed through.

Last of all was a paragraph that would establish the Public Carriage Office's complete authority in the matter of motor cab design. It stated:

"(NOTE: Though the above conditions may have been complied with, yet, if there be anything in the construction, form, or general appearance which, in the opinion of the commissioner, renders the carriage unfit for public use, it will not be licensed.)"

The motoring press welcomed the principle behind the regulations, as they enhanced vehicle safety but the editor of 'Motor Traction' magazine was opposed to the tight turning circle. On reading an advance copy dated March 23 1906, he wrote to Commissioner Henry to voice his opinion on this topic, suggesting a 'more generous minimum' of 30ft or 35ft should be allowed. But Henry backed Bassom and Worby Beaumont and stood firm on the 25ft rule. It is apparent from the motoring press of the previous year that the PCO had considered an even tighter, twenty-one foot turning circle, so the established one was almost a relaxation in itself.

Whatever their reception, the new Conditions of Fitness were timely. Between 1896 and 1905 more than thirty firms making motor cars had established themselves in Britain, although the numbers of vehicles they produced was still small. Between 1906 and 1907 the number of makers virtually doubled. To prosper, car makers had to build cars that were powerful and capacious enough for at least four people, but more affordable to a wider market. From being literally a 'horseless carriage' the car had developed such that it conformed, largely to a standard type, the *Systeme Panhard*, with the engine in front and the driver seated immediately behind and to one side with a wheel for him to steer it. Most importantly for the cab trade, models with engines of around 2-litres capacity and power of around 12-15hp were beginning to appear as a popular size, which proved to be an optimum size for cab work. Now Londoners would see if the motor cab could truly be made viable.

Mann and Overton's Garage

John Thomas Overton was a young man who, at the end of the 19th century was living on his family's farm in Sutton, Surrey. Tom, as he was known, was more interested in motor cars than in farming, so in 1898 he went to the best place he knew to find out about them, which was Paris. There he met a Mancunian, John James Mann, who was buying French and German cars and sending them to sell at his Motor Car Agency in London's Mortimer Street. They joined forces to form Mann and Overton's, to sell German Daimler and French Hotchkiss and Georges-Richard cars from the Victoria Garage in Lower Belgrave Street, Pimlico.

As well as his interest in Mann and Overton's, Mann became the works manager of the Manchester car firm of Marshall and he drove one of their cars in the 1900 1000-mile trial. With these activities keeping him busy, he seemed happy to leave the day-to-day running of Mann and Overton's Garage to Tom Overton. Overton soon came to see that cab work would be an excellent way of testing and promoting motor cars, but what they wanted was the right vehicle. For them it was the 12hp Richard-Brasier, which they introduced to London in 1905. The Richard-Brasier came from the Paris factory owned originally by brothers Georges and Maxime Richard, but that was not the name carried by the first cars to be made

there. That name was Georges-Richard, and it and all subsequent models around this time were designed by Henri Brasier. In 1904 Georges Richard left the company to set up on his own and subsequent models made in the original factory were sold under the name of Richard-Brasier.

The Town Motor Carriage Competition

Between October 15 and 17, 1906 the Automobile Club (soon to become the Royal Automobile Club) held a Competition for Town Motor Carriages at the Wolseley Tool and Motor Company's garage in Waterloo, South London. Mann and Overton's entered two 12hp Richard-Brasiers in class A for vehicles costing up to £600. They were fitted with limousine bodies, one by Bagley and Ellis and the other by a French company, Alfred Belvalette. Another Richard-Brasier was entered by one of Mann and Overton's customers, the City and Suburban Motor Cab Company. This had a French cab body, by La Carrosserie Industrielle. All three put up a respectable showing, with the City and Suburban cab winning a sil-

Far left, J. T. 'Tom' Overton and left, John James Mann, co-founders of Mann and Overton's Garage

ver medal for a Public Service Vehicle. These results were undoubtedly a great fillip for Mann and Overton's business.

Entered also was a 16hp Argyll cab, driven all the way from its factory in Alexandria, north of Glasgow. Since 1900, Argyll had been building cars with a reputation for solidity and reliability. The 1905 Argyll cab was a heavy, close-coupled vehicle with the driver placed above the 16hp engine. It was designed to replace the four-wheeled growler whose domain, because of its capacity for carrying luggage, was the railway station. Despite some intense promotion, the Argyll cab would not be approved by the PCO, as its 30ft turning circle did not comply with the Conditions of Fitness.

It was a sign of the times that the highest placed vehicle in class A was an American Oppermann Electric, with a hansom cab body by Cleaver Brothers. Pitted against internal combustion-engined vehicles, its success was virtually a foregone conclusion, as the judging criteria included smooth starting, absence of fumes and silence in running. However, the Oppermann was not licensed for use as a cab in London and the company went out of business the following year.

Obsolescence For Early Makes

Both the Conditions of Fitness and the progress in motor car design would see off a number of makes. The Herald, with its long wheelbase could not be adapted to meet the turning circle or maximum specified length. Other makes, like the Pullcar, a vehicle designed to mate a simple tractor unit to existing carriage bodies was already an anachronism. The Simplex, too would become obsolete in the face of new, more powerful makes.

Union Approval for Motor Cabs

At this time very few investors seemed to be willing to take a punt with the motor cab business, and the major horse cab masters were opposed to their introduction, fearing the enormous investment required would not yield the return they were then enjoying. However, the London Cab Drivers Trade Union realised that motors were the future, and in January 1905 set up driving and mechanical knowledge classes for their members. Writing in their official publication, the South London area secretary, Will Wright, asked what would happen if, "a company decides to place a fleet of 400 motor cabs on the streets and we don't get our men (i. e. the Union members) on them?"

'The General'

Wright surely knew of something big that was about to happen. Among the spectators of the Town Motor Carriages Competition may well have been the Hon. David Dalziel MP and Edward Cohen, directors of the General Motor Cab Company Ltd., a company formed using a considerable amount of capital from the Paris based Compagnie Generale des Voitures. If so, their interest was because of a massive project of their own, which had been under way since May of that year. Less than six weeks before the competition, the General Motor Cab Company's contractors had begun clearing a site occupied by old houses and overgrown with trees and grass, at the junction of Brixton Road and Camberwell New Road. Using a structure of steel joists covered in red and yellow brick, they were erecting a new purpose-built cab garage.

The building, initially built on two levels but soon extended to three, was the largest of its kind anywhere in the world. It fronted onto Brixton Road, as did the entrance the offices to the northern side, which ran along Camberwell New Road, overlooking Kennington Park. Ramps led from either side of the forecourt to a high-level access road with entrances to the body shop, chassis shop and motor repair shop. Here would be serviced the fleet of five hundred cabs that were on order from Renault in Paris. The General had originally ordered Charron cabs but the maker could not produce a vehicle that suited their needs. Instead, the cabs would the

A young Winston Churchill MP pays the driver of one of the General Cab Company's Renaults.
Churchill was Home Secretary between February 1910 and October 1911. He would be highly unpopular with the London cab trade for refusing to grant a tariff increase

two-cylinder Renault AG, the successor to the single-cylinder models that had been run by the General's Parisian sister company, La Compagnie Française des Automobiles de Place. The first of London's Renaults, part of the biggest single order yet placed for motor cars, arrived in October 1906, long before the building was completed. They were put to work immediately, not for public hire, because they had yet to be licensed, but for private hire work at 7s 6d (37.5p) an hour. This work served to advertise the General's name in advance of the grand opening on March 21 1907. The following day the first cabs, painted bright red with yellow wheels, set out for public hire.

Although the London Cab Drivers Trade Union wanted their members to drive motors, they were totally opposed to the terms The General were offering to their potential drivers. Other motor cab companies were paying their drivers a set wage of around 5s (25p) a day plus 2s (10p) in the pound commission. The General announced that they would fit their cabs with meters and would pay drivers a percentage of the meter reading. The Union claimed that this would result in a reduction in cabmen's earnings. The General's manager, Edward Cohen was intent on driving a wedge between his company and the Union by claiming that the Union were anti-motor and anti-taximeter and, in an attempt to exclude those union members who had learned to drive motors, Cohen set up a driving school for the cabmen who were not in the union.

The Unic 10/12

In October of 1904 Georges Richard left the company he had inherited with his brother Maxime to set up on his own. Fi-

A 12hp Renault, one of the 500 bought for the General Cab Company in 1906. It conformed with the 'Systeme Panhard', having the engine in front, driving the rear wheels, a standard that was gaining popularity with motor manufacturers. The landaulette body set the style for cabs for the next three decades

nanced by Baron Dr Henri de Rothschild he planned a single model, which he would call the Unic. Two years later a new factory was built on the Baron's land at Puteaux in north-west Paris. An economical and serviceable vehicle, the Unic was adopted by many Parisian taxicab operators. It also attracted the attention of Mann and Overton's and they successfully negotiated for an agency. The City and Suburban Motor Cab Company bought four of these 10/12hp 2-cylinder Unics from Mann and Overton's to add to their Richard-Brasiers, and they would buy an-

other 25 the following year. The National Cab Company of Hammersmith bought 250, which they painted bright red. In the capacity of what we would now call fleet manager, the National were to hire the services of a young man who would later make his mark with high performance luxury cars - W. O. Bentley. In his book, 'W. O.: An Autobiography' (Hutchinson, 1958) Bentley acknowledged the important lessons he learned about running motor vehicles in his time with National.

The City and Suburban Cab Company was taken over in early 1907 by The United

Signing up to sell the Unic 10/12hp marked a turning point for Mann and Overton's: this French vehicle was already proving itself as a reliable cab in Paris and would go on to do so in London.
Note the small canopy over the driver, a contrast to the full one fitted to the Renault, illustrated above

Motor Cab Company of Walham Green, Fulham, West London. On the City and Suburban's board were some of the directors of the General Cab Company's French associates. Between 1907 and 1908 City and Suburban bought 224 10/12hp Unic cabs with Christopher Dodson landaulette bodies from Mann and Overton's, considerably boosting the number of Unics on the street.

Conflict over The Conditions of Fitness

The motor industry was disturbed by another aspect of the General's operations. Henry Sturmey, the founder of the Autocar magazine, pioneer motorist and one of the original members of the British Motor Syndicate, examined the Renault's chassis and found that the width between the side members was twenty-six inches, not the thirty-two inches required by the Conditions of Fitness. Sturmey and many others interested in the London motor cab trade were outraged. As a member of the Society of Motor Manufacturers and Traders, he spoke from an informed position when he stated that the Conditions of Fitness were too great an obstacle for motor manufacturers to overcome. Sturmey was also a critic of Worby Beaumont and had criticised his work openly in 'The Autocar'. The reason the PCO gave for allowing the Renaults to be passed was that the vehicles were experimental and that, "in the interests of the public, they should be given a trial." It is possible, however, that as the General began building their premises in May 1906, they may have presented the Renault to PCO for approval before the Conditions of Fitness were anywhere near complete, let alone put into effect.

A New Cab for the Automobile Cab Company

In place of the Fords, Percival Perry supplied the Automobile Cab Company with thirty French 14hp Sorexes, of which the company was the British agent. The Sorex was powered by a 2-cylinder 10/12hp Gnôme engine. These cabs, built to meet the new Conditions of Fitness and fitted with landaulette bodies were paraded on Victoria Embankment on Saturday, October 27 1906. Still aware of the need for the public to identify their vehicles as cabs, the company painted a letter 'A', for 'Automobile', on the glass of the lamps. But there would be other 'French Connections', so to speak that would have a great influence on the London cab trade.

The Rover Cab

The General's initiative was the spur the British motor industry needed to give the London cab market some serious consideration. In the summer of 1907, the Coventry company of Rover launched the Rover Motor Cab Company. Much was made of the fact that the Rover enterprise was entirely British. Indeed, the General Cab Company's chairman, Davidson Dalziel MP had been criticised for his involvement with a French company. (We must remember that the *Entente Cordiale*, the agreement formulated to end centuries of war and discord between England and France had been signed just three years before) Rover promised that 500 cabs would be put into service, not only in London but also in Liverpool, Manchester, Glasgow and other major British cities. This was somewhat optimistic, as their weekly production rarely reached 20, but no doubt they hoped that the cab company would generate an increase in production. Their cab was based on the 10/12 chassis, with a monobloc four-cylinder engine. It had a transverse front leaf spring, a feature that would facilitate the tight turning circle, but would soon be banned from London cabs because the PCO believed it to be an unstable arrangement. Landaulette and closed bodies were offered, the latter being promoted as the Station Cab, with a luggage rack fitted to the roof. Space for a passenger was provided beside the driver and the company would fit all cabs with taximeters. The cabs would be sold to other proprietors through the Rover Cab Agency of Victoria Street at the very reasonable price of £350 or £375 complete with meter. This would be the only cab to be licensed in London that carried the Rover name.

A New Cab Act

The General's operations had upset the Union and the Society of Motor Manufacturers and Traders and now they were to vex the PCO. The General fitted taximeters to their cabs, which were intended to take away the biggest source of complaints that the PCO received from the public about cabmen, that of overcharging. The London Cab Acts, written when all cabs were horse-drawn and without meters, allowed for a hirer to take a cab on a time basis. This practice was permissible for motor cabs but the virtue of a motor was that it was, unlike the horse, tireless. Thus motor cabs were popular for long journeys, when they were hired at an hourly rate, but the advent of a taximeter created some anomalies. There exists on file a letter written to the PCO from a passenger complaining that although he had hired a cab on a time basis, the cabman had attempted to charge him the fare shown on the meter, which was greater than the hourly rate. There was no clear guidance in the statutes as to how the PCO should adjudicate.

The second problem concerned an allegation of fraud. At first, the PCO made no record of which taximeters were fitted to which cabs. The tariff that the General's meters ran on was higher than that laid down by the Home Secretary for London cabs. The General appeared to be acting in this way because the law did not say it could not: there were no specific regulations applicable to either the fitting of taximeters or to specify what tariff they should show. The PCO soon put in place a simple means of recording meter numbers against cab licence plate numbers, which cured the numbers problem, and ensured that the tariff charged was the one that was laid down by the Home Office.

On July 1 1907 the fitting of taximeters becoming mandatory for motor cabs in London. Over in New York City, a new cab proprietor, Harry N. Allen fitted all his cabs with meters and coined a new word: taxicab. It took very little time indeed for

A Bell Punch meter typical of Edwardian times

this word to cross the Atlantic and be shortened to' taxi'.

Another important point to be addressed was that of the number of passengers permitted and where they should sit. The General's Renaults were licensed to carry two passengers, as were most of the earliest motor cabs. They were, likewise also fitted with a third seat beside the driver and there were cases of two of the General's drivers being prosecuted for carrying more than the permissible number of two passengers. This prompted the General's solicitor to write to Supt. Bassom in August 1907, suggesting that their cabs be licensed for four persons, with a third squeezed on the inside seat and a fourth carried beside the driver. Bassom disagreed. He considered that the Renaults were neither spacious enough nor powerful enough and that the small flap beside the driver was "not suitable for a seat but might be useful for ladies' shopping or to put small parcels on."

Bassom's objections were based on safety considerations. He felt that a passenger could distract the driver's attention if seated beside him. He was also well aware of a certain type of person who took cabs. In somewhat picturesque language, he wrote:

"... it must be remembered that cabs are not like private motors where the owner knows the class of person he has beside the driver, but public carriages are frequently used by persons who are more hilarious than wise and one can easily imagine a party of students, young men about town or others leaving a place of entertainment, getting beside the driver and interfering with the mechanism ... so as to be a source of danger to themselves and others using the roads."

New fare tables were printed, one for two-seater cabs and one for four-seater cabs, stating on the table for two-seater cabs that the extra charge of 2d for each additional person above two would apply to four-seater cabs only. The tariff for taximeter cabs was different from that for horse cabs and motor cabs without meters. The rate for horse cabs was 1/- (5p) for the first mile (referred to as the hiring charge) plus 6d (2.5p) for every subsequent mile and waiting time at 2/6d (12.5p) for the first hour and 8d for every subsequent quarter-hour. The rate for a taxicab was an 8d hiring charge (soon to be called the 'flag fall') for the first mile or ten minutes and 2d (0.7p) for each quarter-mile or two and one-half minutes. This would soon create problems, as cab companies, struggling to achieve an operating profit on their considerable investment, let alone return a dividend to their shareholders were powerless to raise extra revenue from metered cab work. Only with private hire

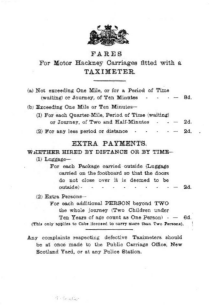

FARES

For Motor Hackney Carriages fitted with a TAXIMETER.

(a) Not exceeding One Mile, or for a Period of Time (waiting) or Journey, of Ten Minutes . . . . — 8d.

(b) Exceeding One Mile or Ten Minutes—
  (1) For each Quarter-Mile, Period of Time (waiting) or Journey, of Two and Half-Minutes . . — 2d.
  (2) For any less period or distance . . . . . — 2d. .

EXTRA PAYMENTS.

WHETHER HIRED BY DISTANCE OR BY TIME—
  (1) Luggage—
    For each Package carried outside (Luggage carried on the footboard so that the doors do not close over it is deemed to be outside) · . . . . — 2d.

  (2) Extra Persons—
    For each additional PERSON beyond TWO the whole journey (Two Children under Ten Years of age count as One Person) . — 6d.
    (This only applies to Cabs licensed to carry more than Two Persons).

Any complaints respecting defective Taximeters should be at once made to the Public Carriage Office, New Scotland Yard, or at any Police Station.

This Edwardian fare table, placed inside a cab shows the extra charges payable for 'each additional PERSON beyond TWO' would companies be able to charge their own rates and this work was seasonal, unpredictable and subject to strong competition.

These matters had already been under the scrutiny of Parliament. The matter of taximeters and other points, such as the placing of a passenger seat beside the driver was put to a House of Commons Select Committee, which sat between March 30 and July 26 1906. Its findings resulted in The London Cab and Stage Carriage Act, 1907, which came into force on February 1 1908. The installation of taximeters had been mandatory on all motor cabs since the July 1 of the previous year. The new Act added the proviso that meters were to be of a type approved by the Commissioner of Police and were to be sealed by both the PCO and the National Physical Laboratory (NPL) to ensure accuracy and the prevention of fraud. The NPL had been opened in 1903 as a National Measurement Institute and thus it was appropriate that it should be selected for this function.

Also under the Act, it would be illegal for a motor cabman to carry a passenger on the driver's seat (still called a 'box' in common with horse-drawn vehicle parlance) and compelled him to take a fare if the distance was under six miles or less

than one hour's duration. Vehicle licences for cabs were set at £2 per annum.

A further part of the Act dealt with the abolition of the privilege system at London's railway stations. This system had been introduced to London in 1839, when an agreement was made for a cab master to guarantee twelve cabs to the London to Birmingham Railway Company's terminus at Euston. Other railway companies soon followed. Despite the fact that the cabmen had to pay, at first, one shilling a day to the railway company it engendered a lot of ill-feeling from cabmen not included in the agreement. Because of the nature of the work, cabs used on privilege ranks were growlers, with capacity to carry the large amounts of luggage that the hansoms could not. With the privilege system abolished in central London, (some suburban ranks were allowed to carry on) station work became available to the motor cab and larger, four-seat vehicles would now be seen on the terminus forecourts.

With this Act and the Conditions of Fitness's stipulation of a twenty-five foot turning circle and a partition between the driver and passengers the criteria for the design and operation of the London cab were set, not just for the immediate future but for the rest of the century and beyond.

Chapter 3

The Motor Cab Comes of Age

By the end of 1907 there were 723 motor cabs on the streets of London, out of a total fleet of 10,512. Of these, 500 were the General's Renaults, and it was the General's operations, coupled with the improvements in motor car design that spurred previously reluctant investors to risk their money in the cab trade. A year on, the number of motor cabs almost quadrupled top 2,805 and the PCO granted type approval to more than a dozen makes of motor cab. Much of the growth was at the expense of the hansom cabs, which were sold off for scrap value and often burnt. By the end of 1908 there were 18 types of cab in service, with 2480 cabs run by just 6 owners. Most makes were French, in particular Renault, Unic, Panhard and Darracq, but the Italian FIAT had a substantial presence. The remaining 325 cabs were run by 169 proprietors, either owner drivers or running fleets of a dozen or fewer cabs. The British makes that would challenge the French dominance in any number were Napier and Belsize, though not one British maker would be producing cabs by the outbreak of war.

The public had now taken to motor cabs, and horse cab drivers began to lose their living. Many could not afford driving tuition. In 1910, the Daily Mail newspaper came to the rescue, setting up a fund raising drive to help the families of horse cab drivers and to organise driving instruction for more than 500 men.

W & G du Cros

The most successful British cab of the later pre-war years was the Napier, run by W & G du Cros. The du Cros family feature prominently in the early years of British motoring history. Harvey du Cros made his fortune in the late nineteenth century by investing in and later becoming chairman of the Dunlop Rubber Co. Ltd. He established contacts with Darracq in France, acquired British concessions for Panhard and Mercedes and invested in, amongst other motor companies, Austin and Napier. However, his health began to deteriorate and in 1908 two of his six sons, William and George took over some of his workload by forming W & G du Cros. This company, based in Acton, West London, would be engaged in a number of activities, including the running of a substantial fleet of cabs.

W & G opened their cab garage in Acton. They preferred to call their vehicles 'hiring landaulettes', as in addition to the cabs there was a large private hire fleet, composed in part of vehicles other than those type-approved by Scotland Yard. Five hundred 15hp 4-cylinder Panhards were ordered through Harvey du Cros' agency. Between five and six hundred of the fleet's cabs, however, came from W & G's London neighbour, Napier, who had already established itself as a quality make and had been made famous by the suc-

A Panhard 15hp of W & G's fleet. The company logo is painted on the door and on the collar of the cabman's coat. This picture is one of a series of postcards, produced for W & G. There is a message on the back of this particular one, written by one of W & G's drivers, Fred Walker, who describes his cab as 'the smartest in the land'.

cessful racing exploits of S F. Edge. The first models were 2-cylinder, 12hp but the rest were 4-cylinder 15hp models. At its peak the fleet numbered over 1000 cabs. With the adoption of 4-seat cabs by the trade, the more powerful 15hp 4-cylinder Napiers were added to the fleet. W & G also ran a small number of Unic 10/12s.

Bodies for W & G's cabs were built in-house and were painted in their own livery of dark green with yellow bonnets and a yellow panel below the door window. The W & G logo, cut out of brass was mounted on the front of the radiator, leading many people to believe that W & G actually made the cabs themselves. The logo was painted on the door panels of the Pan-

hards, but a union flag was painted on the doors of the Napiers to make the case that they were a British presence amongst the dominance the French.

It is understood that Francis M. Luther who would acquire the Austro-Daimler concession for England, assisted with W & G's finance. In addition, Luther had his own cab company, the Coupé Cab Company, running 150 10hp 2-cylinder Napiers, which were serviced by W & G, as well as a substantial number of other private hire vehicles. Although the Coupé Company's Napiers were also painted green and yellow there was no W & G logo on the radiator and the name 'Napier' appeared on the yellow door panel.

W & G's 15hp Napiers carried an identical body to the Panhard, but with one difference: the door carries a union flag, to indicate that the Napier is an all-British vehicle. Just visible is the sharp, inward curve of the chassis, which is to give clearance for the front wheels when the steering is on full lock

The Best of the Rest

Of the literally dozens of other makes, both British and foreign that were licensed, few lasted for very long. We shall see the very serious events that would overtake the fledgling industry a little further on in this chapter, and why some of the biggest either struggled, restructured or simple went under, but we can only speculate on the many reasons why others fell by the wayside. Some produced inferior vehicles, others could not provide the level of maintenance that all too soon was proving vital to successful operations whilst others may have suffered problems such as underfunding, poor management or unreliable component suppliers. The following is a brief summary of some of those makes, listed in alphabetical order.

Adams

Early gearboxes were usually crude, with no synchromesh and were difficult to operate. Thus the epicyclic gearbox, a forerunner of the modern automatic gearbox seemed an ideal feature for London's traffic. Indeed, Henry Ford had introduced it in his new Model T, which helped popularise that car long before its price was reduced to rock-bottom. A British make that used it exclusively was Adams, produced by the Manufacturing Company of Hertfordshire. Entering the cab market in 1911, the company used the advertising slogan, 'Pedals to push- that's all', as its three-speed transmission was foot-operated. They were offered on 10/12hp two- and 12/14hp four-cylinder chassis. The company was renamed Adams-Hewitt and would go on to make larger cars until the outbreak of war, but no more cabs were made after 1911.

Argyll

In contrast to its original 16hp cab, the model that Argyll introduced for London in 1908 was entirely conventional, with a 12-14hp four in unit with the gearbox. It carried a yellow livery, which prompted cab drivers to christen it 'the mustard pot.' It was built from the outset as a four-seater, with two extra seats designed to fold down from the front of the carriage interior so that the occupants sat facing the rear seat passengers. It is claimed that it was the first cab to have these folding 'cricket' seats. In 1910, Argyll built a second, equally conventional, 15hp cab.

Austin

Austin, whose name would become the biggest in the cab trade, made a modest debut in London in 1909. A few years before, in 1905 Herbert Austin had made a centre-drive 15hp limousine that could be used for cab work but it was never licensed in London, being thwarted by the introduction of the Conditions of Fitness. The first Austin cabs licensed by Scotland Yard were also 15hp models, but of a conventional design. Ten of these were run by Urban Taxicabs Ltd. of West Kensington. In 1910, nine examples were introduced by Taxis de Luxe of Hammersmith. In the early years, motor cabs were not particularly well appointed, but the Austins of Taxis de Luxe lived up to their name, having much more luxurious trim.

Ballot

100 Ballot cabs, powered by 4-cylinder 10/12hp engines were operated by the Express Motor Cab Company, an affiliate of

the French Express de Paris, whilst the Quick Motor Cab Company operated a number, which were painted white. Before the Great War, concentrated on commercial vehicles and engine manufacture, with the taxicab their most important vehicle. They ventured sports car manufacture during the 1920s.

Belsize

Belsize was a Manchester company. Originally called Marshall, the firm's new name would see it through until its demise in the early years of the Great War. J. J. Mann was director of the Marshall company. Standing firm against the French invasion, the Belsize was sold as 'the All British Cab'. Its 4-cylinder 14/16hp engine was tough and reliable and the cab enjoyed a good reputation.

Darracq

450 Darracqs were supplied in 1908 to various London proprietors including London United, who ran 250, London and Provincial who had 100 and the Stanhope Motor Cab Company, who operated a single example. The original model was a 4-cylinder 18hp model, but it was considered too large for economical operation. It had gone by 1911, replaced by a more acceptable 2-cylinder, 8/10hp model.

De Dion

The De Dion-Bouton Company operated 2-cylinder 10hp cabs of their own make from 1908. These were replaced in 1909 by a more popular single-cylinder model.

Electromobile

The Electromobile was the last attempt by an electric vehicle manufacturer to enter the London cab trade in the twentieth century. Based in Lambeth, the British Electromobile Company ordered 50 chassis from Greenwood & Batley, a Leeds machine tool manufacturer in October 1908. They were fitted with bodies by several London coachmakers as well as by the

The Manchester-built Belsize was advertised as 'The All-British Cab'.

Performing the job for which it was intended, this Electromobile leaves Euston station, loaded with luggage

Gloucester Carriage and Waggon Company, the firm that had built the second version of the Bersey.

The cabs were operated by the Electric Taxicab Company and they were heavy, bulky 4-seaters with a substantial luggage carrying capacity and a range of 45 miles. These were to work the main London railway termini and oust the horse-drawn growlers, but just 20 out of a hoped-for 500 were delivered. The increased power of petrol cabs, which enabled them to carry four-seat bodies and luggage, plus their unlimited range, would mean the end of electric cabs.

FIAT

The biggest, and the only non-French foreign make represented was the Italian FIAT. The FIAT Motor Cab Co began in 1908 with 37 12/15hp 4-cylinder Tipo 1 cabs, operated from Lupus Street, Pimlico. This number grew to 400, following their move to St. Pancras Road, King's Cross.

FIAT's presence in London was short-lived. This 12/15hp 4-cylinder Tipo 1 was the only model they operated

Gamage-Bell

Cab masters and cab dealers were able to manufacture cabs if they had sufficient financial backing. Gamage's was a famous department store in London's Holborn and in 1909 they announced that they had ordered 250 chassis from BSA in Birmingham. The cabs, the announcement said would have 'all the latest improvements, including electric light, and will be upholstered in morocco.' No proof of the existence of cabs built on BSA chassis has been found, but two body styles built on Napier chassis in 1910 are known to have been licensed. The bodies were built by Horace Bell, who had worked for the General Cab Company. One was a limousine with a fixed head and doors that were hinged on the B-post, rather then hinged at the rear. As a safety measure, wire mesh covered the side windows and accounts for the cab's nickname, the 'birdcage.' The other style was the only open body to be licensed by the PCO for a motor cab. It had a Victoria-type head and although fitted with a side-facing occasional seat was licensed only for two passengers.

Hillman-Coatelen

The Coventry company of Hillman was a latecomer into the cab trade. The talented French engineer Louis Coatelen would become one of William Hillman's sons-in-law. The first cars he designed for Hillman, named Hillman-Coatelen, were big, but a more modest 12/15 model followed and would be the base of a cab which, in 1911 was the last new make to be type-approved before the Great War. Few were built as its arrival coincided with the trade's pre-Great War zenith.

Humber

At the time one of the biggest makers in the country, Humber made their debut in the London cab trade in 1908. Their de Luxe model, a short-wheelbase vehicle with its engine placed underneath the driver, did not operate in London but the conventional 10hp model, designed by Louis Coatelen and built in the Beeston, Nottingham, factory was approved. Humber's Beeston-built vehicles were better ap-

Although few were built, the 15hp Humber cab enjoyed a good reputation

37

pointed and better made than the Coventry-built vehicles and the cab was no exception. The Humber Cab Company ran a fleet of forty-seven in London and another thirty-two were owner-driven. It proved reliable and economical to run and Humber hoped for an expansion in these numbers, but 1908 was a very bad trading year for them and they closed Beeston, concentrating car production in Coventry. They would make no more cabs for London after 1909.

Lotis

Henry Sturmey founded 'The Automobile' magazine, but in 1906 he left to write for a rival publication, 'The Motor'. He also contributed to 'Motor Traction' magazine, possibly influencing the editor's opinion of the 25ft turning circle. Sturmey became a car maker too, building the American Duryea under licence in Coventry under his own name until 1904. Sturmey's opposition to the turning circle was no doubt the result of his desire to enter the motor cab business. In 1908 he introduced a vehicle of his own design and

manufacture, the Lotis. To achieve the turning circle and meet the overall length requirement, the wheelbase was a very short four feet ten inches and its 10/12hp, 1357cc V-twin Riley engine, mated to a two-speed epicyclic gearbox was under the driver's feet. In both cab and private limousine form the Lotis continued in production until 1912. It was the first cab to have a purpose-built luggage space beside the driver.

Vinot

The 14-16hp Vinot was first operated by a suburban proprietor, Oates Brothers of Wimbledon, in 1909, and it was said to be a reliable cab. It is most likely that it was actually a Gladiator cab that was specially adapted for London. Another French company, Vinot et Deguingand took over Gladiator in 1908 and continued to make Gladiator cars with Vinot badges. It was most likely that Vinot et Deguingand continued manufacture of the Gladiator cab, fitted with a Vinot radiator and badge in order to regain some of the investment money.

The 4-cylinder, 8/10hp Wolseley-Siddeley cab, built at the massive Adderley Park factory in Birmingham

Wolseley-Siddeley

Wolseley-Siddeley cars were made in Birmingham by the Wolseley Tool and Motor Car Company and part-named after the general manager, J. D. Siddeley. In 1907, a 4-cylinder 8/10hp model was introduced, featuring a specially built dropped chassis to give passengers easier access. The General Cab Co ordered 250, fitted with two-seat bodies. The cab had a reputation of being difficult to drive, and cabmen used to say that it 'needed humouring', and when four-seat cabs became more common, cabmen refused to take it out.

In 1908 it was replaced by a 2-cylinder 12hp model, using the same dropped chassis. It was fitted with a more substantial four-seat body. The London United Cab Company ordered 250. Subsequent to 1913 they were gradually withdrawn from service.

Farewell to a Pioneer

By 1908 the Herald, the Vauxhall, the Simplex, the Sorex and the Ford were all gone. The remarkable exception was the London Motor Cab Company's Rational. This company had done some very important pioneering work, establishing with little fanfare and no controversy a reliable presence of motor cabs. It is to Heatly-Gresham Engineering's credit that these early vehicles lasted as late as October 1909, but their lack of sophistication caught up with them and they were replaced in the fleet by French Brouhots. Brouhot cabs had been introduced in Paris in 1907 but the company had been in existence since 1898. From 1911, Brouhot abandoned cars and taxicabs and concentrated on agricultural machinery.

The Decline of the Horse Cab

Between 1909 and 1911 the number of horse cabs halved, whilst the number of motor cabs more than doubled. Horses were sold off and horse cabs burned. At the outbreak of war, just 232 hansom cabs survived and a sign that their end was close was marked by the presentation in 1914 of one to the London Museum. The growler lingered on, favoured by elderly ladies who mistrusted both motors and hansoms, and its luggage capacity meant that it would continue to serve railway stations for a while longer. However, the introduction of more powerful four-seat motor cabs eventually consigned the growler to the scrap yard. A handful of horse cabs survived after the Great War, the last disappearing as late as 1948, but seven years after the first Prunel was licensed, the motor cab had reached its pre-war zenith, with almost 8,000 on the streets. It would be another half-century before that number was exceeded.

A New Taxation System

Until 1910, cars over one ton in weight were subject to a 2/17/- (£2.85) annual tax, payable to the Inland Revenue in addition to the road fund licence. Hackney cabs were exempt from the weight tax if they were licensed for the whole year. However, during the London Season, which lasted from May to July many proprietors let their cabs out on private hire, handing in the hackney plate for the duration. An allowance of 7/6d (37.5p) per annum was made if a cab was licensed for part of the year. The London Motor Cab Proprietors Association wrote to the Home Secretary, Winston Churchill, complaining that some cabs were weighed less that 1 ton and not subject to the tax, whilst others were over, but as cabs needed to be stronger for public hire, they would generally exceed 1 ton. As they already paid a 15s (75p) annual licence fee to Scotland Yard for each vehicle regardless of how many months of the year the vehicle carried its plate, the proprietors felt hard done by in having to pay any surcharge.

But it was the Chancellor of the Exchequer, David Lloyd-George who settled the matter. His Finance (1909-1910) Act stipulated that all cars would be subject an annual Road Fund Licence, based on a sliding scale according to a formula devised by the Royal Automobile Club in 1906. Previously, there had been a single rate of 5 guineas (£5.25). under the new regime, the owner of a 6.5hp car would pay 2 guineas, whilst the owner of a 60hp car would pay a colossal £42, equal to the annual wage bill for at least half a dozen servants. The 2-guinea fee for heavy cars was incorporated into the sliding scale, but cabs would pay a flat rate, regardless of engine size. At the same time, the Commissioner of Police would also make an order that would prove extremely unpopular with cabmen. From 1910 he would ban the fitting of full windscreens on cabs. He maintained that a cabman's visibility in London 'pea souper' fogs would be limited by a glass 'screen.

Disputes Over 'Extras'

1911 saw the London motor cab trade's first major industrial dispute. When more than two people were carried in a taxicab, the cabman could charge 6d (2.5p) per person in addition to the fare and 2d (0.8p) for each piece of luggage. These 'extras' became a source of dispute when four-seater cabs came into service. This had not arisen with horse cabs, as no meter and thus no means of registering the extras was in use. The first motor cab masters had calculated their running costs on the horse cab tariff and its 1/- (5p) hiring charge. When the 8d taximeter was introduced, they experienced a shortfall in turnover. This they intended to make up by claiming the extras, as there was no statute to say to whom they belonged. The cabmen had other ideas and the dispute came to a head in October 1911 when the National Cab Company dismissed a driver who refused to hand over the extras he had collected. The London Cab Drivers Trade Union (LCDTU) called a strike and by November 3 some 15,000 drivers, mechanics and cab washers were out.

A Committee of Enquiry had been set up to review the fares situation but the then Home Secretary, Winston Churchill refused to allow a fare increase, despite the fact that London fares were noticeably cheaper than most provincial British towns and cities. Provincial fares were, and still are set by local authorities. 'The Times' claimed that Parliament would not raise London fares because 'cabs were the buses of the Parliamentarians.' Eventually the Board of Trade appointed a Court of Arbitration and on March 12 1912 the cabmen were awarded the extras. The cabmen were also given a set 25 percent commission on the metered fare, and a set price for petrol at 8d per gallon, subject to review should it go up in price by more than 12 percent per annum. (Excise duty had already been imposed on petrol in 1909, but a fifty percent rebate was allowed for commercial users.) The London Motor Cab Proprietors Association was placed in a very difficult position. Already suffering under an inadequate tariff, cab masters were now deprived of the income generated by the extras. The drivers were of course delighted but their satisfaction would be short-lived.

A cause for dissatisfaction amongst cabmen and cab masters alike was that there were, by 1910, too many cabs for the work available. Competition from the new electric trams and the Underground Railway, which provided cheap, reliable transport, took work away from cabs. And not only was the total number of cabs higher than in 1903, but motor cabs could do a job more quickly than a horse cab and in consequence were ranking up for longer-sometimes as much as three hours. Because the Home Secretary refused to increase fares, cab masters promoted private hire business, for which they were allowed set their own rates.

Further Opposition to the Turning Circle

In 1911, Henry Sturmey attended a meeting of the Royal Automobile Club to hear J. S. Critchley read his paper, 'The Evolution of the Motor Cab'. Critchley was a noted automobile engineer and a founder member of both the RAC and the Society of Motor Manufacturers and Traders (SMM & T). Following the reading, Sturmey told the audience that the combination of the 25ft turning circle and the width between the chassis rails had been causing great difficulties for manufacturers. He claimed that many of his colleagues in the SMM & T agreed with him. Whatever the opposition to this regulation, Scotland Yard were not about to change it.

Mann and Overton and a New Unic

1910 saw some significant changes for Mann and Overton's. In March they vacated Victoria Garage and moved to premises at 15 Commercial Road, (now Ebury Bridge Road) Pimlico, which they had been converting from stables for the previous two years. In May they took out a for-

The Unic 12/16hp was the most important cab of the Edwardian era, setting Mann and Overton's up as the most prominent name in the London cab trade. This example was the first motor cab acquired by Birch Brothers Ltd of Kentish Town

mal agreement with Unic Automobiles Ltd., the importers, to sell a new four-cylinder 12/16 cab chassis that was specially designed to meet the Conditions of Fitness. This chassis, which was also sold in France, had a drop in the centre of the side members to give the passengers easier access. The importance of Mann and Overton's deal with Unic was highly significant: here was a cab specifically commissioned and designed to meet the Conditions of Fitness, the introduction of which anchored Mann and Overton's firmly to the cab trade and strengthened their commitment to it.

In December Mann and Overton's acquired showrooms and offices at 10 Lower Grosvenor Place, allowing space at Commercial Road for coachbuilding. Taxicabs would now be Mann and Overton's core business. Sadly, J. J. Mann did not live to see this large expansion. He had not attended a board meeting for some time as his health had been deteriorating. In 1908, at the age of 36, he died, leaving the business in the hands of Tom Overton. After Mann's death, Tom's brother Will joined the company. The 12/16 would prove solid and reliable and Unic became the most numerous make of London cab with 2,500 of it and the 10/12hp in use by 1911.

Two Big Fleets Merge

The United Motor Cab Company in Walham Green, West London and the General had been co-operating with each other but in the autumn of 1908 they merged to form the London General Cab Company. One of the main investors in 'The General' was Associated Newspapers Ltd., who would hold an interest in the company for almost its entire life. United ran 224 10/12hp Unics and 250 Darracqs.

For a while the two companies continued to run independently but the Brixton concern bought Unics as well as 94 Darracqs that they had acquired to replace the Renaults, which had been converted into four-seaters but were underpowered for the job. Besides buying some 2-cylinder 8-10hp Charrons, the General would buy the new four-seat 12/16hp Unics.

The 'Also-rans'

Makers and proprietors both large and small went to the wall after 1911. Much of attrition in numbers can be blamed on the strikes the slump in work and above all, the Home Secretary's refusal to raise fares to an economic level. Here is what is known about those that were lost, either to the cab trade or the motoring world at large.

Cottereau (France)
Cottereau cabs were recognisable by their circular radiator. The company declined and ceased manufacture in 1910.

Charron (France)
Some 2-cylinder 8-10hp Charrons were included in the fleet of the General Cab Co. in 1908 a 4-cylinder model was also licensed.

Adler (Germany)
Adler made cars between 1900 and 1939. The 12hp cab was probably introduced in 1907. Adler was represented in England by coachbuilders Morgan and Co. After WW2, Adler specialised in making typewriters.

Albion (Scotland)
The Albion cab was made by the Albion Motor Car Company, Scotstown,

Glasgow. Albion would cease to make cars from 1915, concentrating on commercial vehicles.

DPL (England)

Made by Dawfield and Philips in 1907, this very compact cab had a 2-cylinder horizontal engine and a 20ft turning circle. It was most likely constructed from proprietary parts.

Leader (England)

Made by Charles Binks & Co. of Apsey, Nottinghamshire between 1905 and 1910, the Leader had a 14/16hp four cylinder engine. Probably no more than a handful of Leader cabs saw service in London.

Marlborough (England)

The Marlborough was made between 1905 and 1910 by T. B. André, who took over the British concession for Malicet et Blin, suppliers of the cab's 15.9hp engine.

Marples (England)

The coachbuilder Stephen A. Marples built the body of the Marples cab in 1907 for the London Improved Cab Co. It probably used a proprietary chassis, fitted with a 2-cylinder 12hp engine.

Mascot (England)

All that is known of the Mascot is that it had a Forman engine and was built in 1907.

Star (England)

Star was a manufacturer of some importance in the early years of motoring, continuing in production up to the mid-1930s. Originally the 12hp 4-cylinder model was adopted for cab work but the 2-cylinder 9hp proved more popular. However, the make's importance was not reflected by its continued presence in the cab

trade and record of its use is not found beyond 1910.

Thames (England)

The Thames Shipbuilding and Engineering Company of London built a 2-cylinder 12hp cab in 1908. It was supplied by C. Grahame-White and Co for the Motor Cab Syndicate of Cannon Street. It was fitted with what was described as 'the Auto-simplex' transmission, of which it was said 'the services of gear-box, chains etc are entirely dispensed with.' Thames abandoned car, and thus cab manufacture in 1910 to concentrate on commercial vehicles.

The Survivors and the Abandoned

According to a list provided by the PCO, cabs licensed in 1909 included; Austin, Belsize, Brasier, , Brouhot, Charron 10hp, Charron (4-cylinder) Cottereau, Darracq 14hp, Delahaye, FIAT, Hillman-Coatelen, Humber, Hurmid, Leader, Marlborough, Napier, Panhard, Renault, Siddeley, Unic 10/12hp and 12/16hp and Vinot. Absent from the list were pioneers and failures alike, including: Adams, Argyll, Adler, DFP, De Dion, Electromobile, Ford, Herald, Lotis, Marples, Mascot, Prunel, Pullcar, Rational, Rover, Simplex, Sorex, Star, Thames and Vauxhall.

The Great Petrol Strike

With fares, and thus income strictly controlled by government, control of expenditure by cab proprietors was critical for survival. Not surprisingly, it was one of those expenditures, the price of fuel that triggered the longest running and most acrimonious industrial actions in the history of the London cab trade and, along with the dispute over extras, heralded the decline of the big fleets. When the price of petrol rose by 70% to 1/1d (5.4p) a gallon the LMCPA decided that drivers would have to pay the full cost. This was a substantial slice out of cabmen's incomes and the Union threw down the gauntlet. Alfred Smith, the Union's president declared that, whilst the Union was happy to abide by the Court of Arbitration's decision, "the men cannot bear the huge increase demanded by the LMCPA... I warn the masters that the time is coming when it will not be a fight to reduce petrol prices but a fight for free petrol."

'The Times' reasoned that if the cab trade was not to be allowed a concession on fuel costs as the oil companies gave the bus companies, then a sensible way to resolve the dispute would be to increase fares. But the paper considered that a fare increase would be highly unlikely. Talks between the Union and the LMCPA on December 30 1912 broke down. The cab masters stood firm and the Union called a strike.

It was during this action that the Union changed its name, to the London and Provincial Licensed Vehicle Workers Union. The strike took place in a time of economic downturn and when the number of cabs, both motor and horse, was in decline. Much of the shake-out was within the ranks of the smaller motor cab companies, but although unaffected by petrol prices, the number of hansom cabs was dropping fast under the inevitable march of modernisation. The financial insecurity of the cab masters would be their undoing, as the Union held firm. By the end of January the London Improved Cab Company gave in and agreed to charge their drivers 8d a gallon. W & G du Cros ac-

cepted the same offer in mid-March and by March 23 the LMCPA agreed that their members would charge drivers 8d per gallon. But the real winners were the bus, tram and underground train operators, whose cheap fares and regular service retained the passengers they had won during the cabmen's strike. The cab masters lost an estimated £1 million and the Union paid out strike pay amounting to £40,000.

The cab masters demanded a fare increase, but Home Secretary Reginald McKenna turned them down. Both cab masters and cabmen suffered. W & G Du Cros re-bodied 100 of their cabs as light vans, hiring them out to organisations such as W. H. Smith and the GPO and converting a section of the Acton works into a parcel depot. Their new company, W & G Express Carriers became a successful business. The London General fared badly, having run up debts of over a half a million pounds against assets of £1.3 million in 1911 and had faced the fuel strike in a weakened position. Nevertheless, the company stuck with its core business. The British Motor Cab Company was absorbed by the London General, whilst FIAT and the London Improved Cab Company closed down. In the short term, cabmen found themselves with no cabs to drive. One of their options was to buy a cab of their own, but PCO regulations put such men in a difficult position. Because vehicles of this age all had very different controls, a cabman had to take a driving test for every vehicle that he wanted to drive. Unless he took time out to pass a new driving test on a different cab, his only option was to buy the cab he had driven from the garage from which he once rented it. To make ends meet, an owner-driver, driving the cab himself with no 'double' partner, was working a seventy-hour week.

The increase in the number of owner-drivers was Mann and Overton's big opportunity to build on the sales of new and second-hand cabs and they took it. Close to 4000 Unic cabs, both 10/12hp and 12/16hp left the factory between 1906 and 1913. It was a joint success for dealer and manufacturer. By 1914 there was only one company making vehicles for the London cab trade, Unic, and there was only one company selling Unics- Mann and Overton's. If the beginning of 1908 saw the design of vehicle established for the rest of the century, then the events of 1913-1914 set the way that the business of running and of selling cabs would be. There would, however be a major hiatus for the nation as a whole, in August 1914, with the outbreak of war.

Chapter 4

Great War, Turbulent Peace

In August 1914 many people in Britain believed that the war with Germany would be over by the following Christmas. For the first few weeks, life in Britain continued much as it had before the declaration. Spurred by patriotism and a spirit of self-sacrifice, private individuals offered their motor vehicles to the War Office, and a significant number of lorries were accepted, often remaining for some weeks in their original owners' colours. But the war continued as opposing forces dug themselves in for a prolonged fight. In 1915 the Chancellor of the Exchequer, David Lloyd George exposed the frightening shortage of ammunition, caused by a complete inability of the War Office to grasp the scale of the war and mobilise Britain's industry. He called upon the Prime Minister, H. H Asquith to increase the production of arms. In May 1915, Asquith created the Ministry of Munitions and appointed Lloyd George as its Secretary of State. Britain finally went on to a war footing, with huge numbers of factories moving over to the production of munitions and material for the armed forces.

The Origins of the Beardmore

Private car manufacture continued in Britain on a very limited basis, but the only make of cab available to the London market was the Unic. As the war escalated, imports of goods from France ceased. With France fighting for her very existence as a free nation, every part of her industry was dedicated to that effort. Mann and Overton's found themselves with nothing to sell, as Unic's Puteaux factory was turned over to the manufacture of munitions. If finding new French vehicles was out of the question, keeping the existing cabs, French or English, on the road during wartime was proving difficult. Napier had ceased making the 15hp chassis in 1914 and the impossibility of finding a cab manufacturer prompted Francis Luther of the Coupé Cab Company to find someone to build a new mode of cab for him.

Luther had been the managing director of the Austro-Daimler concession for England since 1913. He was a personal friend of Ferdinand Porsche, the chief engineer of Austro-Daimler and had returned from a visit to Austria in 1913 with the rights to the 6-cylinder Austro-Daimler aero engine that Porsche had designed. Luther persuaded another old friend, William Beardmore to make it under licence. Beardmore himself was the chairman of William Beardmore and Co. Ltd., the largest industrial complex in Scotland and also the majority shareholder in the Scottish car maker Arrol-Johnston, who in 1911 had relocated to a superb new factory at Heathhall, Dumfries. There was spare capacity in the factory to make the aero engine and William Beardmore and Co. Ltd. entered into an agreement to do so. It would, after a protracted period of development, appear as the 120hp and, later the 150hp Beardmore engine.

With these connections established, Luther and his business partner George Allsworth approached Beardmore's with the proposition of building a cab for London. Arrol-Johnston's old Underwood Works in Paisley lay idle and it was here in August 1915 that the new cab would be built and Superintendent Bassom of Scotland Yard was pleased to advise on its design. But the escalation of the war meant that Beardmore's contribution to the war effort, a major one that already included building over dozen warships for the Royal Navy and the construction of field guns, would increase. The Underwood Works were converted to shell production and work on the taxicab ceased.

The Effects of War on the Trade

The call for troops in 1915 took a great number of Britain's young men, including more than 10,000 cabmen from across Britain, keen to fight for King and Country. When conscription was introduced in February 1916, more cabmen still were taken out of the trade. A large proportion of the young men who went to fight never returned. The cabs, no longer having drivers, were laid up or sometimes used as free transport for wounded or convalescent servicemen.

W & G du Cros' cab operations, already reduced after 1913 would be affected by the war. In July 1914 they appointed their works manager, William Turpin to the board. The works were turned over to

munitions production, making one and a half million shells. For this work, Turpin was awarded the OBE.

London taxis were not commandeered as troop transport, as were Parisian cabs in 1914, when several hundred were commandeered to take reserve troops to the Marne in a desperate and ultimately successful attempt to halt the German invasion. However, many of W & G's Napiers were commandeered for service in the Army, being assembled in Hyde Park and adjoining Kensington Gardens before being rebodied as ambulances and donated to France. Curiously, the Panhards, which of course were French-made were left with W & G for continued use in the cab fleet.

This contributed to the reduction in the numbers of cabs on the streets. and in August 1917, the shortage of cabs prompted the humorous magazine, 'Punch', to print the comment:

"The Home Secretary (Sir George Cave) has determined to put a stop to the practice of whistling for taxicabs in London. It is suggested that he would confer a still greater boon on his fellow-townsmen if he would provide a few more taxis for them not to whistle for."

The shortage would continue: the number of cabs licensed during 1918 dropped to 5,451, the lowest since 1859. There were, in the same year 6,189 drivers.

The introduction of petrol rationing added to the difficulties faced by the cab trade, as cabs were allowed just one and a half gallons per day for singled cabs, i. e. those with just one driver and two gallons for doubled cabs. A number of well-to-do young women became volunteer nurses and it became a tradition at this time for London cabmen to carry them, if in uniform, without accepting any fare. Servicemen on leave created some work, although fuel rationing made it hard to cover it. Women who worked in munitions, nicknamed 'canaries' because of the colour the explosives turned their skin after prolonged contact, began earning considerable amounts of money and they too used cabs when they could be found. For the first time, the PCO allowed women to take the Knowledge, but all who took it, failed to complete the task. In the event, the Knowledge was suspended for the duration of the war.

Inflation made life harder for the cabman who, unable to cover the work either because of petrol rationing or his cab was laid up because it could not be repaired, was faced with rising food prices. In October 1917 The London and Provincial Licensed Vehicle Workers Union demanded a fare increase of 'a shilling a mile, every mile'. The Home secretary refused. Instead, he offered a 6d (2.5p) surcharge for every job. This the union and the whole of the Joint Trade Committee declined and the union called strike, starting on October 17. Although the LMCPA, one of the JTC's members and the owner-drivers' section of the union soon changed their minds and agreed to the surcharge, the union held firm, demanding instead the free petrol they had campaigned for in 1912 and had been promised in exchange for their agreement of a fifty percent fare increase. The government gave way and on December 20 announced that petrol would be issued free to all cabs hired from a fleet.

A second strike in the same year resulted in the abolition of charges to railway stations, which at least was a benefit to the trade as a whole. Now at least every cabman had the opportunity of 'working the rails' when the troop trains came in. The prolonged decline on the numbers of serviceable cabs and petrol rationing put fleet proprietors under great financial pressure. Their drivers operated on a percentage of the meter, so with fewer cabs on the road and fewer drivers doing fewer jobs, their ability to cover the fixed overheads on either their cabs or their premises was severely compromised. Now the Home Secretary delivered a severe blow to all cabmen and proprietors when he refused a fare increase. By the time of the Armistice in November 1918 London's cab fleet had dropped to 3,821.

Edwardian cabs, even models as antiquated as this Renault were still in service after the Great War. Many were run by 'mushers' - owner drivers - like this one, pictured on a family outing at Egham, Surrey in the 1920s

Peace at Last

At the end of the war, David Lloyd George, who had become Prime Minister in 1916 promised that Britain would be "a land fit for heroes to live in." It was to this promise that the armed forces came home, from the mud of Flanders, the sand and flies of the Middle East and the perils of the open seas. And for a short time, Britain's economy promised them much. If £7 million a day could be found to fight the war, then a prosperous peace, it was argued was a certainty. There would be three years of prosperity; indeed of a boom, but war had brought Britain to her knees financially and in 1921 the dream had turned into a nightmare, as the economy collapsed and millions were thrown out of work. Ex-servicemen made up a substantial proportion of the men in the dole queues and the lines at soup kitchens. Many, including the amputees and the blind took to selling matches or busking on street corners.

Cabmen who had signed up for the duration came home with at least the hope of employment, but the war had more than halved London's cab fleet. The Army had commandeered both motor cabs and cab horses and by 1918 the numbers of cabs licensed had dropped from 8,651 to 5,421. Cabmen were bitterly disappointed to discover that some cab masters were profiteering in their time of need, selling off aged, reconditioned pre-war cabs at highly inflated prices. Cab unions had complained that there were some 500 cabs lying idle because they did not comply with the 10-inch ground clearance demanded by the Conditions of Fitness. It is possible that these were the Renaults that had caused such controversy back in 1906. Certainly the numbers were coincidental, but although a demand by the unions that

the 10-inch ground clearance be relaxed was met by the PCO, the cabs were not offered immediately for sale.

There was nothing new in the offing: Ford offered a prototype two-seat cab based on the Model T. It would have been a very cheap cab to buy, but the Public Carriage Office turned it down. The reason for this is not on record, but the Ford had transverse-leaf front suspension, which had already been banned for cabs by the PCO. One must wonder how different the future of the trade might have been if the Ford cab had been passed.

Through the Depression of the 1920s, car companies would concentrate on the far bigger and potentially more lucrative private and general commercial markets. But there must have been some anticipation amongst manufacturers interested in the cab trade that the Conditions of Fitness would be relaxed to keep pace with the advance in car design, but Supt. Bassom did not oblige. The trade would at this time see no permanent change to the rules on ground clearance or the turning circle. In any case, Bassom was engaged in new challenges and whatever makes might have been presented for approval from smaller firms, he knew that there was one from a solid and highly regarded company that had invested heavily and given the utmost commitment to its development - Beardmore.

The Beardmore Appears

At the beginning of 1919, work began on clearing out the 400-odd shell lathes that had filled part of the floor of the Underwood Works at Paisley, to facilitate production of the new Beardmore cab, design work of which had begun in 1915 at Arrol-Johnston. Suggesting either that design work had been laid down in great detail in 1915, or that development had continued throughout the war, work progressed remarkably quickly. Designs were submitted to the PCO on May 14 and approved on May 26. The first chassis underwent road trials on August 18 and a complete cab was tested on September 30. A week later, on October 7 a single example set out for the London works to be type approved. It arrived two days later, 'without mishap,' it was reported, 'or any adjustment having been made'. Type approval was given on October 20. Announced at the London Commercial Motor Exhibition that year under the Beardmore name, it was made known that the cab was the first to be developed in conjunction with Scotland Yard. Its arrival was not before time.

The Beardmore's introductory price of £795 highlighted the extreme inflation brought about as a result of the war. It was quickly brought down to £675, but even this was about twice the price of a suburban house. By comparison, the Unic 12/16 had cost £405 in 1914. The Beardmore was heavily built and, because of the demands of the Conditions of Fitness somewhat old-fashioned looking, but its quality and modern technical specification were claimed to be justification for its higher than average cost. Beardmore's advertising slogan was 'For Comfort and Speed, it's All You Need'.

Its pressed steel chassis - Beardmore were pioneers in this field - had a dropped section adjacent to the passenger doors to allow for easy access and the front of the frame was steeply stepped in to allow for the tight lock. Its 2287cc monobloc five-bearing sidevalve engine was the work of G. W. A. Brown, who had joined Arrol-Johnston from Humber's Beeston, Nottingham factory when it closed in 1908. The engine had a detachable head for easy de-coking, and a modern innovation, a water pump. The four-speed gate change gearbox was separate from the engine to simplify replacement of the leather cone clutch. As was common practice, the hand brake operated on the rear wheels and the foot brake operated on the transmission. Each engine was run in at the works on coal gas using a special carburettor, then the completed chassis were road tested be-

The Mk1 Beardmore was a compact vehicle, with a wheelbase of just 8ft 7in to comply with the maximum permissible length of 14ft.
Each cab received sixteen coats of paint and varnish, in the standard colour of green

fore the bodies were fitted. Beardmore owners could be sure of the cab's reliability and serviceability from day one.

There was a choice of two body styles, the full- or three-quarter landaulette, built in-house of ash. All the body parts were assembled on jigs and sold as separate sections to allow quick replacement with the minimum of fitting after an accident. The company formed to make the cab was Beardmore Motors Ltd and the managing director was Francis M. Luther, with George Allsworth as another director, J. G. Girdwood as company secretary and Sir William Beardmore as chairman. It was sold from Beardmore's own dealership at 112 Great Portland Street, London and serviced at their depot in Hendon, North London. A fleet of 2000 would eventually go into service with Francis Luther's Coupé Cab Company and these numbers helped it to become the most numerous cab in the capital. Despite its high initial cost it was a cab much respected by mushers, who bought some 34 percent of the production run and christened it 'the Rolls-Royce of cabs'. By 1923 the total number of cabs in London had risen,

thanks largely to the Beardmore's introduction, to 7,283. In 1924, 1437 Beardmore cabs were licensed in London. It is a significant reflection of the results of the disputes of 1910 and 1913 that in 1924 there were 440 proprietors with more than 4 cabs, most of them being small businesses with perhaps 15 or 20 cabs, tucked away in corner garages and under railway arches.

Mann & Overton's Reintroduce the Unic

In 1920, Unic resumed production of an updated version of their pre-war cab. Apart from a centre-change gearbox and a modern radiator, it was basically the same Edwardian cab that Mann and Overton's had commissioned in 1910. Already expensive, it was made more so in 1924 with the re-introduction of the so-called 'McKenna Duties' a 33.3 percent duty first levied in 1915 on goods imported into any country within the British Empire. Originally, commercial vehicles were excluded, as they were deemed vital for the war ef-

The post- Great War Unic 12/16 was, mechanically little different from the pre-war model, featuring a 'gate' gearbox with a centre change, a larger radiator and different scuttle .
Dealers Mann and Overton's offered the bare chassis. This example has three-quarter landaulette coachwork by Birch Brothers of Kentish Town

fort. The duties were removed in August 1924 but were reintroduced in June 1925 and extended to cover commercial vehicles, making the Unic very expensive.

The body had a slightly more modern look, with a steel skin covering the ash framework, but the post-war Unic still looked very similar to the pre-war model. M & O also sold bare chassis and at least twenty were bought by North London cab proprietors Birch Brothers, who built their own distinctive bodies for them.

Despite its antiquity and high price, the Unic's reputation ensured that it sold in sufficient numbers to keep Mann and Overton's garage, now in a new home in Battersea Bridge Road in profit. M & O also kept a lot of pre-war Unics on the road too, most likely renovating them where necessary, fitting them with new engines, modern 'gate' gearboxes and other mechanical components and possibly post-war radiators, bonnets and scuttles. It is also possible that fleet garages may have produced 'new' cabs from surviving chassis, using pre-war parts or post-war parts when no pre-war ones were available. By 1924, 1307 Unics were in service in London, although contemporary photographs and newsreels indicate that many of these were renovated pre-war models.

Other, Unsuccessful Makes

There were others who entered, or re-entered the market, some hopeful of relaxed Conditions of Fitness. One attempted re-entry was Fiat, who presented the model IT cab at the 1920 Commercial Motor Exhibition. It was built on the 1912 Tipo Zero chassis, with an 1847cc sidevalve engine. Few Fiat cabs were sold before the vehicle was replaced in Italy by a new model, which did not comply with the Conditions of Fitness. Also at Olympia in 1920 were Associated Motors Ltd., of Fernhead Road, Paddington who exhibited their model. This was a cab of their own manufacture, having a proprietary French Chapuis Dornier engine of 2297cc and like the Beardmore, it had a dropped frame. Its price, £825 reflected the inflation of the time and the cost of producing a low volume vehicle. Although type-approved, it did not go into

Associated Motors Ltd's AML cab was one of several makes that never made it into production.
The radiator, reminiscent of that of a Rolls-Royce Silver Ghost, was typical of a practice many small-scale makers used in trying to gain some kudos from the great names

production, as most likely buyers of new cabs preferred the Unic, which although antiquated was reliable and highly regarded, or the slightly cheaper Beardmore, which by now had seen some service and by now was gaining a fine reputation.

In March 1921 the S. K. A. M, was announced, produced by Skam Motors of Uxbridge Road, West London. A prototype received approval and covered 7000 working miles. The engine was a proprietary 4-cylinder side-valve Dorman of 2613cc, rated at 16hp. It had a constant mesh four-speed Dux gearbox, separate from the engine, designed and built by the British Transmission Co. Ltd. of Portsmouth Street, off Kingsway, London, an associate company of S. K. A. M. The transmission was said to be of a similar design to that of the Whippet light tank, which was also produced by the British Transmission Company. The chassis was of pressed steel with, as 'Commercial Motor' magazine put it, 'none of those sharp bends that weaken the average taxi-cab frame'. It had cantilever rear springing to give a comfortable ride and to eliminate any rear overhang to prevent street urchins

cadging a ride by hanging on the back.

It all sounded very promising, but it would be over a year, in November 1922 before the new cab would be heard of again. It now had a completely new name, the Kingsway and the body had been updated with a full height radiator, level with a modern style scuttle. The British Transmission Company would now be directly responsible for it; the name S. K. A. M. seemed to have disappeared without trace. Very shortly after, so had the cab: priced at £720, just as the economy had slumped, it was not surprising.

Mepward

The Mepward, made by Mepsted and Hayward of Rodney Street, Pentonville, North London, was introduced in 1920, just prior to the collapse of the post-war boom in the British economy. Only twelve were believed to have been made and it was, by contemporary accounts, a very bad cab. It was powered by a 2178cc four-cylinder sidevalve engine, possibly a Dorman and its massive all-wood body made

For 1923, Beardmore altered the cab slightly, adopting the wings of its light van version. The full landaulette body was dropped, with the three-quarter landaulette remaining as the only style available

The Citroën 11.4hp was a cheap cab in comparison to the Beardmore and Unic, but failed to sell in great numbers.
It was fitted with electric lights as standard, although carbide sidelights were retained, as they did not drain the battery like electric lights.
The smart suit worn of the young man with his foot on the running board shows how much pride cabmen took in their appearance

it slow and heavy to drive. The company that ran the cabs foundered. Hayward disappeared from view under, rumour has it, very murky circumstances, but Ernest Mepsted continued in the motor business and we will encounter his name again.

Citroën

Citroën was a new make to its native France. Like William Beardmore, André Citroën made artillery shells during the Great War and when peace came, his factory at the Quai de Javel, Paris, was turned over to the manufacture of cars. But unlike the Beardmore, he made a cheap car claiming, to much ridicule, that he would build one hundred a day. By 1923 he was making more than double that number. From the start, Citroën exported his cars and his Type A tourer sold in Britain for £395. The Type A was even cheaper in France, where it was adopted in 1921 as a taxicab.

It was a modified 11.4hp chassis, based on what was sold in France as the B2 model that London Citroën and Voisin dealer Maxwell Monson introduced as a cab to London in 1923. At £540 it was sub-

stantially more expensive than the private car, but that was because of its chassis modifications and special cab body. Nevertheless, it was still cheaper than the Unic or the Beardmore. Its wheelbase was shorter than the car's and the steering was adapted to comply with the Conditions of Fitness by placing the drop arm inside the chassis instead of outside, setting the drag link at an oblique angle to the frame. The suspension was the same as the car's, with quarter-elliptical springs, two singles leading at the front and two pairs trailing at the rear. At 1453cc its four-cylinder side-valve engine was noticeably smaller than its competitors and this undoubtedly helped its fuel consumption. The gearbox was a three-speed manual with a single dry-plate clutch and the rear axle was a heavy-duty type. The disc wheels were much bigger than the standard Citroën. Besides being required for the specially approved taxi tyres, they also helped provide the regulation ten-inch ground clearance. The body came from Brixton coachbuilders Dyer & Holton. Included in the price were electric headlamps, the first to be offered on a London cab. Although the Conditions of Fitness did not ban headlights outright, it specified that 'headlights of great brilliancy will not be permitted', so it must be assumed that they were of a relatively low power.

Although Maxwell Monson sold cabs on hire purchase to mushers and provided driver training and 'wangle' cabs, (cabs on which Knowledge Boys could practice on for their driving test) it was the London General Cab Company that were the biggest fleet purchasers. Their old pre-war Unics and Renaults were well overdue for replacement and the £625 price of the 'gate' Unic was much more than the General were prepared to pay. The Citroën cab provided the ideal solution and by 1928 the General had acquired 220 examples, almost half the estimated production run.

W & G Try Again

W & G were still running pre-war Panhards and Napiers and were in a difficult financial position. Their Acton premises were acquired in 1920 by A. Darracq & Co (1905) Ltd., who used half the building space to make bodies for Talbot and Darracq chassis. Much of the business conducted there was on behalf of STD, the consortium of Sunbeam, Talbot and Darracq. William and George du Cros moved into commercial vehicle manufacture in 1920 and the cab business was transferred to a subsidiary company, Turpin Engineering Co. Ltd. under the control of William Turpin. The STD connection would bring some hope for the new cabs that the W & G organisation badly needed. An announcement in the Commercial Motor of 22 August 1922, said:

> 'The W & G cab reappears: The W & G taxicab is again to be placed on the market. The chassis of the new model has been designed by Mr. L. Coatelen. The

chassis only, or the complete vehicle, will be sold as customers may require, whilst the price will be competitive.'

Louis Coatelen had already become acquainted with the PCO when employed by his future father-in-law, William Hillman to design the Hillman-Coatelen cab, introduced in 1908. In 1909 he moved to Sunbeam where he became chief engineer and eventually, joint managing director. The chassis of the new cab, made in Paris was a Talbot-Darracq Model DC with a 1597cc 4-cylinder engine. W & G or one of their associates was to supply the body if required. Sadly, it did not get beyond the preliminary stages.

The Yellow Cab

A better and cheaper option, W & G decided, was to buy American, from John Hertz, a man whose name would become a legend in the car rental world. Hertz went into the taxicab business in Chicago in 1910, running cars that the dealer he worked for had acquired as trade-ins but could not sell on. After spending some time studying the London cab trade Hertz built his first cabs in 1915. He called them Yellow Cabs, using them in his own fleet and selling them to others across the USA and Canada. After the war he established an assembly plant in Orillia, Ontario, a small town 55 miles north of the city of Toronto, Canada, to serve the Canadian market. Any goods made within the British Empire that were exported to other empire territories were exempt from the dreaded 'McKenna Duties' and thus the Yellow Cab's price was not handicapped by these additional taxes.

The London version of the Yellow Cab was introduced at the 1923 Commercial Motor Exhibition at Olympia. It was a special model, probably adapted the American '03' model and fitted with the same 2.25-litre Continental four-cylinder sidevalve engine and Brown-Lipe 3-speed manual gearbox. The London cabs were on a 99-inch wheelbase compared to the American's 109-inch, which resulted in the radiator having to be placed in front of the centre of the front axle. There was a certain amount of controversy when it was introduced, not least because of an advert that appeared in 'The Steering Wheel' stating that Yellow Cab were 'manufacturers and operators' and London cab masters feared a big American invasion. Yellow Cab certainly operated cabs in America but the British subsidiary, The Yellow Cab Manufacturing Company of England Ltd., had no intention of doing the same in the UK, preferring to sell to proprietors and mushers alike. The advertised price was £590 complete with body, or £100 down and the rest paid up to five years. W & G would provide the bodies for the cabs, although the first examples that were shipped over were complete vehicles.

Turpin Engineering bought one hundred and twenty Yellow Cab chassis in early 1924 and fitted the ones that followed the aforementioned first examples with bodies similar the American counterparts, although the luggage platform on the London models was left open, where the American version had a door across it.

Turpin would not only be a proprietor, but an agent, selling the cab to mushers, and to proprietors who ran small fleets under contract. Turpin also ran a Knowledge school for aspiring cab drivers, who in return for the tuition would be required to drive Turpin's cabs for a specified period. The bright yellow of the cabs inspired experienced cabmen to call Turpin's new drivers, 'Butterboys'. The term was soon applied to all new cabmen the name and remains in use to this day. Hertz had also gone into truck and bus manufacture and it was this operation that attracted the attention of the American giant General Motors. In 1925 they bought Hertz's manufacturing business, including the cabs. Very shortly after, delivery of Yellow Cabs to London ceased and Yellow Cabs in the USA were produced using Buick engines, on much longer wheelbase chassis, totally unsuited to be modified for London.

The Canadian-built Yellow Cab was operated and sold by Turpin Engineering, a subsidiary of W & G du Cros. just 100 were imported

The Beardmore Super

Despite the depressed economic climate and the troubles that were besetting Beardmore's, demand for the MkI cab was steady, but it was now looking almost as antiquated as the survivors of the pre-war years. It was time for a replacement and in the spring of 1925 it arrived. It was simply called the MkII 'Super' and was based on the chassis of a new 30cwt truck, introduced in 1923 by the Underwood, Paisley factory's works manager, B. Angus Shaw.

The side members of the 9-foot wheelbase chassis were of the new 'double drop' design, obviating the special 'dip' in the chassis by the passenger doors that featured on the Mk1. There was a more modern radiator, and the antique ribbed body was replaced by an up-to-date steel panelled three-quarter landaulette, finished in a choice of green, maroon or blue. A slightly larger version of the four-cylinder sidevalve engine and the separate four-speed gate-change gearbox were carried over, but the brakes were a new design. Both hand and foot brakes operated on the rear drums, with two separate sets of

shoes. Sankey pressed steel artillery type wheels replaced the wooden artillery wheels of the Mk1 and Brolt electric lighting was offered as an optional extra.

Beardmore also made an expensive 12hp car that had gained a reputation for unreliability that a major rework of the engine was too late to change. The Anniesland factory that made it was closed and a new 14/40 car for the private hire market was built at Paisley. Although Paisley was losing money due to the development of the 14/40 and the new commercial vehicles, the taxicab business was a vital one to preserve. After all, Beardmore was the only native British cab maker. In 1925 the Treasury guaranteed a £350,000 loan from the Trade Facilities Act Advisory Committee on the condition that the Underwood Works was run as a separate entity from other parts of the Beardmore organisation. Managing director Francis Luther and fellow director G eorge Allsworth, along with John Girdwood, Beardmore's company secretary, formed Beardmore Taxicabs Ltd. to sell cabs and Beardmore (Paisley) Ltd., to finance sales. The new organisation then leased the Underwood

The Mk2 Beardmore 'Super' used a totally new chassis and radiator, derived from a new range of light commercial vehicles. The body was modernised and the engine produced slightly more power. The steel artillery wheels were also new, whilst electric headlights were an optional extra

works from William Beardmore & Company Ltd, enabling them to make the Super with some degree of financial security.

William Watson and the Hayes Cab

William Watson's name occurs often during the history of the motor car in first half of the twentieth century. He won the 1908 Isle of Man Tourist Trophy race, and he was a close friend of William Morris, establishing, in his native Liverpool one of the first Morris dealerships. (Incidentally, around 1914, Watson's coachbuilding manager was Bobby Jones, who would go on to found Carbodies, the firm that is now the London Taxi Company.) In 1925, Watson entered the London cab trade with an American/British hybrid, the Hayes. The chassis was built in Ontario, Canada by the Hayes Company, a substantial

Despite there being several makers interested in making two-seater cabs, little photographic evidence survives on any, apart from this Berliet, and a Trojan

North American wheel and motor component manufacturer, to avoid paying the McKenna Duties and was fitted with a Continental engine of 2.5 litres. At £425 it was the cheapest on the market, and by contemporary accounts a very good cab. However, it disappeared in 1928, around the same time that Hayes merged with Kelsey and the new company began concentrating on wheel manufacture.

The 'Jixi'

Britain in the 1920s was in the grip of an economic depression. Cab fares had at least been raised in 1920: the flagfall was now 1/- (5p) and 3d for every quarter-mile thereafter: the 'shilling a mile, every mile' that the union had demanded in 1911. But with the inflation the war had engendered, it did little, if any good. Cabmen were often standing idle for seven hours in a ten-hour shift. Piled on top of the lack of work was competition from the newly electrified London Underground and the proliferation of motor buses. But there would be an even more serious threat to both the wellbeing of the cabmen and the development of the cabs. It was the proposed imposition of two seat cabs, which were planned to operate at a lower tariff. These were the machination of Sir William Joynson-Hicks, the Home Secretary in the Conservative government of Stanley Baldwin that was elected in November 1924. 'Jix' as he was known, trained and practiced as a solicitor. He was reputed to be an unpopular and self-opinionated man and had been company solicitor to the London G eneral Omnibus Company when his father, Henry Hicks had been chairman. He was also chairman of the Automobile Association from 1908 to 1923. With this background and his new position as supremo of the Metropolitan Police and thus head of the PCO, (at the time responsible for licensing London's buses as well as taxicabs) Jix thought to revolutionise London's public transport. On representation from a group within the London cab trade, he set up a committee to investigate the possibilities of a two-seater cab that would operate in London at a lower fare.

Jix imposed the plan against great opposition from the trade. Similar vehicles - they would be called 'Jixis' in London - had appeared in the provinces, following an unsuccessful attempt to use motorcycle combination taxicabs. A parliamentary committee was set up in July 1925 to investigate the matter, under the chairmanship of Sir Basil Peto MP. There were four other MPs on the eight-man committee, with Police Commander Pulling of New Scotland Yard as secretary. Arthur Bassom, now a Chief constable, was to sit, but he died suddenly and his place was taken by Frank Elliot. Bassom's experience would be a sad loss, but what his actual contribution might have been and how he might have affected its progress, one can only guess.

The cab trade's Joint Trade Committee (JTC) made strong representations to the parliamentary committee. Already, the JTC said, cabs were ranking for hours on end. They had been demanding cabs that were cheaper to buy and to run but that they should be four-seat vehicles, not two-seaters and should run on the existing tariff. Cabmen and cab masters had invested in four-seat cabs and their investment would be lost if the Jixi were to become numerous. The committee were doubtful of the practicality of having different cabs with different fare structures working alongside each other on the same rank, but this gave the JTC only forlorn hope.

The paradox was that both the trade and the public had made their choice between two- and four-seat cabs almost two decades previously, when motor vehicle chassis became powerful enough to carry four-seat cab bodies. The four-seat cab was endorsed by Chief Inspector Bassom in his evidence to the parliamentary committee that sat over The London Cab and Stage Carriage Act of 1907. The union said quite simply that a four-seat cab could do everything a two-seat cab could do but the reverse was not true. This observation was especially appropriate in regard to railway station work. Did the Home secretary expect the drivers and proprietors of four-seat cabs to exist solely on railway station work whilst the two-seaters ranked up outside in the streets?

In August 1925 the committee reported in favour of two-seat cabs and a two-tier tariff. Jix warned the JTC that lower fares would be imposed if the two-seater cab was not accepted and the JTC had to concede to him. Specific Conditions of Fitness were prepared for the new cabs, specifying a lower ground clearance of 8 inches, a narrower track of 48 inches and smaller wheels and tyres. A smaller passenger compartment was specified too, but the driver's compartment was the same as for four-seaters. Fares were set at 9d (3.75p) flagfall and 9d per mile thereafter and would come into force on May 1 1927.

One voice had spoken wholly in favour of two-seat cabs, that of R. W. Owen, who was a director of White, Holmes & Co., previously known as the National Cab Company (1922) Ltd. This was hardly surprising. White, Holmes & Co. had already built a two-seat cab, the KRC. It took its name from its designers, Kingston, Richardson and Crutchley, who were making a light sports car under the same name. The cab was presented to the PCO a full month before the committee reported its findings and it was put on test as soon as the report, which found in favour of the 'Jixi', was published.

Other makes came forward. One was the Trojan, whose simple, robust and popular two-stroke car formed the base. From France came a 12hp Berliet, which gained type approval in March 1927. Berliet planned to make 200 but only produced a prototype. There was an entrant expected from Beardmore, but that did not appear. Nor, after all the publicity did the KRC. White, Holmes & Co. claimed that the General Strike had affected the motor industry, rendering them unable to manufacture the cab in quantity.

Now the cab trade, having endured the 1926 General Strike on top of an economic depression, suffered another blow. In April 1927 Jix changed his mind and rescinded the order that would have brought in two-seat cabs. He also announced a new lower tariff, even lower than that set for the Jixi. On top of this, the trade were dismayed to discover that he had not actually banned two-seat cabs. He allowed them but by default required that they comply with the Conditions of Fitness for four-seat cabs and compelled them to run on the same tariff. Cab trade representatives withdrew their support for the lower tariff, claiming a complete breach of faith.

After much argument it was agreed that the new fares would be tried for an experimental period but the trade knew the effect would be dire. Inflation had risen by 55 percent since the end of the war. The price of cabs had doubled but fares had only risen once, in 1920 by 17 percent. Cab masters and cabmen were facing bankruptcy and within a month, the JTC asked Jix to reconsider his decision. Jix held firm. The cab trade were told to make the best of what they had been given.

No More Citroëns

The Citroën cab was cheap - its price had been reduced to £325 by 1926 - but it was now in limited supply. Citroën had an assembly plant in England, in Slough, so they could sell cars in the UK without them being liable to the McKenna Duties. The cab's chassis was made in Paris, but the car on which it was based was nearing the end of its production life and Citroën had started building the latest model, the steel-bodied 13/30 at Slough in late 1926. A special seven-passenger model was to be introduced and it would be used in Paris as a cab. It was offered to British provincial cab operators but Citroën was either not able or not willing to provide a modified version of the 13/30 chassis for London.

The Conditions of Fitness Under Review

It may have been a point of honour that Supt Bassom, having encouraged Beardmore to develop their first cab was loathe to pull the rug from under them by letting more modern designs in until they had recouped their investment. The same might be said with regard to Mann and Overton's and the 'Gate' Unic. But Bassom had been involved in new projects, including the study of aviation for police work and in consequence must have had little time to devote to the cab trade. Whatever Bassom's reasoning, the Conditions of Fitness had remained unchanged during the last years of his life.

The simplest, most effective way of keeping passenger numbers and profits up and fares at an economical level was to provide cheaper 4-seat cabs. This was the message delivered to Sir William Joynson-

Hicks, by a rather insidious source, the British Fascist Sir Oswald Moseley of the Unionist Party, who had attempted to side with the cab trade. (Or at least with its non-Jewish membership.) 'Jix' agreed with Moseley and on July 5 1927 wrote to the Commissioner of Police, Sir William Horwood, saying:

> "At the present tariff an owner driver was quite unable to meet the large instalments as they became due on his cab." (*sic*)

Sir William replied,

> "I fancy you will find that the inflated cost of our present taxicab is maintained by the ring of manufacturers, who keep the cost up for their own financial gain, and who, when attacked, use 'the requirements of Scotland Yard' as an excuse."

However, some things were considered sacred at all levels. Sir William went on:

> "One of the things I shall direct Supt Claro *(the new PCO head)* to press for is the retention of the present 'lock' of the taxi-cab."

He then set up a technical committee, under Capt. Douglas Hacking MP, the Parliamentary Secretary of State at the Home Office to 'consider how far the present cost of motor cabs in London is affected by these conditions or other circumstances, and to advise whether any alteration in these conditions is desirable'. Besides Hacking, the Committee of Enquiry was composed of Supt. Claro of the PCO, and three engineers, E. S. Perrin B Sc., AM Inst. CE of the Ministry of Transport, H. C. Clarke AMI Mech. E and G. W. Watson MI Mech E, MIAE. Claro's duties with the committee were in addition to the work he undoubtedly had to do when, in the same year, the PCO moved from Scotland Yard to a new building in Lambeth Road.

The Committee's initial findings were a damning indictment of both the lack of care given to the trade by the government and of Jix's capricious adventure with two-seater cabs. The whole episode of the

Birch Brothers invested in this fleet of Unics in the mid-1920s and fitted then with their own coachwork. They would be made obsolete by the 1928 changes to the Conditions of Fitness

Jixis caused anyone who may have been interested in building a cab for London to shy away. Jix should have been in touch with what was happening on London's streets and in the rest of the country, instead of driving the cab trade up a blind alley.

In 1927 four makes of cab were, in theory available, but the situation was worse than this. The Beardmore Mk2 was readily available but expensive. Unic had stockpiled a quantity of chassis for about a year's sales after production had ceased in 1926 but these of course only guaranteed a limited supply and the cab was fearfully expensive and antiquated. The Hayes was listed but virtually unobtainable. The Citroën was in limited supply, although chassis had been stockpiled.

A major factor for the committee to contend with was that car design had outrun the Conditions of Fitness and the market was too small to interest most UK big makers in making a specialist vehicle. But it was the big makers like Morris, Austin and Singer that could produce, through economies of scale and engineering for production a saloon car of around 12 - 15hp for under £350. How could the big makers reconcile their existing models, all of which were designed with no regard whatsoever for the London taxi market, and yet supply a cab at a price anywhere near cheaper than the Beardmore? The Committee contacted the Society of Motor Manufacturers and Traders to ask them to find any manufacturers who might be interested. Three companies responded, but only Miles Thomas of Nuffield and Ted Grinham of Humber attended, their presence indicating a genuine interest. Humber had introduced the excellent 14/40 but it cost £575. Grinham was not, it seems, committed to the idea, reckoning that they could not make a cab for under £600, which was a serious blow to the PCO's aspirations of seeing cheaper cabs.

Morris had a new Oxford that sold for £240 with a saloon body. Thomas reckoned that they might be able to produce a cab on a production chassis that sold for around £335. But both Thomas and Grinham agreed on what were the main obstacles to their producing a suitable vehicle for the London market. They were the ground clearance, the turning circle and the fuel tank location. Many makers were beginning to site fuel tanks at the rear of the vehicle, which was prohibited for cabs by the Conditions of Fitness.

The Committee finally agreed to lower the ground clearance to 7 inches, and allowed the relocation of the fuel tank to a position under the bonnet. A rear location would still not be permitted. The Committee were split over the issue of the turning circle and the final report declared this, but a minority report by Claro said that 'the mobility of the cab was its greatest asset' and he opposed the change. Advertising on the inside of cabs was also allowed. The new Conditions of Fitness would come into force from April 30 1928. But one of the key players in the market had already responded.

Chapter 5
The 1930s

Britain came out of the Great Depression of the 1920s in poor shape. The 1930s brought some improvement to the economy, albeit inconsistent. The cab trade would see some revival of its fortunes and also see Mann and Overton's take an unassailable position in the market with a marque that had already been licensed for cab work: Austin.

The Morris-Commercial G-Type 'International'

Whilst the old Conditions of Fitness were still in force, two new cabs were being prepared. The first came from William Morris's massive organisation, and it was the Morris-Commercial G-Type. It was not the result of a decision made within Morris Motors, even though Miles Thomas had spent some time giving evidence to the Home Office Committee of Enquiry but the suggestion of George Kenning, a Morris dealer and proprietor of the International Cab Company of Leeds. Earlier in the 1920s, William Morris had seen what he had considered to be potential markets in the British Empire and his truck company, Morris-Commercial designed the Empire Oxford, based on a shortened T-Type 'Tonner' van chassis. Unfortunately, it was too expensive for its intended market in Australia in the face of

competition from cheap American makes, which were built in Canada to avoid paying the punitive McKenna Duties that applied not only to Britain but to her dominions and colonies.

Kenning proposed that the unsuccessful Morris Empire Oxford would make a good taxi for London. The cab took its 'International' name from Kenning's cab company. Produced alongside light commercial vehicles and one-ton vans at the giant Morris-Commercial plant at Soho, Birmingham the first 840, numbered as the 'G-Type' and named the 'International' after Kenning's cab company were converted from unsold Empire Oxfords, using narrower axles to meet the PCO's maximum specified track. The engine was the 15.9hp 2.5 litre sidevalve unit from the 'Tonner'. An overhead worm drive rear axle helped to achieve the ten-inch ground clearance. Originally, the cab was sold without headlights, but later, the new Conditions of Fitness allowed a full lighting system and to replace the twin-shoe rear brakes, a full four-wheel braking system.

The cab appeared in January 1929. The only body offered was a three-quarter landaulette, finished in brown and built in-house at Morris Bodies in Cowley. A further 860 cabs were built from scratch, making a total of 1700. George Kenning originally sold the cab in London but the

A Morris-Commercial G- Type with a two-seat 'Cape' body stands beside a Citroën 11.4hp, around 1930. The Cape body was designed by Mr W. Gowan, a South African, hence its name. Like all two-seater cabs, the Cape never caught on. The idea was revived in the mid-1930s, but failed once more

A 1929 Morris-Commercial 'G' Type International in its original form, with its driver, 'French' Smithy. This cab was owned by Devonian Garage of Carthew Road, Hammersmith. After 1928, most, if not all G-Types were fitted with headlights, front bumpers and front wheel brakes when the regulations permitted them

The Dyer & Holton bodies from the General's old 11.4hp Citroëns were a poor fit on the new, longer wheelbase chassis, requiring a longer body panel between the partition and the driver's door. Smaller diameter disc wheels carried the new 20 x 5inch balloon tyres

concession was soon transferred to William Watson, who moved from Eccleston Place, Victoria into new riverside premises on Grosvenor Road, between Vauxhall Bridge and Chelsea Bridge. The price of the cab in the capital was a highly competitive £377/10/0 (£377.50p) or £465 on hire purchase, with a £50 deposit and 50 shillings (£2.10) per week for four years. Very shortly after, the cash price was raised to £395, which was only a little above the estimate of £355 that Miles Thomas gave to the committee that reviewed the Conditions of Fitness in 1927.

A New Citroën

The second new cab was a Citroën, and it came from the London General. The 11.4hp Citroëns that the General had bought during the 1920s were ageing. The Paris factory had ceased to make its base model, and the General was not prepared to pay the price of the MkII Beardmore and the Unic was no longer available. The General had their chief engineer, P. Gel-

dard design their own cabs with a longer wheelbase chassis than the 11.4hp. To this, he fitted the suspension and axles, radiator and bonnet from the old cabs, the 1.6 litre sidevalve engine from the new Citroën C4 and 20-inch disc wheels, which took Dunlop's new 'balloon' tyres. The old Citroën body was tried on the new chassis and although it made an ungainly, top-heavy vehicle it served the General's purpose well. Geldard also designed a more modern, fabric-covered body with a fixed head. Photographs of them on both chassis survive, but none have come to light of any in service. The remainder of the old bodies were put into storage.

The Beardmore Hyper

Beardmore's industrial empire had been unprofitable throughout the 1920s and some of the subsidiary companies were closed down. One of these was the Anniesland factory where the 12hp light car was made. However, it was from the car chassis that Beardmore developed a

At the left of this picture is one of the London General Cab Company's distinctive fixed-head Citroën body, fitted to the older, 11.4hp chassis. The body may have been an adaptation of the original Dyer & Holton landaulette body, as fitted to the other Citroën cabs alongside it

chassis they could use to build a cab to meet the new regulations. It was possibly the chassis that they had intended for their 'Jixi', though no records exist to confirm this. Beardmore's brochure for the new cab, the Mk3 stated, "The impression that...any reasonably good motor chassis... is suitable for a taxicab... is very far from being the case." However, close comparison of the Hyper's chassis shows a remarkable similarity to that of the 12/30 car, even down to its wheelbase.

The more compact Mk3 was christened the Hyper after, it is said a competition was held by 'Beardmore News', Beardmore's in-house newspaper. The engine was a cast iron four-cylinder sidevalve unit with separate cylinder liners, unique to the cab. Like the previous engine, it had a detachable head and an electric self-starter. Although at 1954cc it was smaller, it was more powerful than the old engine and returned a fuel consumption of over 26mpg. Much of the improvement was due to good inlet port design, which also increased the time between de-coking. The Mk2's separate four-speed gearbox was

carried over so that the clutch, now a single-plate Ferodo, could be changed easily. Also, it was the first cab to be licensed in London with four-wheel brakes. The bodies, either full- or three-quarter landaulette were made in-house, although one example, G F 5001 was understood to have a body by Ricketts. Fuel consumption was further improved by reducing in the cab's weight to 25cwt. Because it was so economical to run it earned the nickname of the 'Farthing Cab', the farthing then being the smallest coin of the realm.

United Motors Ltd and the Unic KF1

Mann and Overton's continued to hold the concession to sell Unic cars and commercial vehicles after the Great War, but in 1922 this was taken up by United Motors Ltd of North West London. Ernest Mepsted, late of the ill-fated Mepward concern joined the company at this time, becoming managing director in 1927. As production of the Unic cab chassis had ceased in

The Beardmore Hyper was a lighter, more compact cab than the Mk2. It came complete with electric lights it was also the first London cab to be fitted with four-wheel brakes. Before, the PCO would not allow them, as they believed they would encourage furious driving, and would jolt the passengers!

1926 and Unic had ceased to supply Mann and Overton's, so Mepsted was free to talk to them about cabs. In the 1920s Unic made the 11cv Type L, with a 1993cc side-valve engine. Mepsted decided that this would make a good base for a cab and so he formed a new company, Unic Motors (1928) Ltd., to build it at premises in Alperton, near Wembley. He would call the cab the KF1. Imported chassis were modified to meet the Conditions of Fitness and fitted with bodies by Jones and Goode and Cooper and, later Gardner Motors of Willesden, who became Unic Agents. The engine, however, was unreliable and sales of the cab did not amount to much, probably less than 100 in four years of production. Sales were not helped by the cab's price: £575, 'fully equipped', according to a letter sent by United Motors to the Motor Cab Owner-Drivers' Gazette. Mepsted's own Fulham Garage at 296/298 Wandsworth Bridge Road ran more than seventy, the bulk of the production run. Very few would survive the Second World War and the last was taken out of service in the early 1950s.

Major Changes Ahead

Although the amendments to the Conditions of Fitness had achieved the results the PCO had wanted, it is significant that the Morris-Commercial, the new Citroën and the KF1 were the result of dealer and proprietor initiatives rather than those of manufacturers. 898 Morris-Commercial, Citroën and Beardmore cabs were newly licensed in the capital in 1929. This was close to the 1000 a year figure that the PCO thought necessary to maintain the fleet, which had grown to 11,000, partly due to the change in the Conditions of Fitness. But no one could have predicted what was to come next.

The Austin 12/4

With the stockpiled 12/16hp Unic chassis now all but used up and the Morris-Commercial and the Beardmore Hyper on sale, 1929 would be a crucial year for Mann and Overton's. Tom Overton had become involved in another family busi-

The Unic KF1 was a very rare and, sadly unreliable cab. Choices of body maker included Goode and Cooper and Jones. This particular vehicle was found in pieces, after it had finished its working life and restored and is the only known survivor of the model

Compare this 'Chinese' Austin 12/4 High Lot of the London General with the Citroën at the bottom of page 57. The body is identical, but it sits a little better on the Austin chassis

ness and his brother Will had taken over control of the firm, along with their cousin, Herbert Nicholls. But Will Overton would not sit, like Poor Jenny, a-weeping over his predicament, for he had the solution in-house, in the company's Manchester premises, where they were supplying the Austin 12/4 to the cab trade.

By the end of the 1920s, Austin was the second largest car maker in the UK. The Austin 20 had been advertised as 'Austin's American Car'. Herbert Austin had run a Hudson through the Great War and for

the 20, adopted the way it had been engineered for production with what Laurence Pomeroy of 'The Autocar' magazine called a 'fewness of parts'. But, like the Empire Oxford the 20 was too big for the UK and too pricey for the British Empire market against cheap, rugged US makes. It continued in UK production but a new, scaled down version, the 12/4, was one of the two cars that saved Austin from collapse in the early 1920s. The other was of course the legendary Seven.

Manchester and other UK provincial

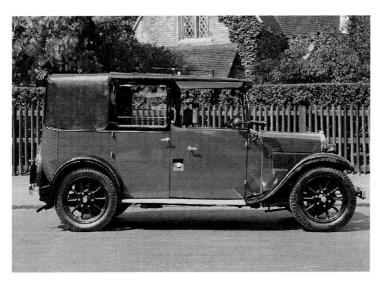

A 1933 Austin 12/4 TT with a Strachan body. The TT had a new four-speed gearbox with synchromesh between third and top gears. The trade gave this model the apt nickname of 'Twin top'. This example was owned by Birch Brothers Ltd

towns and cities could use the Austin 12/4 in standard form because the licensing of hackney cabs in the provinces was, and still is governed by different regulations from London, the Town Police Clauses Act 1847, which is a type of law known as an 'enabling regulation'. This Act allows, but does not compel local police commissioners to license cabs in their area. This power now rests with local authorities, but the Act gives firm rules for the licensing and behaviour of drivers and also give the authorities freedom to choose which type of vehicle to license.

Now that London's Conditions of Fitness had been relaxed, Will Overton turned his thoughts to having the Austin 12/4 adapted to meet them. The chief designer at Austin, Mr A. Harfield was a friend of his and he confirmed that the steering could be modified to meet the turning circle requirement, and brake rods could be substituted for the original cables, as demanded by the Conditions of Fitness. But first, Overton had to get Sir Herbert Austin to agree to the idea, so he went to Longbridge to meet him.

Sir Herbert had a significant number of London dealers to whom he was very loyal and, possibly believing that Overton was chasing yet another dealership, kept him waiting all day, in the hope that he would give up and go home. It was only as Sir Herbert was leaving that Overton confronted him, saying that he was not there on a fool's errand - he wanted to order five hundred specially adapted cab chassis. Sir Herbert recognised Overton's sincerity and agreed to supply him. Austin would gain too. Austin cabs in London would give excellent publicity for the company and gain an advantage over their biggest rival, Morris.

In late 1929, the PCO gave type approval to the Austin 12/4 cab chassis.

Mann and Overton's introduced it in 1930 from their premises at Battersea Bridge Road, and the first vehicle was delivered on June 7. Its 4-cylinder sidevalve engine was already an ageing design, having been introduced in 1922 but it had proved to be a very robust design, that had undoubtedly impressed Will Overton. The cab was also equipped with Austin's new ball-change 4-speed gearbox, which made the vehicle a little easier to drive.

As Austin was only supplying the chassis, Mann and Overton's had to find some coachbuilders. The first 12/4 was fitted with a Dyer and Holton body; probably similar to that fitted to the Unic 12/16hp. Elkington, who were supplying bodies for the provincial 12/4 supplied some more and Chelsea Carriage Co. were known to have provided some too, and Vincent's of Reading were listed in the brochure, but it would be two coachbuilders, Strachan and Jones whose bodies were to prove the most popular in the catalogue. Austin's model code for the cab chassis was HL. The cab trade, fond of nicknames, saw how tall it stood and christened it the 'High Lot'. A healthy 271 Austin cabs were sold in that half-year against annual sales of 535 for Beardmore, Morris-Commercial and Unic KF1 combined.

Of those 271 Austins sold, 196 were sold to the London General Cab Company as bare chassis. The General considered that buying the Austin 12/4 was a much better option than building more Citroëns. They still had the bodies from the old 11.4hp Citroëns in storage and fitted them to the new Austin chassis. The bodies were not a good fit and the General's drivers gave the odd-looking new cabs the nickname 'Chinese' Austins because they had seen how Chinese immigrants mixed western ways with their own culture in ways curious to English eyes. The delivery of more Austin cabs to the General helped Mann and Overton's increase overall sales to 400 in 1931, in contrast to a total of 243 Beardmore, Morris-Commercial and Unic KF1 cabs sold.

A New Morris-Commercial

The G-Type Morris-Commercial International was looking antiquated by the early 1930s, and for 1932 Morris-Commercial introduced the new G2. It was based around the G-Type's chassis but the G-Type's engine was now only available in a 17.9hp version, as the truck for which it was used had been enlarged. This engine would be far too big for the cab, so the 14hp engine from the Morris-Commercial light van was used. This was the Hotchkiss type, Morris's first major production engine and an even older design than that of the Austin 12. The body for the cab was new: it was, like the G-Type's a composite, i. e. pressed steel panels on an ash frame. Because it was lower than the old G-Type, the cab trade nicknamed it the 'Junior'. Availability would be limited.

Morris-Commercial would soon move home, to the old Wolseley plant at Adderley Park and the move would interrupt production.

The Removal of Aged Cabs

Mann and Overton's were not immune to the economic Depression that gripped Britain in the early 1930s: just 309 Austin cabs were sold in 1932 in comparison to 204 others. However, 1933 would be a pivotal year. Now that there were three makers supplying up-to-date models, the Assistant Commissioner of Police, the London Cab Trade's supremo put out a directive, ordering the removal of any cab over fifteen years old from the streets unless it was of exceptional condition. Even then there would be no guarantee of a licence for it if it had been brought up to the standard demanded by the vehicle inspectors. This limit would be brought down to ten years before the decade was out.

For Mann and Overton's, and for Austin, this could not be better or timelier news. Cab masters were now obliged to re-

A Morris-Commercial G2 'Junior' with a factory-built three-quarter landaulette body. A full landaulette body was also available. The full landaulette , with the addition of a full-height driver's door would be fitted to the last pre-war Morris-Commercial, the G2SW

place their aged cabs and Mann and Overton's had a very saleable cab and very little competition. Beardmore Motors had yet to resume production after their move. The Unic KF1 had proved unreliable and would no longer be available and Morris-Commercial production was limited by their factory move. As a result, 834 of the latest model, the TT, with a new four-speed gearbox with constant-mesh between third and top gear were sold against the others' combined sales of 128.

But Austin's success was not due to the scarcity of competition alone. It was a first-class cab in its own right. The big fleet owners liked it because Austin was a big, stable company, the cab was reliable, the spares were readily available and thanks to mass production techniques, its price was kept to a much more affordable level. Crucially, the cab was based on a private car chassis, which mean that Mann and Overton's orders could be fulfilled without interrupting car production. Mann and Overton's could supply a 12/4 cab complete with body for £395, but supplying bare Austin chassis allowed fleet owners to build their own bodies or negotiate a rate with their choice of coachbuilder, which kept their capital outlay low. But what the other makers were not aware of was that Austin were subsidising the production costs of the cab from their advertising budget, and thus undercutting them.

Balloon Tyres

Taximeters were, until, very recently driven by a cable attached to the rear of the cab's gearbox. The reading of the meter depends on the diameter of the wheel and tyre being consistent with the gearing of the meter, and to standardise meter drives, London cabs used a standard tyre and wheel size. Until the late 1920s, the tyre size was 815 x 105, and Dunlop had been making Taxicord tyres in this size, but tyre technology had moved on and the balloon tyre had been introduced. The number of Unics, Citroëns and older Beardmores that used the old tyres were decreasing, but with the arrival of more and more vehicles that used the smaller diameter 20 x 5inch balloon tyres Dunlop would soon cease to make the old types. However, some older cabs were fitted with smaller wheels, to take balloon tyres, enabling those that were still under fifteen years old in 1933 to carry on working. Some actually had, in the changeover period one size on the front axle and another on the rear, because the meter drive was modified to take account of the smaller diameter wheels!

Beardmore Move Home

From the middle of 1929, William Beardmore, Lord Invernairn had struggled to rescue his business empire from collapse. From 1930 onwards, control of the business was taken from him and placed under the control of the banks. In 1932, Francis M. Luther and George Allsworth bought Lord Invernairn's 50 percent stake in the whole taxicab business. Beardmore (Paisley) Ltd. remained within the remnants of the Beardmore group and was reconstructed as a company making high-speed diesel engines for truck and marine applications. They would continue to supply chassis and axles and, for a short period engines and gearboxes. In 1932, Taxi production was moved to the Grove Park, Colindale, North London premises that Luther had taken over when he acquired the Austro-Daimler concession in 1913.

The Beardmore MkIV

Beardmore had a new, MkIV model under development. With the Beardmore engine and gearbox no longer available, Luther and Allsworth turned to William and Reginald Rootes, the Rootes brothers, who were originally car dealers from Maidstone, Kent. The continuing unreliability of their suppliers made them decide to make their own cars, and in 1929 they bought the struggling Coventry company of Humber-Hillman, which also owned Commer commercial vehicles. At the end of the year, they headhunted a new chief engineer, Jack Irving from Sunbeam. Irving had designed Sir Henry Seagrave's land speed record cars, and in 1931, the Rootes brothers sent Irving to Beardmore as a consultant for the MkIV. The Hyper engine was no longer available, but Rootes' new Humber 12 had an excellent 1669cc 4-cylinder sidevalve engine. There was a larger, 1994cc version for a new Commer van, in unit with a four-speed crash gearbox, which Irving recommended for the cab. To accommodate the new power unit,

the Hyper's 9ft wheelbase chassis was altered by replacing the ladder-type cross-members with a substantial X-brace. The front and rear axles were carried over from the Hyper. The new model, christened the Paramount, went on sale in 1934 and its body was a modernised version of the Hyper's, with smart swage lines and domed wings. There would be three body styles available: the full landaulette, the three-quarter landaulette and a fixed-head saloon in a two-door, four-light version for London and a four-door, six light model for the provinces.

Whatever the MkIV's choice of body and specification, Beardmore, like Morris-Commercial lost out to Mann and Overton's Austin, partly because they did not have the production capacity, but with the price set at £435 they had little chance of making any inroads anyway. Capt. Irving had recommended that the price should be higher, but Luther and Allsworth, as directors of the sales company, Beardmore Taxicabs Ltd. knew that the MkIV had to be priced as close as possible to the Austin and the Morris-Commercial.

A new and as-yet unlicensed example of the first Hendon-built Beardmore, the MkIV Paramount, photographed alongside a 1923 Mk1. The man is Stanley Roebuck, who ran a fleet of Beardmore cabs from his Maida Vale premises until the early 1950s

Morris-Commercial Move to Adderley Park

Unlike Austin, whose principal production was private cars with a small number of commercial bodies built on car chassis, Morris placed a greater importance on light commercial vehicles. However, in 1932, they embarked on a new direction and moved the Morris-Commercial factory from its original Soho, Birmingham site where the G-Type cab was built to the old Wolseley plant at Adderley Park, where they would make new, larger trucks and buses. At this time, Morris Motors was experiencing its first ever downturn in business. Britain's economy had slumped once more as a protracted result of the 1929 Wall Street Crash, and Morris's market share was being dented by competition from Ford, Standard and the new Rootes Group. There was little spare cash for new projects and the new engines for the next generation of passenger cars were not yet ready. And, from 1933, all Morris cars of 14hp and over would be powered by six-cylinder engines.

A new cab, the G2S was introduced in late 1934 and would have a sidevalve six of 1938cc, and would be the first London cab to have a six-cylinder engine. The body and chassis were otherwise the same as the G2 and the cab was nicknamed, not surprisingly the 'Junior Six.' Because the Morris-Commercial plant was primarily geared up for truck production, cab production had to be slotted in wherever it could and orders suffered accordingly. Nor would supplies of the specially de-tuned engine, made at the car engine plant, be guaranteed, as the far bigger car market had to be supplied first. After the success of the G-Type, the restriction in supply of cabs would be a disappointment for Watson.

The Austin Low Loader

From 1934, Austin would run down the production of the 12/4 passenger car, whose chassis the cab shared, finally deleting it at the end of 1935. Demonstrating their commitment to the London cab trade, Austin developed a completely new cab chassis from their new Light Six chassis which, although continuing with the original 12/4 engine, rod brakes and modified steering would have an underslung worm drive rear axle and a lower ground clearance than the 7 inches demanded by the Conditions of Fitness. From 1934 this rule was to be eliminated and the change was almost certainly made to allow the new chassis to be type approved. The Home Office realised that they had to compromise with what the motor industry was producing in order to balance the need to keep the cab trade as up to date as possible, whilst keeping faith with those who had invested in the trade and not bring in drastic changes. Certainly, records show that the Home Office did not feel the need to have a full review of the Conditions of Fitness with regard to these changes.

Austin's model code for the new cab was LL, and because it sat lower than the HL and TT, Mann and Overton's described it in the brochure as the 'Low Loading' cab. The trade would call it the 'Low Loader'. Sales were even better than the TT, with 1,111 sold in 1934. Beardmore and Morris-Commercial managed to sell just 302 cabs between them, a reflection of their respective situations. Mann and Overton's were riding high. Tom Overton's son Robert moved from another family business to join Mann and Overton's new finance company, Mechanical Investments Ltd. and Robert's cousin, David Southwell also joined the firm. That

The most numerous of all 1930s London cabs, the Austin 12/4 LL, lined up at the works of the coachbuilder Strachan, in Acton, West London. These cabs are destined for the London General who bought several hundred LLs with Strachan bodies that had a plainer level of trim and an oval back window in place of the standard rectangular one

An Austin 12/4 LL with a standard Jones body, identified by the curls on the front of the roof rack. For a little more money, the purchaser could have the more stylish Jones fishtail body, which had the rear flared out rather than tucked in as on the standard body

As well as the bodies listed in the catalogue, Mann and Overton's would supply a bare chassis. Birch Brothers Ltd fitted this rather plain landaulette body to around 50 LL chassis, for their own fleet.

year the company went public, and changed its name slightly, to Mann and Overton. 1935 would be their best year yet, with 1,178 Austin cabs sold.

W & G go into Receivership

In 1935, receivers were appointed to STD Motors Ltd. of Acton. W. and G. du Cros, which was now part of STD was disposed of. Two years later, William du Cros died, aged 63.

The Beardmore MkV

In 1935 Beardmore introduced a MkV, named the Paramount Ace. The Paisley factory would soon close and there would be no more of the old-type chassis made, so Beardmore acquired a new 9' 6" wheelbase chassis of a similar design to that used on larger Hillman cars, with a beam axle and leaf spring front suspension. The Commer engine was retained, but the crash gearbox was replaced by the four-speed gearbox from Rootes' large passenger cars, which had synchromesh on third and top gears. The MkV exceeded the 14ft maximum length previously allowed by the Conditions of Fitness. The Home Office conceded this amendment with the same attitude as they did the minimum ground clearance rule.

Changes for Mann and Overton and Austin

The Austin LL remained current for 1936 and 1937, with a lower than previous 875 and 659 sold respectively. Although the British economy was once again in recession, Mann and Overton now regained the mantle that Beardmore had taken from them in the 1920s, that of the major supplier of cabs in London, but this time with Austin instead of Unic. Combined sales of the Morris-Commercial and the Beardmore dropped, although gaining an improved share in 1936, with 307 sold. In 1937 they both crashed, with a mere 96 combined. In 1938, Ernest Mepsted sold his Fulham Garage, at 296/298 Wandsworth Bridge Road to Mann and Overton. They would remain in this building for over half a century.

The Austin FL 'Flash Lot'

In 1938, Austin brought out a revised model, the FL. It carried a grille shell similar to the mid-1930s passenger cars and coachbuilders made a 'streamlined' body to match it, with a full height door with a wind-up window. Underneath, however, it was the same LL running gear, the only difference being the relocation of the fuel tank to the rear, as the PCO had decided that it was not such a hazard as they had first thought. Only 213 of these were sold that year, principally for two reasons. In 1934 and 1935, the big fleets had invested in considerable numbers of Austin LLs, which would not need replacing for a while. Much worse, war was looming and the British economy was in recession once more. Cab masters had spent their available money bringing their fleets up to date and would hang on to the rest of their money.

Preparations for war had made considerable demands on raw materials and non-military users found prices already escalating. In 1939 Mann and Overton advertised that their coachbuilders had 'large stocks of materials in hand' but were 'compelled to make the same additional

The last of the 12/4 series was the FL. It used the same design of radiator shell of late 1930s Austin private cars and it was optimistically described as 'streamlined'. This body is the standard Jones landaulette

charge in July of £8/15/0d (£8.75) to cover extra costs'. August 1939 saw Mann and Overton deliver 32 new and 8 reconditioned cabs, which was something of an achievement in the circumstances.

The Morris-Commercial G2SW

Also new for 1938 was the Morris-Commercial G2SW. Morris had replaced the G2S's sidevalve six with the 1818cc OHV six used in the Morris 14 Series III. As permitted by a change in the Condi-

tions of Fitness, the fuel tank was relocated to the rear of the cab. The body was basically the same composite construction landaulette as the G2S, but fitted with a full driver's door with wind-up window to take advantage of the change in the Conditions of Fitness. The G2SW sold for £405 and possibly with this model, Morris-Commercial could have gained a little ground on Austin and Beardmore, but in 1938, Beardmore and Morris-Commercial managed to sell only 65 cabs between them in London. Beardmore suffered from their small production facility and the cab's higher price, whilst at Adderley Park,

This FL carries a 'fishtail' style of body, which was a popular, if slightly more expensive alternative to the standard body. Fishtail bodies had also been available for the Low Loader.
The steel artillery wheels were retained on the FL, as they accommodated the special Dunlop Taxicord tyres

Austin 12/4 FL cabs, some with bodies, some waiting to be delivered to coachbuilders lined up in Mann and Overton's dealership in Battersea Bridge Road. Shortly after this picture was taken, Mann and Overton moved to new premises in Wandsworth Bridge Road

Morris-Commercial were still placing priority on high-profit commercial vehicles and now military vehicles, as war loomed over Europe.

The Beardmore MkVI

The last pre-war Beardmore was the MkVI Ace of 1938. It was not, the brochure announced 'an entirely new Beardmore. Just an up-to-date production embodying twenty years' practical experience in cab building, with such additions and refinements as the modern trend demands.' These 'additions and refinements' earned Beardmore the nickname of the 'greengrocer's barrow', as, it was said, 'all the best was in the front!' The MkVI carried on this tradition, offering a full driver's door window, although for this feature the purchaser had to pay an additional £5. The Ace also had an all-synchromesh gearbox, developed for the new 1939 Hillman Minx. The price was £480 for the single landaulette and £485 for the three-quarter landaulette. Production was tiny, and in January 1939 Beardmore Taxicabs Ltd., the sales company was liquidated in preparation for a new liaison with William Morris's Nuffield Organisation.

Private Hire Licensing and Cheaper Cabs

The first real challenge to the licensed cab trade's method of operation came in 1938, when a type of private hire car, fitted with taximeters set at a lower rate than taxi fares and called 'Streamliners', began operating in outer London. The instigation of a suburban cab driver's licence to try and provide some local competition angered private hire operators, who felt that the suburbs were their domain. Many 'streamline' groups were opened, sometimes employing licensed cab drivers and paying them a set wage. The Joint Trade Committee asked the Home Secretary, Sir Samuel Hoare to investigate with the view to licensing private hire. He commissioned the Hindley Report, which was published in January 1939 and recommended that the private hire trade should indeed be licensed.

The report was not acted upon, and fuel rationing during the Second World War crippled the operations of the 'Streamliners'. Part of the report looked the possibility of seeing cabs being replaced at more frequent intervals than ten years, which, it suggested, would be achieved by manufacturing vehicles to sell

An illustration from the Morris G2SW 'Super Six' brochure. Like the MkVI Beardmore and Austin FL, the driver's door had full glass

at a cheaper price. By saying that 'there would be no economy in using vehicles as lightly built as the ordinary mass-produced private car of similar horsepower', the Commissioner was mindful of the hard work that a London cab did. But he was aware that cab riders would prefer to ride in up-to-date vehicles. As for price, an Austin 12 cab cost around £395 when the new Austin 12 private car sold for around

£200. Building a slightly less robust cab to sell at around £300, and thus introduce a lower tariff, might he felt, result in 'a permanent increase in hirings', and would be 'in the best interests of the trade'. The economic and political situation did not improve through 1939 and the debate over cheaper cabs was swamped by the more urgent demands of war.

The MkVI Beardmore Ace. The extra length of the new chassis meant a bigger passenger door could be fitted and the back axle was moved to a position behind the rear seat instead of slightly in front, giving the passengers a more comfortable ride. A three-quarter landaulette body was also available

Chapter 6
The Second World War

When, in 1939 war broke out again, one lesson had been learned from the Great War, and that was that it would involve every citizen and the whole country was mentally, if not altogether materially, ready for a long fight. Rearmament had been under way since 1938, the Territorial Army had already been mobilised and when war finally broke out children were evacuated to the countryside and everyone carried gas masks in preparation for German aerial gas attacks. In reality, very little happened at first, either in the way of actual fighting or to the civilian population at home. The British Expeditionary Force (BEF) was sent to France to assist the French against a German invasion but stood by, waiting, in what was known as the 'Phoney War' as Germany conquered Poland and Norway. Then in May 1940, the Germans crashed through Belgium, drove the BEF out of France and in July launched an aerial attack on Southern England. With this attack, the Battle of Britain and the Blitz that followed, the war was brought to Britain's doorstep. London's cab trade would be in the thick of it.

Beardmore and a New Nuffield Cab

In the first few months of the war, the cab trade, like the rest of the country carried on as normal an existence as possible. Beardmore ceased manufacture before the outbreak of war and the Colindale works were turned over to the manufacture of

The Oxford prototype, photographed at the Wolseley factory at Ward End, Birmingham after completing its trails with Beardmore Motors. Note the one-piece windscreen, the first ever to be fitted to a London cab and the new, smaller, 18-inch wheels

aircraft components, gun parts and electronic gear for rockets. Their showroom at 112 Great Portland Street was demolished in the Blitz, and business was transferred to 167-169 Great Portland Street, which had been the offices of Francis Luther's Austro-Daimler Concessionaires.

Beardmore were still interested in the cab trade, and Francis Luther negotiated with Nuffield to replace William Watson as the London agent for Morris-Commercial cabs. Before the outbreak of war, Nuffield had begun work on a new cab. Whereas the previous models had come from, originally Soho and later Adderley Park, the new vehicle would be a product of the Wolseley factory at Ward End, Birmingham. It had a new solid box-section, X-braced chassis, designed by Charles van Eugen, a Dutchman who had joined Riley from Lea-Francis in 1938, only to find Riley taken over by Nuffield. To power the cab, the engineers in the Marine and Commercial Division of the newly-formed Nuffield organisation built a unique derivation of the XP series engine used in the Morris 10 and MG Midget. It had a capacity of 1.8 litres and a dry sump with an oil tank mounted below the cab's radiator. In 1940, the chassis was fitted with a conventional coachbuilt landaulette body by Jones Brothers of Westbourne Grove, painted dark blue. This prototype, registration no EOM 844, was presented for approval on July 15 1940.

Based at Beardmore Motors' depot in Kentish Town, North London the cab covered some 300,000 miles throughout the war at the hands of Roy Perkins who had become, just after his 21st birthday in 1938 one of the youngest men to hold a cab licence. Perkins had been exempted from National Service on medical grounds, as he had suffered an injury as a child that left him with a permanent limp. To enable

Perkins to cover sufficient mileage, Beardmore drew petrol from the ration of other cabs in their fleet. Perkins would record every detail of every job he did and even such details as how many times he stopped at traffic lights. With the help of his wife Alice, he collated this information and presented it to Nuffield in the form of regular reports. Naturally, Nuffield took a keen interest in the cab's development, with Wolseley's chairman, Charles Mullens making regular visits to London to check on progress. Perkins would pick him up from, and return him to the railway station, which gave Mullens a chance to ask Roy about the cab's progress and to discover first hand how it was running.

Cabs and Cabmen in the Auxiliary Fire Service

Before 1938 the British government followed a policy of appeasing the Fascist dictators in Europe and made no formal preparations for war. Only individuals and private organisations had the foresight to make such preparations. One such exception within government was A. L. Dixon, the Assistant Under-Secretary of State with responsibility for the Police Division of the Home Office. He had recently been given responsibility for the new Fire Brigades Division. He knew of the 'Blitzkreig', the lightning war that the Nazis had prosecuted in the Spanish Civil War and he had recognised the damage that concentrated aerial bombardment had caused to towns and cities. In partial preparation for the possibility of similar action against Britain, he instigated the design of fire pumps, either for installation in boats and lorries or mounted on a trailer. By early 1939, 2,800 pumps had been made and deployed.

A 1935 Austin LL belonging to the London General Cab Company, newly equipped with London Auxiliary Fire Service equipment. It may not actually have entered service as a fire appliance when this picture was taken, as it still has a meter fitted. Later, all requisitioned cabs would carry the grey livery of the Auxiliary Fire Service, but already the cab has white paint applied to the wings to make it more visible in the blackout

In 1938 an Act of Parliament was passed to allow the formation of the Auxiliary Fire Service. This enabled fire brigades throughout the UK to enlist volunteer fire fighters and commandeer, where appropriate suitable vehicles. The London Fire Brigade (LFB) knew that with its peacetime strength it would not have the slightest chance of dealing with a major series of air raids. Before the trailer pumps had been distributed, it had been assumed that there would be enough lorries and large cars available for the AFS to commandeer to tow them. On further investigation, it turned out that there were not. The Cab Trade Committee of the Transport and General Workers' Union foresaw this and in 1938 wrote to Herbert Morrison, a prominent MP and the former leader of the London County Council. They suggested that the AFS recruited cabmen and their taxicabs. They argued

The five-man AFS crew of this MkV Beardmore look very smart. The cab has yet to be painted in AFS livery so this picture may well have been taken around 1940. It may possibly be part of an AFS division stationed in Hendon, even attached to Beardmore's own factory

that if the route to a blaze was blocked through bomb damage, the men would know the quickest way around, and the cabs could, it was anticipated, be able to tow the pumps.

Morrison spoke to the head of the LFB, Sir Aylmer Firebrace, who liked the idea. He contacted departments of the government to see if they already had any plans to commandeer cabs for their own use. They had not, so immediately after the Act came into force, the LFB borrowed an Austin 12, BYV 35, from the London General and fitted it with a tow bar and bracket, designed to tow a trailer pump. Described as a 'sound engineering job,' the tow bar was passed by the PCO in November 1938. In 1938 a list was compiled of all London fleet proprietors and the cabs they owned, to assess how many would be available. Then in January 1939 the LFB began to requisition a significant number of cabs and cabmen to drive them. All the cabs would come from fleets so as not to risk the property of owner-drivers. The AFS would offer cabmen a wage of £3 per week for 12-hour shifts, which would ally the fears of those who knew of the difficulties faced by their older colleagues in the Great War.

At first, the scheme called for 2000 cabs, which was a significant slice of the 10,000 or so that were then licensed. Towing brackets for different types of cab were designed and made, but it was decided that the AFS would use the Strachan-bodied Austin LL, the most numerous type of cab in London, to simplify the design of the towbars. Cabs were requisitioned from eight of the largest proprietors and the first batch of towing brackets were sent to them, with orders that they should fit them. W. H. Cook of Chiswick surrendered the most, 54 with Taxicabs (London) of Hammersmith giving up 50 of

their cabs, the London General and The Great Cambridge Garage, E4 giving up 25 each. Further brackets were sent to Birch Brothers of Kentish Town and later to up to 30 different garages by August 1939. The cabs' proprietors had to surrender the licence plates, as the vehicles would not be suitable for hire. A total of 1,782 plates were surrendered, one sixth of the cabs in London. Most of those remaining were owner-driven or were either older, less reliable types or those whose bodies were of such a design that would make fitting the towing brackets difficult or uneconomical.

On September 1 1939, the day the Germans invaded Poland, the AFS was mobilised, and, two days later when Britain declared war on Germany, London's auxiliary firemen were told to report to their stations. They were formed into crews, five to a Trailer Pump (TP) unit consisting of cab and trailer and were posted one to each of London's street fire alarms. For the first few weeks the crews were stationed on street corners, with no food or shelter and they had little in the way of protective clothing or equipment, save a tin hat, some rubber boots, a gas mask and belt with an axe. But soon, sub-stations were set up, often in whatever buildings could be requisitioned and proper equipment and uniforms were provided for the crews. Between ten and twenty cabs were housed in a sub-station, alongside larger appliances, such as Heavy Units (HUs), turntable ladders and Escape Carrying Units, (ECU) all crewed by up to a total 30,000 auxiliary firemen and women. Some fire stations in London had more than 1,000 auxiliaries attached, so large was the anticipated scale of the air raids. The proposed twelve-hour shifts were replaced with a three-watch system, with 24 hours on, 48 hours off and the firemen were paid £2/18/5d (£2.92) per week. The cab proprietors were paid £1/17/6d (£1.87) a week for the hire of the cabs.

The period of the 'Phoney War' gave the AFS time to mount exercises to train the crews. It was on one such exercise, on Hampstead Heath that the AFS discovered that the Austin 12 was not powerful enough to tow the trailers. When the cabs failed to climb Haverstock Hill, Hampstead the crews were ordered to get out and push! However, some better-off AFS volunteers offered their own private cars for towing trailers, which the AFS accepted with alacrity, especially as most of the cars were large, including many American models that were much more powerful than cabs. Some, if not all of these were converted to vans and pickup trucks. In view of the severe petrol rationing, the owners were glad to see the cars put to good use rather than be laid up for the duration, if not lost forever. The result was that at the end of 1940, 2124 of the 2381 cabs that had been taken out of work were returned to their owners, leaving just over 257 with the AFS.

Despite the government saying originally that they had no specific need for cabs in wartime, the AFS would not be the only users. Over and above the number retained by the AFS, 14 were requisitioned by the LCC and some London boroughs, which were fitted with ambulance bodies. 12 were used for rescue and demolition work and 64 were designated for what was described as 'staff care'. In 1940 the remaining AFS cabs were painted grey to match the other vehicles.

On September 7 1940, the first night of the Blitz, the AFS went into action, employing nearly 1000 appliances, including the cabs. The Luftwaffe would cause extensive damage all across London, and indeed the UK, with huge areas sites devastated. These larger fires could truly

be handled by larger appliances, but the true value of the trailer units was in containing smaller fires that would be inaccessible otherwise.

The AFS continued serving throughout the Blitz until its end in May 1941. In August 1941, all local fire brigades in Britain were nationalised, to form the National Fire Service and the AFS was incorporated into the new organisation. The NFS served throughout the war, dealing with the V1 and V2 rocket attacks of 1944 and 1945. Whilst AFS volunteers were originally thought of as men who were trying to avoid conscription into the armed forces, their critics were quick to recognise the dangerous work they did. Prime Minister Winston Churchill described them as 'the heroes with grubby faces.'

Mann and Overton Struggle On

At the outbreak of war, Mann and Overton were able to supply new cabs. Indeed, there were a significant number awaiting delivery. As the war progressed, shortages of materials made delivery more and more difficult. Prices were gradually increased, and in 1940 purchase tax of 33.3 percent was levied on the wholesale price of the vehicle. By March 1941, a new Austin cost £451. In late 1941, what were described as 'government restrictions' on the supply of raw materials curtailed manufacture. From then on, Mann and Overton increased the capability of their machine shop to make or recondition such spare parts as they could. They ventured, for the only time in their existence, into the fleet business, running their own cabs, buying, in 1944 the Star Garage and Parsons Green Garage, both near to their Fulham premises. An advertisement placed by

Mann and Overton in 'The Steering Wheel' in April 1945, just a month before VE Day, advised of the expected supply of mechanical and body components for cabs of more than ten years old.

Wartime for Cabmen

The London cabman was as a much victim of the attention of the PCO in wartime as he was of the bombs of the Luftwaffe. The laws governing the blackout were strictly enforced, and rightly so, for any light from the ground might make a target for the enemy. To maintain a total blackout, street lights were not turned on at lighting up time and motor vehicle lights had to be masked. Special headlight masks were made and it was compulsory for them to be fitted to all motor vehicles, taxicabs included, from January 22 1940, but Joseph Lucas, the manufacturer had neglected to obtain approval for them from the PCO for use on cabs. Thus until the masks had been approved, cabmen had to suffer the ludicrous situation of having

An evocative picture of a 1936 Austin LL, turning south around Trafalgar Square. This picture may have been taken early on in the war, as although the cab has headlight masks, it does not have white paint on the wings

Carriage Officers order them to remove the headlight masks, rendering them liable to prosecution by the police.

Petrol Rationing was introduced on September 16 1939. Posters urged people to consider the question, 'Is your journey really necessary?' but for the cabman, who would sometimes provide a far better service than public transport could offer, the initial limit of 2 gallons a day was punitive. It was barely enough for a one cabman, let alone a double team and this, along with the short-lived fiasco of the headlight masks drove cabmen to work days in a time when the blackout made their availability to provide safe transport at night all the more desirable. Ken Drummond, chairman of the Motor Cab Owner-Drivers' Association (MCODA) pushed for more, claiming with justification that petrol was the cabman's 'bread and butter'. In December 1940, just after the start of the Blitz, an extra 20 gallons of petrol per month was made available. This, at the request of the Secretary of Mines was further increased, to an additional 30 gallons per month. Although far from generous, this would be recognition of the valuable work performed by the cab trade throughout the war when public transport had been steadily reduced.

When air raids were imminent, the cabmen themselves often wore army-type tin helmets (one imagines that some of these were relics of the Great War, worn by the very cabmen who had served in that conflict) and at the sound of the air raid sirens, would be prepared to take cover in the nearest air raid shelter. The difficulty of driving in virtually total darkness is hard enough to imagine, but these were compounded by the constantly changing hazards and road closures caused by bomb damage and by pedestrians, who themselves were struggling to find their way through the darkness with torches, the lenses covered in brown paper. A 20mph speed limit imposed for the duration was an important rule in maintaining safety, but it is to the cab trade's credit that the accident rate actually fell during the war.

The war forced changes to the licensing regime. The restricted, and eventual non-availability of new cabs prompted the Commissioner of Police to suspend the practice of the PCO 'inviting' cab owners to scrap their vehicles when they had reached ten years of age or the end of their tenth plate. The Commissioner also allowed owner-drivers who had laid up their cabs for the duration should be allowed to have a full tens years' service from their cabs, to be counted from the time the cab was laid up.

The large number of American troops stationed in and around London after 1941 provided a harvest for cabmen in a number of ways. The Americans were described, rather sourly as 'over-paid, over-sexed and over here'. Their much higher wages allowed them to become regular cab riders, the only downside being that they loved the 'cute' fold-down heads of the landaulette bodies, and in warm weather insisted on lowering them. This upset a lot of cabmen, as the joins between the fold down part and the fixed part of these roofs had been sealed to stop them leaking in the rain and these enthusiastic and boisterous GIs were ripping open the seals!

The 'over-sexed' amongst them, most of whom were barely more than boys, with pockets full of money, very little if any sexual experience and the realisation that they may not live to see the next day were eager custom for girls intent on a good time, professional or otherwise. A cab, with the discretion afforded by its landaulette hood provided a convenient place for what we might call 'intimate transac-

tions'. There were stories of a small number of cabmen who supplied their cabs for such work on a regular basis. In Lisle Street, Soho was the Beaufort Club, where these cabmen could play snooker or billiards and generally take a break. The Shaftesbury Theatre, next door had been bombed and the site was surrounded by hoardings. The ground was used as a car park, with space for perhaps a dozen vehicles. The old boy who worked there would, with the cabmen's blessing allow the empty cabs parked there to be used by the 'ladies of the night', ensuring that the cabs were returned clean and that the cabman received a tidy sum of money, perhaps as much as £20 for the use of the cab. It was certainly safer than driving in the blacked-out streets and they didn't have to use a single drop of petrol!

THE OWNER-DRIVER AND M.C.O.D.A. GAZETTE.   SEPTEMBER 1940.

POLICE NOTICE

ACTION TO BE TAKEN BY DRIVERS OF CABS DURING AIR-RAID WARNINGS.

1. Cab drivers who decide to take cover when an air-raid warning is given should:

   (i) stop as soon as they come to a suitable place where they and their passengers (if any) can find shelter, and park their vehicle in an unobstructive position on a rank, or by the kerb, or in a garage, or open space off the highway if possible;

   (ii) see that no article of value is left in the cab;

   (iii) immobilise the vehicle by taking away an essential part of the mechanism or by locking the steering wheel;

   (iv) switch out all lights except the side and rear lamps. If on a cab rank, only the front and rear vehicles need be lighted.

2. Cab drivers who decide to continue to ply for hire must clearly understand that they are bound by the charges shown on the fare table inside the cab. As in the case of other forms of public transport, no additional charges may be made on account of an air-raid warning.

If a driver decides to remain with his cab on a cab rank he will be regarded as plying for hire; he must therefore accept hirings just as if the air-raid warning had not sounded.

The Commissioner will take serious notice of any case where it is established that drivers, when plying for hire during an air-raid warning, refuse to take passengers except at special rates.

At night, drivers must not use headlights during an air-raid warning.

New Scotland Yard,
6th September, 1940.

The Public Carriage Office maintained as high a level of discipline during the war as it did in peacetime; perhaps even higher, as this notice shows

The Home Guard

At the beginning of the war, conscription took a substantial number of young men in their twenties from all walks of life, including the cab trade. After the retreat from France, Britain and her Allies began rebuilding the armed forces. Call-up would be extended to men in their thirties and, later in their forties. Not only that, but cabmen who had other skills were transferred to industry and other jobs known as 'reserved occupations' to help with the war effort, which, although vital in keeping the front line troops well supported further depleted the numbers of working cabmen.

Some of the men remaining went into the Home Guard, the fighting unit originally formed in May 14 1940 as the Local Defence Volunteers, whose task was to act as a rear guard against a German invasion while the army formed the front line. Home Guard personnel consisted of men too old or too young for enlistment but who would nevertheless be fit enough to defend their country, as well as those in reserved occupations. Home Guard battalions were formed from all walks of life, including small communities, factories and trades. In the spring of 1941 a London Taxicab Battalion was formed, recruiting cabmen and others in the cab trade. The Home Guard London District Commanding Officer, Brig. J. Whitehead wrote to the MCODA Gazette, saying:

"In response to the many enquiries which have been made, I desire to confirm that the men enrolling in the 59th County of London (Taxi) Battalion, Home Guard, will be called upon only when an emergency arises for the sole purpose of driving (or maintaining) taxicabs according to the declaration made upon their Enrolment Forms.

There are no parades, guards or drills for the men of this Battalion, who will be required for work in connection with the local defence of an area where their particular knowledge will be invaluable in the circumstances which may prevail.

It is for this reason that an urgent appeal is now made to taxicab drivers throughout London to enrol in this Battalion for this particular work, in order that we may be fully prepared to meet the emergency when it arises."

There would be provision for payment of up to 10/- (50p) per day when called up for full time service as a compensation for

Dad's Army: cabs of the London (Taxi) Battalion on exercise with a detachment of the County of London Home Guard

loss of normal earnings.

Proprietors who loaned their cabs to the Home Guard were paid 9d (3.75p) per mile for the use of the vehicle, plus an extra petrol ration. Cabmen have always been notoriously difficult to organise, but despite a very shaky start the Taxi Battalion grew, according to one of its members, Simon Kogan, into 'an efficient body of men, disciplined and well trained.'

Coping with Difficult Times

As the war progressed, the shortage of spare parts and the loss of vehicles to bomb damage became more acute and the ten-year life of a cab was extended by the PCO to minimise that loss. Shortage of tyres was also a problem with, at one point, cab proprietors having to obtain consent from a Carriage Officer to have a tyre retreaded. Fuel availability resulted in other road users calling on the cab trade to help them out. Some cases were from those in genuine need but others were from those all too happy to take advantage. There were stories of wealthy women sending cabs to collect their shopping instead of using their own cars and companies using cabs to make deliveries when they wanted to save their own petrol ration. The Motor Fuel (Cab Service) Order, 1942 would prevent private individuals from using cabs to make long journeys for which they would have used their private cars. The order did this by restricting journeys made by cab to those 'within the area in which they are licensed to ply for hire plus a distance not exceeding five miles beyond the boundary of the area.'

Tributes for Wartime Cabmen

When the war finally ended in August 1945, many members of the public expressed their gratitude. One letter in 'The Times' said,

"When handing out awards for gallantry is finally made, I hope the London taxi driver will not be forgotten. Invariably cheerful, invariably when wanted, night or day, he will take you anywhere and appears to have no thought at all for his personal safety. Post offices close down, banks cease to function but after the crash of the bombs comes the starting up again of the taxi's engine."

Columnist Oliver Stewart of 'The Tatler' wrote:

"I think that most Londoners will join me in paying tribute to the taxi men. At many times they are the only above-ground transport that keeps at it."

But however hard the trade had struggled and whatever accolades its members received, London's cab fleet had suffered as much damage as it had in the Great War. It would take at least as long to rebuild as it had in the 1920s.

Chapter 7

Steel Bodies and Diesel Engines

As 1945 began, Britain and her allies were confident that it was not a matter of whether the war would be won, but when. The parts of the British motor industry that had survived the conflict were already gearing up to produce their pre-war models, as an interim measure before introducing any new products that they were able to develop. For once, the cab trade would be ahead of the industry in introducing new models: not because it chose to, but because it had to, as all the pre-war models were out of production.

The Oxford Cab

By mid 1945 Nuffield were happy with the way the Oxford had performed in its protracted test and decided that they wanted to put it into production. The Home Office had been considering a review the Conditions of Fitness, so Jack Hellberg of Nuffield's Marine and Industrial Division wrote to them, asking if they were going to do so, as any changes might severely compromise the new cab. He was told that the regulations would stay the same, with the exception of that the landaulette body would be prohibited, as they decided that they now wanted cabs to resemble, as much as was possible modern saloon cars although, as they stated there must be 'demarcation between car and cab'.

By a great effort Nuffield's engineers, under the guidance of chief experimental engineer Charles Griffin got the cab type-approved by the PCO in late 1946. A four-door hire car version would also be made.

At the end of World War II, the Taxicab Fleet Operators' Federation commissioned this body on an Austin FL chassis to illustrate the kind of body they thought would be most suitable for post-war operations, considering the PCO's requirement to have cabs that more closely resembled private cars. The landaulette hood was gone and the lines were much simpler

The prototype of the production Nuffield Oxford, photographed at Ward End. The wheels are 18 inch, although still of the steel artillery type

The cab would have a completely new composite body, of pressed steel panels over an ash frame with a fixed head. The first new cab to be offered in peacetime, it was put into production in 1947 at Nuffield's Ward End factory, with some made at Drews Lane, Birmingham until 1949. Production was then transferred to the Morris-Commercial plant at Adderley Park, Birmingham.

The engine was the prototype's 1803cc dry-sump unit, with a four-speed manual gearbox and the channel section chassis, made by Rubery Owen in Birmingham had semi-elliptical spring suspension all round. With William Watson's retirement, the way was open for Beardmore to take over the dealership. Further, Beardmore had secured steel allocations, which were very difficult to come by in the post war years. The government had issued the decree that Britain must 'export or expire', and the biggest exporters would receive the biggest amounts of steel. But the London taxi, being for a specific, non-export market would be exempt from this ruling. The deal was that Nuffield would receive Beardmore's steel allocation, which would

The hope of future prosperity can be sensed in this publicity picture of the Series I Oxford, taken near Regent's Park in the winter of late 1947

enable them to build the Oxford, in exchange for Beardmore selling and servicing the cab. Also, Beardmore would recondition as many of their own 1930s models as they could get hold of, and sell them on to cab drivers desperate to get at what little work there was in the austere post-war years.

The war had caused a considerable amount of inflation, and the purchase tax of 33.3 percent that had been levied on all new private cars and cabs in 1940 still remained in place. The new Oxford would cost £780 plus £217/8/4d (£217.42p) purchase tax, a total of £997/8/4d (297.42p) , more than double that of its predecessor, the Morris-Commercial G2SW. At that price, the cab trade could not afford to buy enough Oxfords to replace the cabs lost during the war. Petrol too was more expensive, fares were stuck on the tariff of the 1930s and there was very little money in people's pockets to spend on luxuries and little business going on for people to need cabs, let alone afford cab fares. The trade would struggle on for a good few years, driving repaired pre-war models, some built as far back as 1930.

The Austin FX and FX2

With the 12/4 chassis out of production, Mann and Overton had no new model to sell. They had managed to buy in a number of pre-war cabs in almost new condition that had been requisitioned by the AFS, but apparently had not been used, which met some of the demand. Leonard Lord, the head of Austin, assured Robert Overton that he was committed to the London cab trade. Lord had registered the name 'Taxicar' with the Society of Motor Manufacturers and Traders, but thankfully he decided not to use it. Of

more practical use was the new cab chassis that Austin produced in late 1945. This was numbered, in line with Austin's numbering system as the FX. It had a 14hp, 1.8-litre sidevalve engine, being an overbored version of the current 12hp unit. Mann and Overton fitted the chassis with a pre-war body and put it on test, but it was not up to the job. By the end of 1946, Phil Baker of Austin's chassis design department had designed a new chassis that, according to Austin's J. W. R. Penrose,

"caused some considerable amount of work for our drawing office over and above new models the Company is introducing at the moment."

The new chassis was numbered FX2 and it was a conventional 'double drop' with semi-elliptical springs, a beam front axle, lever-arm hydraulic shock absorbers and rod-operated brakes. Even this late, Austin had not adopted hydraulic brakes, so it was no surprise that they were not about to experiment with something new to them for a vehicle with such a limited market. The gearbox was a rugged four-speed manual with synchromesh on second, third and top gears. What was an innovation for Austin was the overhead valve engine, which was a 1.8-litre four-cylinder version of the 6-cylinder, K-Series 3.5 litre lorry engine, and the PCO gave type approval to the chassis on March 9 1947. This engine had not started life as a passenger car or light commercial engine at all: it was actually developed as a power unit for a British version of the legendary Willys Jeep. When the Jeep had begun to arrive in the UK from the USA, the Atlantic convoys were suffering huge losses and it was felt that Britain needed to produce its own version. But the Battle of the Atlantic, where the Nazi U-boat menace was quelled, resulted in far greater quantities of American hardware and the project

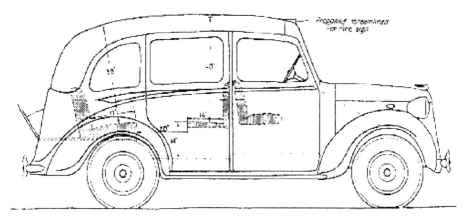

'The Cab you will operate in the Future' is how Mann and Overton announced the new Austin 14 in 'The Steering Wheel' trade paper of January 12 1946. Although slightly more modern than the FL of 1938, it was still very traditional in appearance

was delayed until after the war. This left Austin with a very useful engine for passenger car and light commercial use. Fitted would be an hydraulic Jackall system which would jack up any or all of the wheels of the cab without the need of a separate jack.

Then there was the matter of the body. A traditional coachbuilt body was out of the question. Even if the labour could be found, it would be far too expensive, timber to build it was scarce and repairs would be costly. An all-steel body was what was wanted but Austin would be struggling for manufacturing capacity for their passenger car bodies. They certainly had no room to build around fifteen bodies a week for the cab. Luckily, Joe Edwards of Austin knew just the people who could help. During the war, Austin needed

The Austin 14 FX chassis as delivered to Mann and Overton in December 1945. This was the first cab since to have disc wheels, although it is not possible to establish whether they were 18-inch, or the newer 16-inch that would be fitted to the FX2 Just visible under the wheel arch is the cylinder of the Jackall hydraulic jacking system

some expertise in making aircraft fuselage panels and got together with Carbodies, a company on the west side of Coventry who had supplied MG with bodies and had gone on to provide special coachwork for the Rootes Group and Rover.

Under Lend-Lease, Carbodies had been supplied with press tools and metal-working tools, plus a remarkable material called Kirksite, a low-melting point alloy from which press tools for limited production runs could be made at an economical cost. Edwards got the Ministry of Supply to invite Robert Overton of Mann and Overton to a meeting at the Ministry of Supply where he met Carbodies' managing director, Ernest Jones and works manager John Orr. With Kirksite tools, Carbodies were sure they could build the body at a realistic price, and a deal was struck to develop the cab. Austin would supply the chassis to Carbodies, who would build the body, mount it, paint and trim it and deliver the complete cab to Mann and Overton in London. Mann and Overton would provide 50% of the money, with Carbodies and Austin supplying 25% each of the balance. This gave Mann and Overton the major share in the cab as well as the exclusive right to London sales.

Carbodies produced a coachbuilt prototype body on the FX2 chassis, and on the 20th of May Robert Overton and Herbert Nicholls of Mann and Overton and vehicle inspectors from the PCO went to Carbodies to look at it. They were generally pleased with the light and airy appearance of it in comparison to the pre-war landaulettes. To compare it with pre-war cabs, the additional windows were blanked out with a board, but it changed the appearance from '...an up-to-date modern appearance to that of a drab, old-fashioned vehicle...' so the new design was kept, although the privacy valued by certain passengers at night had not been completely abandoned. Darkened glass was to be used in the small back window, and no interior driving mirror would be allowed.

The FX3

The FX2 received type approval in June 1947, but the following October Austin announced that they would not be making the 14hp and 18hp cars they had first planned, but an interim 16hp model with a 2.2 litre engine, which would now be supplied for the new cab. In October 1948

The FX2, photographed by Carbodies Ltd.'s managing director, Ernest Jones at one of his favourite locations, Charlecote Park, near Warwick.
This vehicle had a coachbuilt body clad in aluminium. It would remain in service until the 1970s in York

a second prototype was built with a pressed steel body and was given a new model number- FX3. Mann and Overton announced it to the cab trade on June 11 1948 and two steel bodied examples went out for trials. JXN 841 went to Central Autos of Chelsea and the steel bodied cab, JXN 842 went to W. H. Cook of West London. The FX3 had its formal introduction at the 1948 Commercial Motor Transport Exhibition at Earls Court that November alongside its four-door FL1 hire car version. It was offered in standard black cellulose for £936, including purchase tax at 33.3 percent, with alternative colours at extra cost. Thirteen more FX3s were commissioned in London between December 1948 and January 1949. The FX2 was registered as JXN 841. No record exists of who bought it, although it did end its service life in the 1960s in York, fitted with a Standard diesel engine.

The cabman was given a bit more comfort than he had in pre-war days. Retained would be the the window in the driver's door, as was seen in the Oxford, but new was a one-piece windscreen, plus a sliding glass partition to the cabman's left, which would go some way to cutting down the chill winter winds. This was described as 'enclosed drive. Nuffield had intended to put this on the Oxford, but lack of money prevented it. Now, as soon as the new Austin came out with one, Nuffield fitted a similar partition to the Oxford.

Now the London cab trade had the choice of two cabs, but sales were slow. London, along with the rest of the country, was still struggling to recover from five years of war and greatly increased living costs. Fuel costs had almost doubled since the late 1930s and fares would not be increased from pre-war levels until 1951. To add to the misery, the Austin's big engine returned 18mpg compared to a 12/4's 25mpg. An attempt to improve fuel consumption was made by fitting a higher ratio back axle and a smaller, 1 1/2 inch carburettor, but its effect was minimal. The FL1 retained the original carburettor.

Double Purchase Tax on Cabs

In 1951, Britain had troops fighting in the Korean War, was attempting to put down political insurgence in Malaya and was rearming to face the threat from the Warsaw Pact countries on the other side of the 'Iron Curtain'. The Chancellor of the

An Early FX3, fitted with wheel trims. Previously they were forbidden so that when Carriage Officers made inspections at cab ranks they could see if all the cab's wheel nuts were in place. Other early improvements included the substitution of plastic headlining for a wool cloth one and a rubber floor mat

93

Exchequer, Hugh Gaitskell used the Budget of April 1950 to raise some £830 million to fund military expenditure. One of his measures was to levy double purchase tax on luxury goods and new cars and cabs. This put the price of an FX3 up to £1210/3/4d. Not surprisingly, this brought sales of new cabs down from 960 in 1950 to 698 by the end of 1951. Almost a one-fifth of the cabs on the road were over sixteen years old, and these price hikes reduced the likelihood of proprietors replacing them in the near future. To ensure there were sufficient cabs on the road, the Assistant Commissioner allowed that an inspecting officer could not refuse a licence to an aged cab if it fulfilled all the requirements required for that licence.

One small ray of hope was a 33 percent fare increase, brought into force on June 1 1950, with the flagfall raised to 1/3d. (6.25p). This was the first increase since 1933, and, remarkably a second increase, small by comparison came into force in June 4 1951. But the benefit of both was cancelled out in January 1952 when the price of the FX3 was increased to £1309, a restriction of 30 months was placed on a

hire purchase period (this was actually a concession to the cab trade- the repayment period for HP on a private car was 18 months) and the retail price of petrol was raised to 4/3d (21.25p) a gallon. Also, it was not permitted to include the cost of the purchase tax in the sum borrowed, so the tax had to be paid up-front. Cab sales crashed, with just 132 licensed in London in 1952. The previous lowest figure was 105, and that was in 1940, the first full year of the war. Even in the darkest years of the 1920s, peacetime sales had not dropped that low.

Series II and Series III Oxford

In 1950, Nuffield introduced the Series II Oxford, with pressed steel wheels to replace the old artillery-type. They would still take the old 18-inch tyres, rather than the new 16-inch that were fitted to the FX3.

Later, a revised Series III was introduced, with an extra side window, to give passengers the same brighter interior they got with the Austin.

The Series II Oxford differed only slightly, externally from the Series I in having pressed steel wheels

Birch Brothers Ltd and Diesel Power

Along with some other commodities such as sugar, fuel had continued to be rationed after the war due, the Labour government said to the dollar shortage, which limited their power to buy supplies. There was a rise in the amount allowed in the spring of 1949, but after the 1950 election, when Labour's majority was slashed they realised that rationing would no longer be tolerated and in 1950 they ended it, saying that two American oil companies had come to a deal to supply oil in return for buying British goods.

But in 1950 the wholesale price of a gallon of petrol, which is what the fleet proprietors paid rose to 3/3 ³/4d. (16.5p), partly due to an increase in fuel duty. With the FX3's thirst, this increase hit every cabman but particularly the fleet proprietors who were paying up front for the fuel, which was recovered as part of the drivers' cab rental. The London Cab Drivers Trade Union had demanded and got 'free petrol' in 1917, but in reality this was an illusion. The cab masters simply increased the percentage of the meter reading they charged the cabman, even though a cab drivers' strike succeeded in raising their share of the meter from 25 percent to 37.5 percent. The proprietors needed something drastic to help out with this double blow, as most of them were operating at a loss. But there was an answer in the offing.

Diesel road fuel, DERV, was slightly cheaper than petrol and a diesel engine returned far greater economy, albeit at the expense of acceleration and speed. Bus and truck operators had already begun to use diesel vehicles, but the engines available were, with one or two exceptions, big commercial units. The small diesel, suitable for a light or car-based commercial vehicle, let alone a family car did not, in 1950s Britain exist. Only Borgward and Mercedes-Benz in Germany and Citroën in France produced such engines, and these were slow, heavy and noisy. At the end of the Second World War, the Standard Motor Company signed an agreement with Harry Ferguson to design and make a new tractor, using the new 2.1 litre Standard Vanguard petrol engine. This tractor would become famous as the 'Little Grey

The Series III Oxford on display at the 1951 Commercial Motor Show. Centre is Francis M. Luther, the man behind all Beardmore cabs, talking to Wolseley's chairman, Charles Mullens. On the right, with his back to the camera is Roy Perkins, who was at this time a salesman for Beardmore's and had driven the prototype Oxford throughout the war

John Birch, newspaper in hand with his chief engineer. Mr S. Stewart. The cab, an Austin FX3, was the first London taxi to have diesel engine. The picture was at a photo session to launch the diesel engine

Fergie'. Farm or 'red' diesel was tax-free and for obvious reasons farmers preferred a diesel tractor, so Standard developed a diesel version of the Vanguard engine for the new tractor.

Cab and bus proprietors Birch Brothers of Kentish Town, North London had been pioneers of diesel power in their buses since the 1930s, valuing the diesel's fuel consumption and longevity. John Birch, the general manager had bought FX3s from their introduction, but like every other proprietor found the high fuel consumption totally unacceptable. As soon saw the announcement of the diesel tractor was in 1951, he approached Standard to see if the engine could be fitted into an FX3. The engine was about the same size as the Austin both physically and in cubic capacity and it fitted neatly into the FX3's engine bay, requiring only a re-routing of the exhaust and some other minor engineering tweaks to install it. This particular diesel engine had been de-

The 2.1 litre Standard diesel, fitted into an FX3. note the twin SU electric fuel pumps, installed to keep a steady fuel pressure to the injector pump

veloped for agricultural use and only developed around 20bhp, which was inadequate for road use, so Birch, with the approval of Standard's technical director, Ted Grinham engaged the services of A. Freeman Sanders in Penzance, Cornwall to improve the power output. This was done by fitting a camshaft from a Vanguard petrol engine, stronger valve springs, a redesigned inlet manifold and a new injector pump.

The Standard diesel, nicknamed the 'Fergie' after the tractor was tested in an FX3, registration number KGT 109 and Birch made several runs to and from Freeman Sanders in Cornwall, on one occasion through a snowstorm and another in torrential rain, which served to establish the engine's durability and adequate power output. It also enabled Freeman Sanders to examine the engine first hand, fresh from roadwork. This, the very first diesel powered London cab was approved in August 1952 by the PCO and approval was given for 25 in total, Birch's entire fleet to be converted and run on an experimental basis. All these were completed by the first week of January 1952 and showed to be returning a consistent 30mpg, virtually halving the fuel bill. Birch attempted fit the Standard engine into an Oxford for a Plymouth taxi operator but the engine fouled the steering box and the project was abandoned. There were other enquiries, from all over the country about conversion of private cars including an Austin 16 and an Austin A70 that were not followed through, as Freeman Sanders held the patent for the combustion chamber design and was adamant that he would not issue a licence to Birch to fit the engine in anything other than a London taxi. He would only sanction Standard's to do other conversions. There was a discreet enquiry in early 1953 from the Austin Motor Company, who wanted to Birch to install a diesel engine in an FL1 Hire Car, for evaluation purposes. For the sake of diplomacy, John Birch fielded the enquiry to Standard's Ted Grinham. It is not known if Grinham and Austin's took this any further.

PCO approval for Birch to install the engine in fifty cabs belonging to other proprietors was given in February 1953, but before he was willing to convert any cabs for others he made sure his fleet were running satisfactorily first, including the correction of excessive oil consumption by the fitting of different pistons. By the end of April, Birch was able to carry our conversion on other cabs, including the fleet of W. H. Cook at an initial price of £285 per cab.

Once word had got around of the economy of the diesel cab, requests for conversion came in thick and fast, from individuals and fleet owners alike, both in London and as far afield as Manchester, Bristol and Glasgow. To accommodate the London enquiries, Birch requested, and received approval from the PCO to have the numbers of converted cabs increased to 75.

Diesel power had well and truly arrived in the London cab trade and other organisations were already jumping on the bandwagon. Both the Hackney Transport and Engineering Company and Dives of Stockwell adapted the 1.8 litre Borgward Hansa engine to fit the FX3 and Perkins offered their big 3-litre P4C diesel in the FX3 and the Oxford for £280, claiming a net saving of £266 over 50,000 miles. However, the Perkins, at 3 litres was a physically large engine and although at first Mann and Overton expressed concern over its effect on the transmission they later advertised the conversion.

The London General had experimented with the Mercedes-Benz 170 and the Borgward diesel, but found that both were underpowered. For them the 'Fergie' was the best, and in the second half of 1953, after having been trained in the method of installation at Birch's premises they converted their entire fleet in their own workshops. Soon their FX3s were lining up at the new diesel pumps on the garage forecourt in Brixton Road, with filler caps painted yellow to ensure they were filled with the right fuel. The General's fleet manager, Geoff Trotter, described the conversion as "an economic necessity - we couldn't do it fast enough."

Associated Newspapers, who were major shareholders in the London General Cab Company ran a fleet of FX3 delivery vans for the London Evening News. They

An Argo taximeter, as fitted to cabs in the 1950s. With the exception of some internal illumination, meter design had changed little since Edwardian times. Likewise, fares had failed to keep up with modern times and this was one of the main points to come out of the Runciman Report

had an initial conversion on a new van in late 1953. All this business enabled Birch to bring the price of the conversion down to £270 for individual cabs and as low as £235 for multiple orders.

The Runciman Report

The cab trade was expressing great concern over its financial difficulties, and in August 1952, the Home Secretary, Sir David Maxwell Fyfe asked Viscount Runciman, the newly-appointed President of the Chamber of Shipping and Chairman of the General Council of British Shipping;

> "To consider the effect of the present economic and fiscal circumstances on the taxicab service (particularly in London) and to report what changes if any in the present system of taxation, control or organisation are desirable in the public interest."

The report was published on February 6 1953 and found that the cab trade was indeed in deep financial difficulties. Two major causes of the difficulties were highlighted. The first was the high cost of new cabs, which was greatly inflated by the imposition of double purchase tax, and the 30-month restriction on the hire purchase period, which had already resulted in a dramatic number of new cabs sold. Second was the ever-increasing cost of fuel, particularly in the light of the high fuel consumption of the FX3. All this was reflected in the submissions given to the committee in relation to profit and loss. Every fleet proprietor, no matter how diligent he was, was losing money every single day his cabs were on the road.

The committee examined the case for a rebate on petrol duty, fare increases, amendments to the taxation of cabs and ways of reducing the number of unengaged miles, particularly with reference to additional cab ranks, the ratio of cabs to drivers and the use of radio. It recommended that both hire purchase restrictions and purchase tax of any kind should be removed altogether from the price of a cab that complied with the Conditions of Fitness. The committee also recognised that diesel engines might prove to be the answer to the fuel problem, but considered that it was far too early to say whether the ongoing trials of diesel cabs (Birch Brothers were not mentioned by name) would be successful.

Heartened by this, Robert Overton and representatives from the LMCPA and the TGWU lobbied extensively for the removal of purchase tax on cabs. In the April 1953 Budget, the Chancellor of the Exchequer in the new Conservative government, R. A. Butler not only abolished its application for cabs but also laid down legislation that banned the imposition of such a tax on cabs approved by the PCO. The effect of this was that sales of new cabs began to increase once more. At last the pre-war cabs still surviving would be withdrawn from service. Some of these were sold to students, who took them on tours of the UK, mainland Europe and sometimes much farther afield.

A New Austin Diesel Engine

Some large fleet proprietors were not happy about the 'Fergie' engine. It made the FX3 slow and there had been problems with starting in cold weather, high oil consumption and occasional failures. They pressed Robert Overton to ask Austin to build their own diesel engine. Mann and Overton accepted the importance of John Birch's work in keeping the cab trade prof-

itable. Indeed, they were happy to finance such conversions on existing cabs through their own finance house, but thought that making such a conversion ought to be an unnecessary expense. At first, M & O's David Southwell approached John Birch with an idea that Austin might install the Standard diesel on the production lines rather than depend on an aftermarket conversion, but soon after, Robert Overton spoke to George Harriman of BMC about Austin producing their own small diesel. In December 1953 Austin announced that they were going to develop such an engine from the 2.2 litre petrol engine and engaged engine specialists Ricardo to do the job. This had an immediate effect on Birch's business, especially as some of the performance figures put out by Austin showed that an FX3 with their engine performed as well as a petrol cab but with similar fuel consumption to the Birch conversion. This was mollified in some respect as rumours (ever a danger in the London cab trade) got around that the Austin engine was proving troublesome in trials. By mid 1954 the new engine, also of 2.2 litres but with a different bore and stroke from its petrol 'parent', was fitted in a small number of FX3s. The conversion received type approval and went on trial for a period of six months. It returned a similar 30mpg to the 'Fergie', almost halving the operational fuel costs of the petrol engine. The production version, the FX3D was announced at the 1954 Commercial Motor Exhibition. It price was £942. This was £80 more than the petrol cab, and less than one third of the cost of a Birch conversion. In consequence, Birch's orders for engines all but dried up for short period.

However, the Austin engine suffered teething troubles. The blocks tended to split and if the injector timing went out it would fire before the top of the stroke and send the engine into reverse, pumping out clouds of smoke. For a while at the end of 1954, Austin stopped delivery of petrol FX3s in, according to John Birch an attempt to prevent customers buying petrol cabs and having Standard engines fitted. The problems with the new Austin engine prompted Birch's customers to continue specifying conversions on existing cabs and by the summer of 1954, he had ordered over 100 more engines and by April, 1956 had installed over 1500 engines in FX3s and FL1 Hire Cars, both in London and in the provinces and supplied almost two dozen London cab fleets.

Austin soon had the injector pump modified to cure the reverse running problem and the diesel FX3 became by far the most popular option. Mushes as well as fleet owners had Austin diesel engines fitted to their FX3s, including some that previously had Ferguson or Perkins conversions. The ultimate success of the Austin diesel effectively ended Birch Brothers Ltd's conversion. Birch himself tacitly admitted that the Austin diesel was more powerful than the Standard when he suggested to Ted Grinham that he should send an engine to supercharging experts, Shorrocks. And openly he said that his conversion project could only be an interim measure.

John Birch was hailed in the national press as 'the man who saved the cab trade.' Modestly, he brushed aside this accolade, even though his initiative did bring the trade back towards profitability. One thing he can be credited with is certain, and that is that he started a practice that lasts to this day; the use of the diesel engine. The fuel rationing that was an outcome of the 1956 Suez crisis was confirmation that diesel power was here to stay and that both Birch and, soon after, Austin had made the right decision in adopting diesel engines.

The Beardmore MkVII

Beardmore Motors were in a pretty comfortable position. They had a viable vehicle, the Oxford to sell with no real worries about production, because it was made by one of the biggest car makers in the UK, the Nuffield Organisation. It was, as former sales manager Roy Perkins put it, 'a licence to print money'. Then it all went wrong. In 1952, the Austin Motor Company and the Nuffield Organisation merged to form a new organisation, the British Motor Corporation, (BMC). After initially taking the post of chairman of the new firm, William Morris, Lord Nuffield, the owner of the Nuffield Organisation retired and Leonard Lord became chairman and managing director. This gave Lord the opportunity to make Austin the dominant partner over his long-time rival. The Oxford cab, production of which had been moved to Ward End to make room at Adderley Park for tractors and transmissions, was one of the first casualties of Lord's restructuring. Why, Lord reasoned should he be making two very similar vehicles for such a small market, especially when Austin had such a dominant position in that market? The Oxford would go, he decided, in favour of the more modern FX3. Around 1926 Oxfords were made by the time production ended in 1953.

Beardmore learned that they were about to lose the Oxford in a telephone call from BMC. They would have a year's grace before it finally ceased production, but were not given the opportunity to buy the rights to the Oxford and continue building it themselves. Beardmore was left with three options: one, to continue servicing existing Oxfords until spares ran out and then cease trading; two, to see if a new manufacturer would be interested in entering the market or, three to design and

The first design of body for the MkVII Beardmore, distinguished by its flat bootlid and downward curve to the bottom edge of the rear side window. Only five bodies would be made in this style

make a cab of their own. The first option, abandoning the business was out of the question, certainly for the managing director, Francis Luther and his long-time business partner, Georg e Allsworth. Beardmore Motors had been their life since the end of the Great War. Seeing how profitable their connections with Nuffield had been, they investigated the second option, to get someone else to build a cab for them to sell. They approached Fiat of Italy, who were happy to entertain their proposals, but wanted a minimum run of

10,000 vehicles per year. This was out of the question, of course. Less that one tenth of that number were bought by the London trade annually, with provincial sales making up only a small additional number. Next, Beardmore's approached Vauxhall's in Luton. All seemed to go well at the meeting, until one Vauxhall executive declared that if his company did business with the London cab trade, he would resign on the spot. In his experience, he said there never were such a bunch of thieves and vagabonds! Exit Vauxhall,

PLB 555, the second MkVII Beardmore, and the one used for publicity photographs. This cab has the same flat bootlid and rear side windows as the cab picture opposite. Note the depth of the windscreen in comparison to the later cab, pictured overleaf

101

leaving Beardmore's with the third and now only option, to build the cab themselves.

Although Beardmore could not have the entire Oxford, they could use its chassis, which was made by Rubery Owen. Throughout 1953, Beardmore's works manager, Jim Bates designed a new cab around it, with modern running gear. Ford had introduced two new OHV engines, a 2262cc 6-cylinder for the Zephyr and a 1508cc 4-cylinder for the Consul. Beardmore's, ever conscious of fuel economy opted for the Consul and the first pre-production chassis was fitted with this engine. The rear axle was the ENV type used on the MkVII Jaguar saloon but with a lower differential ratio and the brakes were Lockheed hydraulic, also of the type supplied to Jaguar. By contrast, the front beam axle came from a milk float. The Burman worm and nut steering box was specially built, to cope with the turning circle. There were also telescopic dampers, coming into use on motor cars but as yet unused on London cabs. The Oxford's engine had a dry sump but the Ford engine had a conventional wet sump with the well

at the front. Rather than have Ford make a new sump with the well at the rear, which would be an expensive job for the small numbers required, the Beardmore's front springs carried the front axle three and a half inches further back than the Oxford's.

The PCO were not against the introduction of modern technology, but approval was needed for what Beardmore wanted, despite the fact that all these features were commonplace in contemporary cars. The PCO's vehicle inspecting officers were still serving policemen who had been trained up for the job. Their primary concern was for public safety and it was still their way to err far too much on the side of caution in respect of the introduction of new technology, with the result that London's cabs lagged behind what the rest of the motor industry considered to be standard practice. Part of the reason for this was because it could take a long time to get something approved and that time and the money it cost was often thought not worthwhile. On October 22, 1953 Bates, along with Francis Luther's son Jack, at the time a director of Beardmore motors met Mr Harold Gould, the Superintend-

The happy cabman is Mr A J Skinner from Camberwell, who had just won this MkVII Beardmore in a competition

ent of the PCO, and outlined the specifications they planned for the new cab. Gould was open to innovation, provided it did not compromise passenger safety or convenience. He expressed concern that the linkage of steering column gearchange might jam in the new cab as it had begun to do in Ford cars, but he was not opposed in principle to these 'innovations', and work began on a first prototype.

Next, a body was needed. Like the FX3, the design would be of pre-war appearance, rather than modern. The board's claim was that the new MkVII would be the lightest, most economical purpose-built London cab yet made. They also said they were single-minded in that it would be hand built by craftsmen from the finest materials to ensure long life and be a first class investment. It has been said that Luther was very much a traditionalist and wanted an old style cab but in truth, Beardmore had little option but to choose a traditional-style coachbuilt body. They could not afford the considerable tooling costs for an all-steel body, they did not have any of the production facilities that existed at Carbodies and steel was still

scarce. Nor was there the room at Hendon for high enough production run to recover the kind of outlay needed.

Thus it was decided that Beardmore's North London neighbour, Windover would make a traditional coachbuilt body. Although Windover had been making bodies for luxury cars for half a century they had abandoned this type of work after the war, as there were very few car makers left that needed the services of coachbuilders and there were fewer customers to buy what were built. Now, Windover were concentrating on bus bodies and had no design pattern for a modern, full width car body. The ash frame of the cab's body would be clad in aluminium which, although more expensive than steel, was at the time far more readily available, and lighter. This would reduce the cab's overall weight and thus help its fuel consumption. However, Windover did at least have the Oxford body as a pattern, which complied with the dimensions specified in the Conditions of Fitness and of course fitted the chassis. In May 1954 a cab was submitted for type approval. The PCO described the body as 'of a very ordinary cab design,

In the 1950s, as in decades before a cabman was unusual in having personal transport, in the form of a cab at his disposal, and there have been many family snapshots like this one to preserve that status. Clear from this picture are the distinctive features of the MkVII Beardmore's Windover body: the near-vertical boot line, the horizontal bonnet line and the opening windscreen

with an all weather driving compartment.' Naturally, a glass sliding partition was fitted to the driver's nearside. The PCO found eighteen minor detail faults, but there was nothing that Bates could not remedy.

Ford was very supportive of Beardmore's, but thought at first that the Consul engine would be inadequate for the cab and wanted them to use the Zephyr engine. Keen to keep Ford on side, Beardmore set aside another pre-production chassis and fitted it with a six-cylinder Zephyr engine, but instead of fitting a full cab body to it, Windover's were asked to fit a pickup truck body, to act simply as a test bed for the engine. This truck was fast, but heavy on fuel compared to the Consul chassis, confirming Beardmore's original choice of the Consul engine.

On May 13, 1954 Francis Luther died at his home in Sussex of the effects of lung cancer. He was 71. He had been the driving force behind the company since 1919 and had been involved in its genesis at the start of the Great War. With his death the company, already in decline began moving slowly towards collapse. To replace him, the board invited Francis Allsworth, the son of the George Allsworth, to return from the USA to take over as managing director. The younger Allsworth had been managing director of the Coupé Company before going to America to study production methods. Despite wanting a modern-style body, Francis Allsworth had to accept that it was too late to make major changes to the MkVII. Application for type approval went ahead and given to chassis number BM/7/1 on November 10 1954. Approval was granted the next month for the complete cab, in time for the cab's debut at the 1954 Commercial Motor Exhibition. This was delivered on February 4 of the following year, registration number PXF 762. It cost £895.

Beardmore began to make changes to the design of the body almost immediately. A modified body on chassis BM/7/6 was submitted to the PCO for type approval on December 12 1954. It had a different back end, with a defined 'notch-back' boot, a shallower windscreen and rear side windows of a revised design. Type approval for this style of body was given shortly after on chassis BM/7/7. Only chassis numbers 1 to 5 would have the original body style, and from Chassis no 7 onwards all production MkVIIs would have the new back. The aluminium roof was difficult and expensive to form. In the June of 1955, some time after the first MkVIIs had been delivered, a glassfibre roof and wings, made by the Semtex company had been given type approval. The wings continued to be tested over the next eighteen months and fitted from January 1957 but the new glassfibre roof would not be seen on production MkVIIs until fitted by Weymann from 1958.

Chapter 8

Towards Modernity

It was clear that although almost all pre-war cabs had been removed from service by 1956, the three models of post-war cab were very much of a pre-war design in comparison with modern cars. And one model, the FX3 was lagging behind in technical specification. The next five years would see attempts, successful and otherwise to remedy that situation, but would be thwarted or constrained by regulation, misplaced ambition, inadequate funding and poor development.

The Birch Cab

Letters John Birch received from owners of large saloon cars, wanting to know if the Standard engine would fit in their particular model proved there was a growing demand for a diesel car and the installation of the Standard diesel in the FX3 also enabled Standard's to evaluate it for possible use in the Vanguard saloon. Standard's chief engineer, Ted Grinham, who had been overseeing his company's part of the FX3 conversions, suggested to John Birch in early 1953 that the Vanguard saloon or estate might make a good taxi for London. Grinham, it will be remembered represented his old company, Humber at the Committee of Enquiry on the Conditions of Fitness in 1927, and was surely calling to mind his experiences from that time. Birch advise him that the Vanguard's 94-inch wheelbase would be too short for the job, but if Standard's were to make a suitable chassis, then he was prepared to

The Birch cab. Park Royal Vehicles' design engineer Alfred Hill took the cab's front end styling from the contemporary Standard Ten. The severe lines of the body reveal that it was designed by a bus and caravan builder

Three passengers could be seated across the back seat of the Birch cab, with the fourth tucked alongside the driver, facing rearwards

consider the idea of making a cab of his own, so in early 1953 he approached Standard with a plan to build one. An agreement was made whereby Standard's would loan Birch Brothers Ltd a specially modified chassis, Birch Brothers would arrange for the fitting of a suitable body and operate it in their fleet to evaluate it for suitability as a cab, returning it to Standard's from time to time for their own assessment.

Grinham arranged for a specially-modified chassis, number X541 to be made, which had a longer, 107-inch wheel-base, was narrowed at the front to enable the turning circle to be achieved and had the steering column set at a more upright position to suit a different body. The engine would be the Standard diesel, type number DEC 479E mated to the Vanguard's three-speed gearbox. It had the Vanguard's independent coil spring and wishbone front suspension and the hydraulic brakes were modified to dual-circuit operation to satisfy the PCO's needs for public safety. During 1953, Standard's engineer, Lewis Dawtrey worked on the construction of the new chassis, and was

The luggage compartment of the Birch, accessible through a substantial full-height door. For all the space it offers, the load height is much greater than that of a contemporary FX3 or Beardmore

also supplied with an FX3 chassis for comparison. However, it would not be until late November 1954 that Birch Brothers finally took delivery of the chassis. It was presented to the PCO for approval in February 1955. It is not known if its hydraulic brakes and column gearchange were questioned, because the PCO had already seen such innovations on the MkVII Beardmore, but a list of over dozen minor faults were presented for correction. As soon as they were done, it was time to build and mount a body.

John Birch decided that the cab would mark a major change. It would certainly not be one that the PCO could describe as 'very ordinary', as they had the Beardmore! The natural choice for the body maker would be Park Royal Vehicles Ltd, a west London firm who specialised in bus bodies who were at the time building one of their 'Royalist' luxury coaches for Birch Brothers. Park Royal's chief designer, Alfred Hill, would draw up the plans. The four passenger seats and the luggage compartment were set out in an unusual, if not entirely new arrangement, where three passengers sat on the back seat and the third in a rearward-facing fixed seat alongside the driver, separated from him by a partition. A survey made just before the Birch cab was designed showed that only one in ten cab journeys were made by more than one person, and Birch knew from the meter readings of his company's cabs that the vast majority of those journeys were short, so he decided that a fourth passenger could put up with a less comfortable ride. The offset seat was an American idea that had been introduced as a conversion for sedan cabs in the late 1940s by San Francisco De Soto Dealers James F. Waters, but whether John Birch was aware of it is not known. Novel, though was the luggage compartment,

which was accessed by a single, full height door on the nearside rear. No records appear to survive telling of the construction of the body, but it is quite likely that it was coachbuilt, as that was how Park Royal Vehicles built all their buses at the time.

John Birch was considering calling the cab the 'Essbee', from the initials of Standard and Birch and also put the idea to Standard of using the chassis for other unspecified, commercial applications, as an increase in production volume would reduce the unit cost of each chassis. The cab, painted blue and white was licensed by PCO on December 21 1955, and it was put on a six-month test starting on April 18 1956, with the plan to send it back to Standard from time to time. 'Motor Transport' Magazine road tested it and liked it. Compared to the Standard-powered FX3 it was smooth, thanks to improved engine mountings and it was pleasant to drive. Acceleration was modest, but far more important was the fuel consumption, which was an average of 37mpg. Following the articles in 'Motor Transport', and other periodicals, Birch received several enquiries from potential buyers, but he had to tell them that it was at present still a prototype, but estimated that it would cost around £1000-£1100. More than six months on from its introduction, John Birch was pleased to report to Ted Grinham that the cab had performed almost faultlessly, returning an average fuel consumption of 34mpg. the only fault was with the front springs, which had to be replaced with heavy-duty ones.

Unfortunately, through no fault of the cab's design, Standards would not put it into production. They had introduced a diesel version of the Vanguard, using the same engine as John Birch had put in both the FX3 and the 'Essbee'', but not fully understanding the fuel supply requirements of a diesel engine, had made a poor job of the installation, and blamed the engine. Also, they had let their licence on Freeman Sanders' patents lapse, which effectively ruled out the engine use in the Birch cab and thus killing the project stone dead. Nevertheless the cab ran for several years in Birch Brothers' cab fleet before being used as an inspection vehicle for the motor coach side of business, based at the town of Henlow Camp, Hertfordshire from where the company ran a service in and out of London. From there it was most likely scrapped.

A Beardmore Diesel

Beardmore were not far behind Austin in offering a diesel option. In 1955, after making enquiries about a Ricardo version of the Standard diesel, the 2.3 litre 23CV they settled on a new Perkins engine, the four-cylinder 4.99 for the MkVII. This 1.6 litre engine - its capacity in cubic inches was 99, hence its type number - had been tested for some months in chassis number BM/7/4, with the specially sought registration, RYT 99. (RYT for 'right', and 99 for the engine) But reliable as it was, the Perkins was noisy, and not quite powerful enough for the job. Besides, it made the cab heavier by a full hundredweight, which, apart from demanding that an extra leaf be fitted to the nearside of the cab, further handicapped performance. Not surprisingly, the take-up was low, with something less than one in ten diesels sold, compared to the reverse with the FX3. Quite a few diesel MkVIIs were eventually converted back to petrol power.

A New Coachbuilder for Beardmore

In 1956, exactly a century since Windover was founded, the company was bought out by rival coachbuilders, Weymann. Since the decline in the market for coachbuilt cars after the end of the Second World War, Windover had made the transition into bus body building, but Weymann had been building bus bodies since 1929. Weymann took what they needed from Windover's, moved it to their factory at Addlestone in Surrey and sold the premises to Henlys, the big chain of motor dealers. For Beardmore's the changeover appeared seamless, with the first cab with

The boot of the Weymann body fitted to the MkVII Beardmore has a gradual slope, compared to the more upright profile of the Windover, as can be seen on this restored example

a Weymann body being delivered in November 1957, one month before the last one by Windover. This, however could have been simply a matter of what body maker's plate was fitted to each particular cab. Weymann would also fit the new Semtex roof and glassfibre wings, the latter having been submitted for type approval in 1955 and but not found to be of good enough quality until further developments had improved the techniques.

The body that Weymann built would be outwardly similar to Windover's, but Beardmore's decided that this would be an opportunity to introduce a new model. The lines were streamlined a little, with a more graceful slope of the rear panel and the line of the bonnet altered so that it sloped down to the radiator shell instead of being horizontal. The opening windscreen, prone to water leaks was replaced by a fixed one and electric windscreen wipers replaced the vacuum Ford ones.

To keep the MkVII's price competitive with the FX3, Beardmore's profit amounted to a mere £50 per cab. The use of the finest materials and the employment of the best craftsmen cost the company dear. Company secretary Ken Jaeger would say, many years later that the MkVII was far too well built to be a cab. In fact the only compromise they seemed to make towards cost over quality was the use of Rexine for the seat facings instead of leather. At a production average of two cabs per week, the profit didn't cover the wage bill. Jaeger tried in vain to make the board understand that the cab was not generating any profit for future investment, and the ultimate survival of the company. All they could see was the excess of the assets set against the liabilities on the balance sheet. Unfortunately those assets were fixed, and could not produce cash. When cash was needed, some HP

agreements were sold to an outside finance house, which gave them the purchase price of the cab immediately. Cash sales netted the company virtually nothing. If Luther's death heralded the end of the company, Beardmore's board were beginning to hasten it.

The Austin FX4

In 1954 Carbodies' owner, Bobby Jones, sold out to BSA and retired. Jack Hellberg moved from Nuffield to become Carbodies' commercial manager and in March 1955 he was asked by Mann and Overton to get together with Austin to plan a new cab. To take account of the great increase in development costs, Austin's engineer Albert Moore and chief draughtsman Charles Benlow began with the existing FX3 chassis. They fitted it with the independent front suspension from the larger contemporary BMC cars and the Austin Westminster rear axle and the 2.2 diesel engine from the FX3, mated to the Borg-Warner DG150M automatic gearbox that would be tested successfully in the FX3 from 1957. There would be dual-circuit hydraulic brakes, using parallel master cylinders, mounted under the floor, with one master cylinder operating the front brakes and the other the rear. Neither a petrol engine nor a manual gearbox were to be offered - the cab masters' wishes for an automatic cab had been granted exclusively.

At first, the cab was given the model code ADO6, (ADO standing for Austin Drawing Office) but this was soon changed to FX4, using Austin's pre-BMC numbering system. Austin's chief designer was Ricardo 'Dick' Burzi, an Italian who had fled his native country in the 1920s after insulting the fascist dictator, Benito

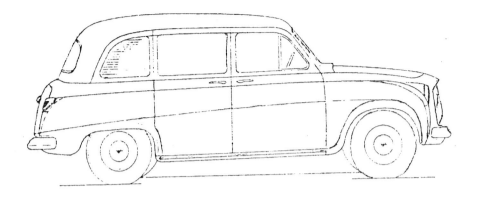

Austin design draughtsman Eric Bailey's first outline drawing for the FX4. Bailey has been quoted as saying that he was aiming to produce a design that was not, in his own words 'offensive to anyone', but he surely would not have imagined that he was developing what would become one of the world's most recognisable motor vehicles

Mussolini. Burzi was busy finalising the design of a new small Austin car, the Metropolitan and also hard at work on another new small car, the 'Farina' A40, so Austin's chief design engineer, Jim Stanfield, gave the job of designing the new cab to one of the younger men in his department, Eric Bailey. A surprised and delighted Bailey received guidance from Phil Baker, a senior chassis engineer, who had worked on the FX3 and was able to give Bailey guidance on the mysteries of the PCO and the Conditions of Fitness. A full-size mock-up of the cab's interior was set out to the PCO's requirements, but for the styling, Bailey was given a free hand. Rather than copy the designs Dick Burzi had used on previous Austin family cars, Bailey decided he should produce '... a pleasant shape that not cause offence to anyone.' For some of the lines of the body he relied on the work he had produced for the Vanden Plas Princess, including in-board headlights. Bailey had also worked

The first pre-production FX4, registration number VLW 431, which went into service with York Way Motors during the summer of 1958. It is pictured here outside one of the gates of South Park, Fulham around the corner from Mann and Overton's garage

on the design of the A30, so it is no coincidence that the front wing line of both the FX4 and the A30 have some similarity.

On June 4 1956 Mann and Overton's David Southwell and the PCO's Mr Gould went to see the wooden first mock-up that had been produced by Austin. Despite the modern mechanical specification, the cab's three-door body was an anachronism and having examined the Birch and approved a full body with a fourth door, (albeit of an unconventional design) he recommended that the new Austin should be of such a modern appearance too. Curiously, Gould did not like its upward-opening 'crocodile' bonnet, even though such a design was used on the Birch. Neither did he like the headrests fitted to the rear seat, which he thought were unhygienic. He disliked the fixed windscreen, believing that an opening windscreen gave the driver better visibility in the 'pea soup' fogs common in London before the clean air act, but he was persuaded to approve it, as he had done for the Weymann body fitted to the MkVII Beardmore.

Bailey then produced the FX4 shape now recognised the world over. He thought his original design for the sides was too plain, so he introduced the now familiar feature line along the side, which gave it more character, producing a wide line where a moulding strip could be applied and also a natural division for two tone paint, which was very much in vogue at the time.

A full size wooden model was made, complete in every detail, including opening doors, full interior detail and a jacking system that allowed it to be raised and lowered to simulate the ride height when the vehicle was loaded or empty. It was painted red and white, using the feature line to provide the separation of the colours as Bailey had envisaged. He also produced some artwork for a design with some styling differences, coloured yellow and white and it included a wrap-around rear window, another innovation that was gaining popularity with car designers now that the technology in the manufacture of glass had undergone a revolution. But Robert Overton took such a liking to the red and white full size model that the artwork for the yellow and white version was not shown to him. With the PCO's approval, it was signed off.

From here the design went to Carbod-

Although the London General Cab Company were very critical of the FX4, they were obliged to buy them in order to keep their fleet up to date and up to strength. This is possibly the first one they bought.
Note the original door handles, which were too fragile and were replaced with much sturdier ones

ies, where chief engineer Jake Donaldson developed the design for production. He hinged the bonnet and grille on the scuttle in one piece and designed the inner and outer front wings and the lower body sills so that they could be unbolted for ease of replacement. For durability and ease of cleaning, the interior trim panels were one-piece plastic mouldings. Leather was retained on the seat facings, despite Beardmore's decision to use Rexine throughout.

The need for a new cab was pressing: the number of cabs in London had, at the end of 1952 dropped to 5,437, less than the number licensed in 1946 and even at the end of 1958 it still had only risen to 6,157. All of Mann and Overton's and much of Carbodies' and Austin's hopes, and indeed the trade's rested on the new Austin. Application for type approval for the FX4 chassis was submitted to the PCO on January 10 1958, and the first complete prototype, VLW 431 was presented on June 27 and passed on July 14.

But when cab trade representatives had their first glimpse at Carbodies' factory they were very disappointed. They disliked the way doors were hinged at the back edge: several accidents had been caused, both to pedestrians and to the doors themselves by passengers carelessly opening the doors before the cab had stopped. An American serviceman had been fined for the damage he had caused by such behaviour, and an FX3 had its doors hinged on the B-post as an experiment. The PCO had reservations about hinging the doors this way round, claiming that it allowed people to run off without paying, as a driver might be able to hold back at least, the offside door. (For some unexplained reason, they did not consider that a bilker might prefer to use the safer and more convenient nearside door to make his es-

cape.) There were, apparently no adverse comments from passengers, but Mann and Overton's managing director, David Southwell would not approve the conversion for the FX3 without a directive from the PCO, possibly on the grounds of unnecessary expense. Thus, the FX4 was presented to the trade with these rear-hinged doors. Geoff Trotter, the managing director of the London General called the cab 'a recipe for disaster' and described the bonnet as 'diabolical'. Barnet 'Barney' Davis, the taciturn managing director of Felday Cabs called it 'a bloody awful vehicle.' Robert Overton, dismayed with the cab's reception, wrote in his diary, "what a headache this is going to be!"

VLW 431 was tested by York Way Motors of Kings Cross, and was used that year for promotional photographs and films. The FX4 was announced to the trade in September 1958, and shown at the Commercial Motor Show. The FL2 hire car version was exhibited at the Earls Court Motor Show. Type approval was granted on 25th November 1958, and the cab went on sale at £1198.

An article in 'BSA News' predicted London sales of 50 a week, which turned out to be optimistic in the extreme. Production difficulties, due to inadequate press tools caused hold-ups right from the start. The tools were designed by works manager Percy McNally who was known to be talented in man management, but had a limited knowledge of pressing sheet metal and he had designed what turned out to be some truly awful tools. Faulty roof pressings had to be rectified by outside contractors at considerable expense, the bonnet was proving to be almost impossible to make and the boot lid was proving difficult too. In June 1959, after a total of less than 200 cabs had been delivered, David Southwell of Mann and Overton wrote to the PCO to apologise for the delay. The PCO were then applying an un-written ten-year rule on cabs, and if a pro-prietor wanted to run a cab for longer than the prescribed ten years, he would have to apply for an extension. Because of the delay in delivery of new FX4s, Gould agreed to extend the working life of quite a number of FX3s in order to maintain as many cabs as possible on the streets.

To sort out the problems, Carbodies brought back Bill Lucas, who had worked on the FX3 but had left when Carbodies sold out to BSA, to design new press tools for the roof, bonnet and boot. But not all was well when those cabs were delivered. In the first couple of weeks, the bonnet of a cab on its way to Heathrow airport flew open, causing an accident. Representatives of Borg-Warner showed members of the London Motor Cab Proprietors' Associa-tion (LMCPA) some damaged compo-nents from returned gearboxes and blamed the damage on bad driving. They had some justification, as older drivers had no experience of automatic gearboxes

and, out of ignorance were treating them very badly, but further investigations by Borg-Warner showed that the gearbox was a mismatch for the engine. A diesel engine has inherent torsional vibration in the crankshaft, a product of its high compres-sion. This vibration would be absorbed by a torque converter, but the DG had a drive lock-up, which transmitted the vibrations to the internal components of the gear-box, wearing them out prematurely.

In September 1961 type approval was given for the new four-speed synchromesh gearbox from the Austin Gypsy to be fit-ted as an option to the automatic and Borg-Warner's new Model 35 automatic replaced the DG in 1964. In 1962, when the fittings for a manual gearbox were available on the chassis, the 2.2 litre petrol engine, which had been the original power plant of the FX3 was introduced as an op-tion. No automatic gearbox was offered in the UK market with the petrol engine, ei-ther for the FL2 or FX4, although a spe-cial petrol automatic was built for trials in New York City, USA.

Although the London General Cab Company was very critical of the FX4, buying was, for them and almost all other cab fleets, Hobson's choice. Here, an early example goes through the cab wash the company installed around 1960. Note the darkened 'purdah' glass in the back window, installed for the sake of passenger privacy

A New Engine and a New Home for Beardmore

The Mk2 Ford Consul, introduced in March 1956 came with a larger, 1703cc engine, but it was not until May 1958 that the new engine was fitted to the Beardmore. In October of 1958 Beardmore's general sales manager, Ted Vaughan, wrote to the PCO, advising them that early on in the new year the assembly of cabs would be transferred from Hendon to the Weymann factory in Addlestone. Colindale was to be closed. Vaughan also wrote to all owners concerning the move, advising them that servicing in London would be carried out by an associate company of Beardmore, Graham Terrace Motors. It was an economic necessity to move body production down to Weymann's bus building factory in Addlestone, but Beardmore could not have guessed where this association would eventually lead.

John Birch's Standard Atlas Taxi

The FX4 had only just been type-approved when John Birch, the man who had put the first diesel engine in an FX3 condemned it outright. It was too big and too thirsty, he said - 26mpg against 31mpg for the diesel FX3. 'This has almost destroyed the advantages of the diesel,' he wrote on January 20, 1959 in a letter to A. E. Coaley of Standard, when he requesting drawings of their new Atlas van, as he believed that he could build a cab around it. He had noticed that the Atlas had a turning circle of 29 feet, and he believed he could get down to the mandatory 25 feet demanded by the Conditions of Fitness. He already reckoned that an Atlas taxi would weigh half a ton (508kg) less and than the FX4

and return 30mpg with its original 1-litre Standard petrol engine. Best of all, Birch thought it would sell for about £1000, almost £200 less than the Austin. The main drawbacks of the Atlas was that the front suspension was by a transverse leaf and the front track was narrower that the rear track, both of which were not allowed by the Conditions of Fitness. However, Birch knew that the Assistant Commissioner had discretionary powers to over-rule any part in the Conditions of Fitness if he felt that it were in the public's and the trade's interest so to do, and Birch felt that he had a chance. "If I can't persuade him," Birch wrote to Frank Higham, home sales director of Standard, "nobody else can!"

The Atlas chassis was in two pieces, with a straight rear section that ran from under the seats to the rear and a front subframe, holding the suspension, engine and gearbox that could be unbolted from the main chassis and removed for ease of maintenance The main chassis would be too high for passenger access, so in March, 1959 Birch got Willowbrook, a Loughborough, Leicestershire firm who had built bodies for Birch Brothers' bus fleet to make a new rear chassis with a dropped section of over 7 inches to allow a lower floor.

Standard and Birch continued to cooperate with the project throughout 1959, but what didn't help the project was the poor reputation that the Atlas was already earning for itself. It was underpowered, slow and front-heavy and also it rolled and pitched, which was not helped by the design of the front suspension. It had been designed as a town delivery van, which is why it was given a tight turning circle and side-loading doors, but a lot of operators saw its capacious body and decided to use it on longer distance work, for which it was unsuited.

114

The Assistant Commissioner of Police took a dislike to the chassis and would not give Birch a clear answer to his request for a relaxation of the rules governing the suspension and track. In another letter to Frank Higham, Birch, tellingly wrote;

> 'If I keep nagging I might get dispensation to operate an experimental vehicle and that is why I have decided to build a body. If I can demonstrate a complete vehicle I am sure that our chances of getting even this limited approval will be very much enhanced.'

He intended to send a small deputation of engineers to the Assistant Commissioner to try and persuade him, rather than 'continue to write letters which remain unanswered.'

Birch met with Gould and F. W. Perrett of the PCO on November 6 1959. The PCO men were of the opinion that the narrow front track of the Atlas would make it unstable, if the front spring broke, the steering would be lost, a point that John Birch considered as ridiculous, because it had never happened to an Atlas van. Birch also maintained that the rules in the Conditions of Fitness were antiquated in the light of modern engineering know-how, especially in regard to buses (Birch's other line of business) and that the

Atlas had been approved by the Ministry of Transport as a minibus. Sadly, he found Gould and Perrett intractable. This would not deter him from his aims, but it meant that it would be delayed for some time.

The Winchester

The lack of a viable alternative to the FX4 prompted the Owner Drivers' Society (ODS) to enter the manufacturing field. For decades they had run the Westminster Insurance Society for owner drivers. The consulted their membership and in 1960 put in hand the design of a new type of cab, called the Winchester. A new company was formed to build it, Winchester Automobiles (West End) Ltd. and its managing director was Ken Drummond, a leading figure in the ODS and Westminster Insurance.

The Beardmore MkVIII

In 1957 Beardmore's managing director, Francis Allsworth put in place the design of a new model, the MkVIII, but a chassis was not set aside for the prototype until February 1960. Its wheelbase was

The first chassis for the Atlas taxi, with a 1-litre Standard 10 engine and the very awkwardly placed gear lever. The need to make a lowered centre section made the construction of the chassis very complex

longer by two inches, but the beam front axle and cart springs were kept. Outline plans were submitted to the PCO in February 1961 for a full width shape, and a prototype body in GRP was built at Hampshire Car Bodies (HCB) of Totton in Southampton. Allsworth declared his intention of taking 50 percent of the market with it.

In March 19 1961, F. W. Perrett, the Chief Inspecting Officer of the PCO, visited HCB to look at the MkVIII. He saw that it complied with the Conditions of Fitness, but the restrictions of his job limited the way in which he could express his disappointment with what can only be described as a truly ugly vehicle. He criticised the shape of the wheel arches as being too acute and the grille as being too flat. That the passenger doors were hinged on the central B post was noted, although not objected to. The roofline, which added three inches over the MkVII's 76-inch height, was criticised for being too bulky. This report was a disappointment, but they pressed on.

To find development money for the MkVIII, Francis Allsworth approached the London General Cab Company. His idea was to set up an arrangement similar to the one that existed between Austin, Car-

bodies and Mann and Overton, with the General as the main dealer. In the summer of 1961 The General's board went down to Weymann at Addlestone. The visitors were horrified as the factory doors were drawn back. Their opinion of the MkVIII was decisive. They hated it. It was not the compact cab they believed the trade needed. They had no option but to turn down Beardmore's invitation.

New Power for the Atlas Taxi

The announcement of a more robust version of the Atlas, the Atlas Major, powered by the 1.67 litre Standard Ensign engine gave Birch's cab project a new impetus. This was further driven by his fulfilling a contract to install Perkins 4.99 engines in the Standard Ensign saloon and estate car for export. There were some engines left over when the sales of the diesel Ensign dried up, and following the introduction of the Commer 15cwt van, which was direct competitor for the Atlas Major, he offered to install the remaining engines in the Atlas Major. He also redesigned his cab with a new chassis and the Perkins 4.99 engine and had a body built, based on the Atlas van and in March 1961 and

Unloved and unlovely, the MkVIII Beardmore was Francis Allsworth's hope for the company's future. Persuaded by his sales team to put it in the showroom to gauge the cab trade's opinion, the brickbats it received convinced Allsworth he was backing a loser

The last chassis produced by John Birch for the Atlas cab was fitted with a Perkins 4.99 diesel and a far more convenient remote control gearchange, but still the PCO would not pass it, because of the front suspension arrangement

asked the Assistant Commissioner if he could present it for inspection. Birch's offer was accepted, but in May 1961 the Assistant Commissioner passed the PCO's verdict in a letter to Sir Austin Strutt of the Home Office. He said:

> "Last Monday Mr. John Birch produced his Standard Atlas motor chassis… for our inspection. We did not care for the de-sign."

However, the authorities did appreciate the need to be seen to be playing fair, saying:

> "…failure to deal with and accept this vehicle would cause immediate criticism."

But already, thanks to something totally unrelated to Birch's enterprise, all hell was about to break loose.

Chapter 9

Upheaval, Uncertainty and Innovation

In 1957, Prime Minister Harold Macmillan claimed, 'Lets be frank about it; most of our people have never had it so good.' He was right: there was full employment and most people had more money to spend than they had ever had.

The Minicab

Along with the prosperity came a growing demand for cabs, but by the end of 1958, a mere 6,157 cabs had been licensed in London from the low of 5,437 in 1952. FX4 production had been held up by tooling difficulties at Carbodies and Beardmore's MkVIII, Birch's Atlas and the Winchester were only in the development stage, and even if none of three makers could produce the vehicles, the PCO could not put enough cab drivers through the Knowledge of London examination in good time to drive them. Speaking in Parliament in November 1960, Rupert Spier MP criticised the London cab trade for being outdated. He also called for a central telephone system to enable the public to book cabs and for a smaller, cheaper type of cab. Dennis Vosper MP, the minister responsible for cabs, answered by saying that smaller cabs would not be viable, nor would they stand the wear and tear. There was, however, someone who sided with Spier. He was Michael Gotla, a law graduate and the proprietor of the private hire firm, Welbeck Motors. In 1961, with financial backing from Isaac Wolfson of the Great Universal Stores Group, he put a fleet of red Renault Dauphine hire cars on the streets. He called them minicabs and with them he planned to circumvent London's hackney carriage laws.

It was, and still is an offence for the driver of a minicab to accept a street hiring in the same way that a taxi driver does. Minicabs have to be pre-booked, but Gotla announced that the public could approach any of his drivers and pre-book the minicab with the office via a car's two-way radio. The drivers were under instruction not to take the passenger without making such a booking, but this instruction was routinely ignored. The cab trade was in uproar over this blatant abuse and when cab drivers caught minicab drivers plying for hire, a violent situation often followed, as the minicab drivers, who were recruited from types who could, shall we say, look after themselves, retaliated with equal force.

Eventually, the courts ruled that the way that Gotla had instructed his drivers was illegal. Unsuccessful attempts were made by the cab section of the Transport and General Workers Union to outlaw minicabs altogether. Reforming the laws governing the plying for hire, or at least setting out a clear legal definition of it would have strengthened the police's hand in dealing with the minicab drivers' activities, but the Home Secretary, R. A. Butler, decided against it, feeling that the minicab was adequately controlled by existing law. Gotla's business went bust not long after, but the die had been cast. The minicab trade boomed and eventually spread throughout the country, with minicabs outnumbering taxis many times over.

But that was not the end of the matter. The call for cheaper cabs continued. Remembering the 'Jixi' fiasco, the trade were very concerned about any changes to the Conditions of Fitness that might be made. Feeling that they would undermine the introduction of the new cabs that were under development, the LMCPA's secretary, J. E. T. Welland, wrote to Butler, suggesting that he set up an advisory body before making any decision. In response, Butler set up the Hackney Carriage Advisory Committee, with Dennis Vosper MP in the chair. The Committee's task was two-fold: to examine the present Conditions of Fitness and to advise the Assistant Commissioner, consistent with the need to safeguard the public, if and how they ought to be modified and also, on request to advise on the technical points which may arise in the course of his consideration of any specific proposals for a new design on taxicab.

Cab Trade Reaction to the Advisory Committee

Now the MkVIII Beardmore, the Winchester and Birch's Atlas cab, all designed to meet the existing regulations were put on hold. Of these, only the Birch was a smaller, cheaper vehicle and although the Home Office had a very low opinion of it, John Birch soldiered on, presenting his new Atlas Major taxi chassis with its Perkins 4.99 engine to the PCO in April 1961. That his initial optimism was now turning to frustration is clear in a further letter to Standard's home sales director Frank Higham, when he hoped that 'they (the Home Office and the Assistant Commissioner) would be more sensible.'

In a letter to Standard's engineer, Harry Webster in June 1961, Birch wrote about the:

> - tumult in London at present regarding the design of London taxis triggered by Gotla ... all this comes on top of a sudden appreciation by the cab trade that the Austin FX4 taxicab is complete failure.'

He told Webster at Standard's that he had submitted a modified Atlas chassis for approval and was waiting for it to be inspected and tested. He said, 'the Assistant Commissioner is "entirely wedded to the Austin" and is opposed to my relaxation of the regulations.' He added that he had been told a year before by Mr Gould that he would be allowed the front suspension, but the decision had been reversed and they 'intend to make their stand on this feature on the grounds of safety.' He asked Webster for any production figures and any reports of suspension failure in the Atlas, but no record of any reply by Webster in relation to suspension failures has come to light.

By this time, Standard Triumph had been taken over by Leyland. Birch knew Donald Stokes, the then sales director of Leyland, as Birch reminded him, 'the firm of Birch Brothers Ltd was Leyland's oldest customer'. In a letter in July 1961 to Stokes, Birch said that that Home Office have been told that Leyland were tired of the procrastination on the part of the Commissioner and would probably do something at very high level. He was worried too that the Japanese might break into the taxi market.

Beardmore's Francis Allsworth was worried too: he had on order enough components to make 250 examples of the new cab. In July 1961 he wrote to the Commissioner of Police, saying,

"...We would appreciate any information you can give us as to this committee's progress and when their findings, at least interim ones, can be expected. We already have in stock some £100,000 of specialist components as the basis for the first trial run of our new taxicab... With consistent and growing rumours that the new Assistant Commissioner will allow metropolitan taxicabs of substantially inferior specification that the present standard, we are reluctant to take on more liabilities... (and) much of the material might well have little more than scrap value..."

In August, parties with vested interests were invited to submit their case to the Committee. Allsworth's written submission supported the status quo, but he asked that manufacturers be allowed 'sufficient latitude to enable them to take rapid advantage of technological progress.'

In September 1961, manufacturers and proprietors alike had the chance to offer their opinion in person to the Hackney Carriage Advisory Committee. John Birch hoped to make a two-pronged appeal, one for the retention of the Conditions of Fitness and a second to ask them to sanction his new design. He was told that he cold only make his case for the first point, and that he would have to wait until the committee published its findings before his new vehicle could be considered, which Birch considered to be extremely unfair, especially as the Assistant Commissioner had been sitting on Birch's submissions for a considerable length of time without deigning to make a decision either in favour or against the Atlas cab, and could quite easily make such rules that would outlaw it without Birch making any representation.

With progress toward a conclusion perilously slow, Beardmore's Francis Allsworth pressed the matter further. Writing to Mr. Perrett at the PCO in April 1962, he told him;

"We are already committed to a new production programme of 'conventional' taxicabs, and our financiers will not guarantee support for its implementation until they are assured that the existing regulations will, in general substance, continue in

A Renault Dauphine minicab of Welbeck Motors. Air France were early advertisers but withdrew when disputes between the cab trade and the minicab operators and drivers, both legal and physical, became headline news

force."

Robert Overton too made strong representation to the Committee to preserve the status quo, and eventually, the Advisory Committee decided to update the Conditions of Fitness, but retained the regulations demanding the 25ft turning circle and the separation of driver and passengers. They did, however, remove the requirement for a separate chassis, citing that only luxury cars such as Rolls-Royce and Daimler used them. The new rules would come into force on January 1 1963. Certainly, the prominence of Mann and Overton and the FX4 played a crucial part in influencing the Advisory Committee's decision. Tellingly, the Committee said in an internal memo referring to result if the regulations had been altered too drastically;

> "We would be in danger of upsetting our major supplier, Austin."

Alternative Vehicles

At lest two cab makers were not to take the threat of a relaxation of the Conditions of Fitness lying down. The most successful post-war chairman of BSA, Carbodies' owner was John 'Jack' Sangster. He developed a great affection for Carbodies and when he retired he kept a close watch on the company. Reading of the economics of Welbeck Motors in the Financial Times in January 1961, Sangster realised that if the Conditions of Fitness were altered to any considerable degree, Austin's and Mann and Overton's dominance of the market, and Carbodies' profit would be seriously affected. He decided that his best strategy was 'if you can't beat 'em, join 'em'. BMC had recently introduced the Morris Mini-Minor and Austin Se7en, the legendary 'Mini'. If the demand

would be for small, economical vehicles, why not, Sangster reasoned, make a cab out of Britain's smallest proper car and make a real 'Mini-Cab'?

Hooper's, widely considered as the world's finest coachbuilders had been a part of BSA, but had been almost defunct since BSA sold Daimler to Jaguar in 1960. Sangster asked Hooper's chief designer, Osmond Rivers to adapt an Austin Se7en, telling him Rivers to give the new vehicle as much headroom and legroom as he would the passengers in a Daimler limousine. Rivers did just that, adding sliding doors for easy access and well-upholstered seats. When the Hackney Carriage Advisory Committee made its recommendations, the 'Mini-Cab' was scrapped. As a footnote, Rivers' fee for designing the vehicle, £84, was paid for by Carbodies.

Beardmore Motors too were working on an alternative. Their connections with Ford led them to choose a Cortina, which they fitted with a heavy-duty clutch and shock absorbers and a dog-leg partition similar to that fitted to the original Birch. Both experiments were abandoned when the Advisory Committee announced that the Conditions of Fitness would be left largely unchanged.

The Winchester is Introduced

In October 1962, when the dust created by the review of the Conditions of Fitness had settled, the Winchester was finally introduced. Its price was £1,165, compared to the FX4's price then of £1,171. It was the first London cab to have a glass reinforced plastic (GRP) body, which was built by James Whitson of West Drayton, Middlesex' who were pioneers in the manufacture of fibreglass bodies and were supplying the body for the Peerless sports car. Winchester chose fibreglass for the body for two reasons: one, producing press tools for a steel body for such a limited production run would make the cab too expensive and two, it was hoped that fibreglass would be less expensive to repair than steel and thus ease the burden on the parent insurance company. The inclusion of an upright radiator grille rather than a horizontal one now almost universal on contemporary cars was, probably a deliberate nod to the FX4, so that the public would recognise the Winchester as a taxi right from its introduction.

The body was made at Whitson's factory at Yiewsley, Middlesex. It was mounted on the Rubery Owen chassis inherited, via the MkVII Beardmore, from the Oxford and power was from a Perkins 4.99 diesel engine. The same Rubery Owen front axle and ENV rear axle as the Beardmore's were used, although the sump of the Perkins engine, which hung down at the rear, allowed for the location of the front axle further forward and thus a slightly longer wheelbase. Completed bodes were then shipped from Whitson's to Winchester's premises in Lot's Road, Chelsea for finishing and delivery to the customer.

Unfortunately the Winchester was a poor product, despite the best attempts of those involved. Much was made in the publicity of the internal 'running board' of the Winchester, which was revealed when the doors were opened, but in reality it was a necessity, because the chassis was so high that the step had to be put in to enable passengers to get in the cab. This was also the case with the MkVII Beardmore, but the Beardmore's external running boards prepared the passenger for the step inside the door. This hidden step earned the Winchester the nickname of 'the pick 'em up and pull 'em out' cab, because passengers often fell flat on their faces when they didn't realise that the step was there! The high chassis also made for an awful driving position. The driver sat almost on the floor, unable to raise the seat high enough without the steering wheel cutting into his legs, and operating the pendant pedals from such an awkward position as to cause serious back ache.

Now there was a choice of three cabs, but in reality the picture was not so rosy. With a tiny production run of an average of one vehicle a week, Winchester had no financial clout, and could not buy in their supply of components is quantity. As such,

The Mk1 Winchester was produced in a two-tone grey finish. The built-in roof sign says 'Taxi For Hire'

the cab was almost a home-made job, with no two vehicles completely identical. When a cab was ordered, they simply went to the local main agents or motor factors and bought the minor components such as the lights and other electrical parts over the counter! Neither the Winchester nor the ageing Beardmore could match what the Austin could offer the cab masters in terms of availability or serviceability. For the same reasons the Austin remained the preferred choice for mushers too.

The End of the MkVIII Beardmore

Despite Francis Allsworth's hopes, the MkVIII Beardmore was wholeheartedly disliked within Beardmore Motors. To convince Allsworth that this design was a lost cause, the sales staff persuaded him to place it in the Great Portland Street showroom and invite comments from cabmen and the public at large. It took very little time for the message to sink in. Allsworth convened a meeting at their London showroom and taking the London General Cab Company's and the PCO's comments into consideration as well, killed off the exist-

ing MkVIII design. They commissioned a new design and a mock-up was constructed at Weymann in Addlestone. It was a full-bodied vehicle with all four doors hinged from the front, but it was to be built on the original MkVIII chassis. They still needed a financial backer, and once more approached the London General, now a wholly owned subsidiary of Associated Newspapers Ltd. In the summer of 1963 the General's board were invited to view the new cab, but again, they said no. With this rebuff, Beardmore gave up the idea of developing a new taxi.

The End of the Atlas

John Birch was now also ready to make progress with the Atlas cab and presented his latest chassis to the PCO for inspection. Eight detail faults were found, seven of which Birch knew he could remedy with little or no difficulty or considered to be unjustified. He outlined his opinions in a letter to the Hackney Carriage Advisory Committee. To the PCO's last comment, that 'the chassis is not very pretty' he simply wrote, 'Comment: None.'

To try and improve sales against com-

Alongside one of the London General's early Austin FX4s, MCW's mock-up of the revised Beardmore MkVIII looks massive. Its rather bizarre interpretation of American styling influences is a sharp contrast to the traditional lines of the MkVII, or indeed the conservative styling of the FX4

petition from Bedford, Rootes, Ford and BMC, Leyland upgraded the Atlas, and in 1963 a larger version, the Standard 20, with a choice of a 2.2 litre petrol engine or a 2.3 litre diesel was introduced. Birch wrote to Donald Stokes, asking him for advice on which chassis to use, the 15 or the 20 and whether he should discuss the building of a special body with Park Royal Vehicles, or go elsewhere. In the event, Birch went to Park Royal, who produced a conversion of an Atlas body with the original front end and a raked-back rear window, similar to that adopted for the Beardmore MkVIII. It was tilt tested at London Transport's Aldenham Works in October 1963, but from there, it disappeared without trace and not long after, Birch Brothers eventually gave up their century-long involvement with London the London cab trade.

The MkVII Beardmore Four-door

With the MkVIII scrapped, Beardmore's only option was to update the MkVII by fitting a fourth door across the luggage platform. Even that apparently

simple change was delayed to excess. In December 1963 a modified cab was presented, but the PCO didn't like the handbrake, which was relocated to a position between the driver's seat and door. This meant that it would be cable operated, unlike the Austin cabs' handbrake rods. (The PCO referred to the cable as a 'wire rope') It would take two years before the cab was passed with a handbrake cable, and Beardmore sales suffered as a consequence. A more crucial handicap to sales was 21-week strike in 1964 at Weymann's, which followed Metro-Cammell's purchase of the company the previous year.

In the mean time, new engines were tried, because of changes by the respective makers. A second Perkins diesel, the 4.107, was tested in 1962 in RYT 99. This engine was adopted for marine use, (one famous installation was in 'Gypsy Moth IV', the yacht that Sir Francis Chichester sailed single-handed around the world) but it would lead to the choice, in later MkVIIs, of the more powerful 4.108. In 1964, a 1.6 litre Hillman Minx petrol engine was tried, as the in-line Ford engine was due for replacement by a new V4. The Hillman engine never went into a production cab, but contacts were maintained with the Rootes

The four-door version of the MkVII made the cab a little more comfortable to drive, but for a vehicle built in the 1960s its style and construction was now very old-fashioned. Two-tone paint was an extra-cost option

Group.

With no new cab to develop and sales of the MkVII slowing, Beardmore were facing the end. In more modern times a ruthless board of management would have cut the losses, shut the company down and made everyone redundant, but this was not Beardmore's style. They were a small company that had a strong loyalty to its workers and its customers. Beardmore company secretary Ken Jaeger would recall much later that Beardmore were like a happy family.

The Winchester Mk2

The Perkins 4.99 engine had made the Series I Winchester slow and very noisy and so for the Series II, introduced in 1965 a 1600cc Ford Cortina engine and four-speed gearbox was fitted, with the option of the larger Perkins 4.108 diesel. The job of building the body, now finished in black, was transferred to Wincanton Engineering in Old Woking, Surrey, who also took over the building of bodies for the Peerless, because Peerless's management had serious issues regarding the build quality of the Whitson's body.

The Metro-Beardmore

In 1965 Beardmore's entire production was transferred to Metro-Cammell-Weymann's factory in Washwood Heath, Birmingham. All the cabs produced there were fitted with four doors and a four-speed gearbox, with the option of the 1.7-litre Ford petrol or Perkins 4.108 diesel engine. Sales of this now obsolete vehicle were very slow. Only loyal customers, or those that would not deal with Mann and Overton at any price, stuck with Beard-

more.

In the same year Metro-Cammell-Weymann's Works manager, Mr D. D. Boote, sent drawings of a new prototype, with simple, modern lines, and referred to as the 'Metro-Beardmore', to the PCO. No details of whose chassis would be used are now known but its wheelbase was identical to that of the MkVII Beardmore and was intended that a Rootes engine would power the cab. But the London General Cab Company examined the Metro-Beardmore and, seeing that it was, overall marginally longer, higher and wider than the MkVII considered it simply too big and heavy. Once more they rejected any offer of a deal.

Winchester Automobiles' publicity people were quick to latch on to the fact that the Mk2 cab shared the same Ford Cortina engine as this Brabham racing car. The cab was now built by Wincanton Engineering

The Metro-Beardmore was MCW's first attempt at designing their own cab. It is hardly an attractive vehicle: the London General Cab Company's board rejected an invitation to invest in it, considering it to be too big and too heavy

A First Try at an 'FX5'

With the virtual disappearance of Beardmore and the poor sales of the Winchester, Mann and Overton were able to dominate the London market with the FX4, but by 1965 a replacement was due for consideration. Mann and Overton had consulted with the trade, and one proprietor, Ronnie Samuels of Great Cambridge Garage provided a list of the features he would most like to see in a cab. He wanted a smaller, cheaper-to-run vehicle, with simple servicing and a built-in taximeter and a separate chassis, but also sliding doors and forward control, which were part of John Birch's ill-fated Atlas cab. It was assumed that the new cab would be numbered FX5 and the general chassis drawings were begun, but ideas as revolutionary as Samuels' were, not surprisingly disregarded.

The fact that Carbodies had not been profitable from the time of the BSA takeover until 1963 worried Mann and Overton. This, plus a quote of £350,000 from Carbodies for a body for the FX5 prompted Mann and Overton to talk to other body manufacturers. The introduc-

tion of the Winchester opened the possibility of a glass fibre body and the sports car makers Jensen and Keeble Cars, (the latter being a company that grew out of the commercial collapse of Warwick, the successor to Peerless) were both consulted. As a young man, Andrew Overton remembers well being driven around in a Gordon-Keeble sports car, a luxury sports coupé with a Chevrolet V8 engine by his father, Robert, who had been lent one by Gordon-Keeble's management. The quality of both the Gordon-Keeble and the Jensen were without question, and Jensen certainly had the capacity to make as many cabs as Mann and Overton could sell, but Joe Edwards of BMC recommended that Mann and Overton stayed with pressed steel. He believed that GRP was still not developed enough for such heavy usage and the idea was abandoned.

The Winchester Mk3

The Series III Winchester was introduced in September 1966. The ENV axles supplied to older Jaguars would no longer be available and so Winchester fitted a new model, the MkIII with the Ford V4 Transit engine, four-speed gearbox, rear axle and brakes. Along with the axles and brakes came fourteen-inch wheels, which sat the MkIII a fraction lower on the ground.

The End of Beardmore

With the Great Portland Street show-room closed, the last MkVII, NUU 466E was delivered in January 1967 from Beardmore's own Threeway Garage in St. John's Wood to Messrs T. V. W. Spencer and N. T. J. Hopley. The company continued to maintain the existing cabs from Threeway garage, but as the end drew near, regular customers invited to go to Threeway and for £100 a head, the foreman filled their cabs up with as many spares as was wanted. Once genuine Beardmore spares ran out, problems began to occur. The PCO would not allow repairers to use pattern parts for fear that they would be sub-standard. Owners had no option but to sell their cabs out of service and drive Austins. Beardmore ceased trading in 1969, but as there were no creditors, the company was not liquidated, and still existed on record at Companies House until the late 1990s.

The Winchester Mk4

When Beardmore announced that they were ceasing cab production, Rubery Owen stopped making its chassis, which put Winchester, whose chassis was a derivative of the Beardmore's in a difficult situation. Fortunately, they found a new chassis maker, Keewest Engineering in Southampton, who was also responsible for making the chassis of the Gordon-Keeble high performance GT car. The new chassis needed to have the same ground clearance as the original, with sufficient clearance for the Ford Transit axles, which were carried over from the Mk3. What Keewest made for Winchester was a simple, even crude affair of welded, square-section steel tube, a marked departure from the sophisticated Rubery Owen chassis. The optional Perkins 4.108 diesel was carried over too, but the Transit V4 petrol engine was replaced by the new 1.6 litre Ford Cortina 'Crossflow' and full synchromesh gearbox. No automatic transmission option was offered.

There would be completely new, very modern-style body too, built by Wincanton Engineering, who had supplied the bodies for the Mk2 and Mk3, and for that matter the Peerless sports car, built by

The 14-inch wheels of the Ford Transit running gear set Mk3 Winchester slightly lower on the ground. This particular cab is the pre-production model and has a petrol engine, as indicated by the external fuel cut-off tap, placed high on the front wing

John Gordon, one of the two men behind the Gordon-Keeble sports GT. But where the Gordon-Keeble was luxurious, the interior of the Winchester was as austere as previous models, with details like the door handles and fittings often of the cheapest type. The lines of the body suggest a very hurried job, possibly one that had been chopped up from a previous design. But it still required some planning financial investment, and this raises a question. Sales of Winchester cabs had been notoriously poor and Winchester Automobiles could not have made very much profit out of sales, and thus been able to put aside much development money, so the question arises of where the money, or indeed the design for an all-new body may have come from. It may well have come from Keewest, the successor company to Keeble Cars, which was one of the companies approached by Mann and Overton with a view to building a fibreglass replacement body for the FX4. No documentation has been found to substantiate this idea. But whatever its origins, the cab came too late to make any impact on the FX4, which was being improved year on year.

Gas Power for Cabs

The big issue over fuel in the 1950s was its price, but in the late 1960s, concerns over exhaust emissions began to arise. In 1970, fleet owners W. H. Cook and Sons of West London invested in a fleet of petrol FX4s that they converted to run on liquid propane gas. Although the petrol FX4 returned about 18mpg, there was no fuel duty on LPG, so fuel costs of a gas-powered cab were about two-thirds that of a diesel cab. A pressurised gas container was fitted above the petrol tank so that it protruded into the boot floor, displacing the spare wheel, which was bolted to the partition in the luggage compartment. At first, the project went well, despite some early problems with exhaust valves burning out due to the higher combustion chamber temperatures, but matters turned bad for Cook's in 1972, when the government announced that it would put duty on LPG, doubling the price from 11p to 22p a gallon. (2.42p to 4.84p per litre). Managing director Vernon Cook wrote to Parliament, saying, 'we regret that any excessive excise duty would kill off the project and

Perkins' publicity photograph of the Winchester Mk4. Note the Perkins logo on the grille.
Two other prototypes were built, both petrol, registered as VLT 613G, and VLT 611G, which was white and used for tilt testing at the Transport Road Research Laboratory at Crowthorne

with it the end of hopes for a cleaner city.' The rise in duty would do more than kill of Cook's hopes. In September 1976, W. H. Cook pulled out of the cab trade after 108 years.

FX4 Facelift

Mann and Overton's 1965 plans for an 'FX5' had been scrapped, but still the cab trade expected, with some justification, a replacement for the FX4. Instead, in 1967 they got a face-lifted 'MkII' version of the FX4. This treatment was being administered to all BMC models, so it was no surprise to the trade. The new version earned itself the nickname of the 'new shape' amongst the trade and it did at least address some of the complaints made about the cab. The hated roof-mounted limpet indicators were replaced by the taillights from the MkII BMC 1100 and indicators and repeaters were fitted on the front wings. The inner panels of the front wings were redesigned to include rain channels. Previously, rainwater had collected under them and in the space of three or four

years would rot through the metal and pour onto the driver's right foot!

Under-bonnet soundproofing was fitted, making driving less tiring and communication with the passenger a little easier. The FX4's original driver's compartment was designed for an older generation, but many younger cabmen were noticeably taller, and found it cramped. The partition from the FL2 Hire Car, which was angled back to house its forward-facing tip-up seats was fitted, although a new design of rearward-facing seats was used in the FX4. This new partition allowed the driver's seat to be reclined, thus giving a little more legroom, but it also gave some taller drivers chronic backache. The horizontally sliding glass in the FL2's partition replaced the vertically sliding pane. The water pipes that fed the original passenger compartment heater ran under the cab, but in winter, when it was needed the cold air cooled the water in the pipes, making the heater virtually useless. The heater unit was relocated to under the driver's seat and hot air discharged from a circular grille between the cricket seats.

Two of the 'new shape' Austin FX4 models, introduced in 1967. The rear window was made of clear glass and an interior rear-view mirror was at last allowed

Enter the Metrocab

Following the Metro-Beardmore project, Metro-Cammell-Weymann's managing director, Tony Sansome, considered by some to be of the most forceful and dynamic people in British industry at the time, decided to revive the idea of making taxis. MCW's Metrobus had failed to make the inroads into the newly opened up London bus market that he'd hoped, and Sansome wanted to keep his production lines going by making a cab. In September 1968 MCW sent the PCO drawings of 'Project HO 10180', named the Metrocab. Two weeks later the PCO accepted it, remarking only that the wheel size had not been marked on the drawings, and criticizing the excessive hump in the floor.

A scale model was made for MCW by Specialist Mouldings of Huntingdon, after which MCW produced a full-sized mockup at their Washwood Heath, Birmingham factory. As the London General Cab Company had been involved with Beardmore, Sansome invited their board to look at it, with a view to them becoming purchaser and possibly dealers if he put it into production. The General declined, saying it was a 'box on wheels' and much too big.

However, they accepted MCW's invitation to act as consultants and possible purchasers of a revised model.

The General's board then viewed another new model, built by Haring Conti Associates of Sandy, Hertfordshire. The following October 17, Messrs Whomersley and Gupwell of MCW went to the General's Brixton premises to discuss the project with Geoff Trotter, Joe de Ciantis and the General's chairman, Sir Neil Cooper-Keys. The General's board felt that MCW's new cab would end up too much like the over-large FX4 and wanted MCW to investigate one of three options; a front engine with front wheel drive, a rear mounted engine with rear wheel drive or a monocoque construction. They felt that unless MCW followed a more modern approach, they should"

'...not counsel Metro-Cammell to proceed any further along such a conventional and similar design as defined by the FX4... a revolutionary design would reduce weight, improve performance and make the Metrocab marginally different.'

For their part, MCW felt that the General's ideas were 'impracticable, too expensive and time consuming'. Having seen, even in the very early days of motor cabs that it had become uneconomical to

The Metrocab prototype was some fifteen inches shorter than the FX4 and a more compact vehicle than the Metro-Beardmore. It is certainly a far more modern-looking vehicle than the Austin FX4. The appearance and the recognisability of a London taxi would be the subject of much debate in the years to come

130

adapt even an entirely conventional motor car design for London taxicab work, one can sympathise with MCW's position, despite the General's desire to keep a close rein on the running costs of a cab. Eventually, they reached a compromise whereby MCW would develop a conventional prototype that was smaller and lighter than the FX4. Along with Geoff Trotter and Joe de Ciantis, the PCO's Chief Inspecting Officer Mr Collins went to see an interior mock-up of their latest idea on January 9 1969. Collins was reasonably satisfied with what he saw, and the General agreed that MCW should produce a running prototype.

At Metro-Cammell's railway engineering department, engineering director Frank Bonneres' team produced three designs of simple box-section frame, all X-braced for strength and rigidity. They were submitted to the Motor Industry Research Association for strength testing, and the best design selected for the prototype. A Perkins 4.108 diesel engine was fitted, and a Ford Transit all-synchromesh gearbox, back axle, steering box and beam front axle. The GRP body was a contemporary design by Haring Conti Associates, and built by Henlycraft in Southampton. Although the driving position was a little

cramped for tall drivers, the visibility through the big, curved windscreen was excellent. It was fifteen inches shorter than the FX4 and some 56lb (25kg) lighter. Some of the features on the cab, including a steering crash link, telescopic shock absorbers, an alternator and full servo brakes were not found on the FX4, highlighted just how far behind the times the Austin was.

But MCW were to fall foul of the Conditions of Fitness from the outset, on one crucial point; the type of steering ball joint fitted. The rules demanded that the ball joints should be non-pendant, i. e. fitted with the bolt going downwards into the steering arm to which they are located. The PCO maintained that the tight turning circle put excessive loading on pendant ball joints, causing them to wear quickly. MCW were determined to have pendant ball joints, arguing that they were used with safety on buses and lorries. The argument delayed progress until the Transport Road Research Laboratory convinced the PCO to change their mind.

A prototype, finished in blue to match the General's pre-war livery submitted to the PCO in December 1969. When presenting the prototype, MCW made the mistaken assumption that the PCO would

The Metrocab prototype's interior was functional but not unpleasant

By contrast, the driver's compartment was very basic. Most components were sourced from the Ford Transit

accept the same sort of rough and ready finish that motor manufacturers considered normal for early prototypes, producing what they considered to be the physical equivalent of a 'rough draft'. However, MCW soon found out that virtual production standard was what was wanted if type approval was to be granted.

The PCO found a list of no less than fifty-eight faults, the most serious being the front axle, which they condemned outright. In order to get the track arrow enough to fit, (although not of course for production) MCW had cut the Transit front axle into two shortened halves and butt-welded them together. PCO Chief Inspecting Officer Jack Everitt was not going to accept this at all, and was backed up by a decisive statement from Ford. Mr Collins wrote to MCW stating his disappointment over the condition of the Metrocab. He concluded his letter by saying,

"You can be assured of our continued co-operation, but I feel that in the past some advice has gone unheeded."

In February 1970 the Metrocab was introduced to the trade at the London General's filling station at Southwark Street, Southwark. However, type approval would not be given until July 31, after three more attempts by MCW. Even then it was on the understanding that it was

'... to be regarded as a prototype for experimental purposes, and that further modification would have to be made before the cab goes into production.'

The Metrocab immediately went into service with the General. There was some uncertainty from the public about whether it was a taxi and because of this, the General's drivers were offered a lower rental as an inducement to drive it. In nearly three years' service and 100,000 miles the engine was trouble-free, delivering excellent fuel consumption. Despite some signs of localised starring in the gel coat, the GRP body stood up to the job very well. Certainly it was encouraging to the makers to see that it, as a prototype, could do the job at least as competently as an FX4. In some ways it did the job better; the brakes were much better and the body was draught proof, leak proof and rust proof.

Now, Tony Sansome now wanted to know whether the General would place a significant order for the cab. He wanted to have it as a standby line in the bus body factory when there was a pause in bus production, but the unions at MCW were making some uncooperative noises, wanting the cab to be a full-time production vehicle. For the General's board the task of appraisal was agonising, because they had been, in Geoff Trotter's words, 'surrogate fathers' to the cab, right from Beardmore's first approach to them in regard to the MkVIII. It at least followed their ideal of a cab in that it was lighter and cheaper to run, but it was an unknown commodity in a market that was already in the firm grip of Mann and Overton's FX4. And in order to service both types the General would have to carry two completely different sets of spares, and employ trained craftsmen, or train new people to repair the GRP body. By now, the improved 'new shape' FX4 had been on sale for two years and the fleet drivers agreed that they would rather have it than the Metrocab.

Sansome did the only thing he could do, and pulled the plug on Metrocab. There was a second prototype built, which was much better finished, and if it had gone into service it might possibly have affected the General's decision, but it was not to be. The Metrocab was doomed to the same fate as the Beardmore and the Birch - the history book.

Chapter 10

Monopoly by Default

The trade was angry that, since the demise of the Metrocab and the Winchester they could not foresee any replacement for the FX4, either from Austin or any other source. Comparisons with modern saloon cars like the Ford Zodiac, which was much better equipped and sold for about the same price, had been made in the trade press from 1972. To make matters worse, the price of the ageing FX4 price rose steeply as a result of the inflation of the 1970s. An FX4 cost around £1,200 in 1971. Thanks to inflation, it could be sold three years at a profit, as could a 1980 FX4, which would be selling for more than its £7,000 price at three years old.

Stories about collusion between Mann and Overton and the PCO, of how they were supposed to contrive to keep the market sewn up and the customer pinned down became rife. Pressure from trade bodies resulted in an investigation by the Monopolies Commission, but Mann and Overton were not found to be engaged in any illegal or improper activities. The market was open to anyone who could build a cab that met the Conditions of Fitness. The trouble was, no one else wanted to. For the PCO, preserving the status quo was the safest option for the trade, even though it meant the perpetuation of an ageing vehicle, with neither a replacement nor a competitor in sight. To alter the Conditions of Fitness and allow cabs based on other production vehicles might

in theory have given the trade more choice, but to do it when there were no viable alternatives in the offing would be irresponsible. The damage caused to trade confidence over the minicab debacle of 1961 was warning enough.

But in writing and enforcing such strict rules as the Conditions of Fitness, the PCO brings upon itself a responsibility to the trade to ensure that there are so framed as to allow manufacturers to produce vehicles that comply with them. If no manufacturer were to come forward, the PCO may well have to reconsider the regulations. The very existence of the FX4 and the Winchester and the brief appearance of the Metrocab proved that they could be met satisfactorily, and there if were just one supplier, then the PCO could say with some degree of justification that it was possible to meet the regulations and there was no need for them to be altered.

However, many circumstances, including inflation and a slump in world trade meant that there were not only no vehicles other than the FX4 that complied, but no contenders had made efforts to produce a cab, despite ideas from some European and American makers for purpose-built or adapted vehicles that appeared in the cab trade press. Thus, for fifteen years the FX4 would be the only cab made anywhere in the world that would satisfy the Conditions of Fitness. Not that Carbodies didn't want to make one.

The British Leyland LM11

The 'new shape' FX4 was considered by the trade to be a stopgap, and at British Leyland, progress was being made towards producing a new range of models and the older models that provided the components used on the FX4 were being phased out. Alec Issigonis, the man who had created BMC's Mini, and David Bache, who had styled Rover's 3-Litre and 2000, began designing a new cab based on the proposed replacement of the Austin-Morris JU250 15cwt van. The project, numbered LM11, seemed sound in theory. The JU250's beam axle allowed the 25ft turning circle to be easily achieved, and the development costs would be relatively low, which, considering that Austin-Morris was losing a great amount of money was a definite advantage. However, as talented as Bache and Issigonis were in their own fields, the cab they produced was, in the opinion of the people at Carbodies a disaster. Carbodies designed a new mock-up, and Issigonis and Bache had to admit that it was an improvement and gave it the go-ahead. However, Mann and Overton saw no reason to invest in a vehicle that they considered as unnecessary, especially as it was not an improvement on the FX4. The LM11 was abandoned.

A New Engine for the FX4

At the end of 1971, Austin-Morris introduced the AE250 1-ton van, to replace the ageing Morris LD. The 2.2 litre diesel that powered the LD was the same as the FX4's but the new van would have a more powerful 2.52 litre engine. This would meet forthcoming exhaust emission regulations and was fitted in the FX4, giving the cab much better acceleration and, with a higher ratio differential a top speed of over 70mph. With the engine came an alternator, a negative earth electrical system and a single 12v battery. The price increase was a modest £40.

When BSA sold Daimler to Jaguar in 1961, they had no more in-house Daimler limousines to call on to transport visitors, so commissioned this FL2 limousine, painted gold with the BSA 'piled arms' symbol on the door. Pictured from left to right are BSA's company secretary H. R. Niven, Carbodies' director and general manager Bill Lucas and Carbodies' engineering director Jake Donaldson

Carbodies Become Complete Manufacturers of the FX4

The Austin-Morris division of British Leyland was losing money at a serious rate, and Standard-Triumph's managing director George Turnbull was transferred to Austin-Morris to try and make it viable. Part of his task was to close or rationalise uneconomical factories, and one of these was Adderley Park, where Morris-Commercial cabs and, for a time the Nuffield Oxford was produced. Now only FX4 chassis was built there. Turnbull offered the assembly plant to Carbodies and director and general manager, Bill Lucas, who accepted, provided he could transfer the entire, albeit small workforce to Coventry and not have to make anyone redundant. The tracks, jigs, overhead cranes and all the other equipment were moved in their entirety, with virtually no upset to

taxi production. In fact, the people building the chassis actually earned more money working for Carbodies than they were at Adderley Park! With this change, Carbodies became complete manufacturers of the FX4, in practice if not in title.

A New Owner for Carbodies

BSA, who owned Carbodies was a huge concern. It encompassed some of the best names in the British motorcycle industry, including BSA, Triumph, Ariel and Sunbeam. It had owned Carbodies since 1954, but when its most effective and influential post-war chairman, Jack Sangster retired, his successors failed to meet the challenge of the Japanese motorcycle industry and the combine went into free fall. Worried that the British motorcycle industry would collapse, the government asked

Mann and Overton's Robert Overton, (second from right) and David Southwell (centre left) talk to Leyland's George Turnbull (right) and Carbodies' Bill Lucas at the 1970 Commercial Motor Show at Earls Court. Later at this event, Turnbull would offer the FX4's chassis manufacturing plant to Carbodies

The chassis assembly shop at Carbodies' factory in Coventry

135

Dennis Poore, the chairman of Manganese Bronze Holdings (MBH) to help. MBH owned Norton Villiers, a combine of Norton Motorcycles and Villiers, who had produced engines for many of Britain's independent motorcycle manufacturers. Poore was at first reluctant, but the government threatened to nationalise the remnants of BSA. Poore did not want to have a government-owned competitor and so in 1973 authorised Manganese Bronze Holdings to buy the remnants of BSA. Along with it came Carbodies Ltd.

The news of BSA's impending demise caused a great deal of worry at both Carbodies and Mann and Overton. Would the new owners close Carbodies down? By now the FX4 was virtually the only cab available, the Winchester all but defunct. If BSA's new owners discontinued the FX4, the Conditions of Fitness might have to be abandoned, the whole industry thrown into a downward spiral and the unique London cab would be a thing of the past. Their worries were unfounded. Manganese Bronze's head office was in the City of London and Dennis Poore was great user of cabs. He was delighted to be the head of the company that made London taxis and the FX4 continued in production.

European Vehicle Regulations

In 1973, Britain joined the European Common Market and would be subject to many and varied new rules and regulations. Not least of these governed vehicle design. The 2.2 litre Austin petrol engine that had been available in the FX4 and FL2 since 1961 would not meet the European exhaust emission legislation. These models were now the only vehicles using this engine, most of which were FL2 Hire Cars, which was a very moderate seller. Rather than spend money that it didn't have in modifying the engine to meet the regulations, BLMC scrapped it, leaving the 2.5-litre diesel as the only engine available for both models.

New European safety rules demanded the fitting of protective steering and anti-burst door locks and the requirement that all vehicles, either new or of an existing design had to be crash tested. These regulations would have an effect on the two makes of cab on the market. One would be improved, the other, lost for good.

Despite being deeply in the red, Austin-Morris were obliged to engineer the FX4 chassis changes required to enable it to pass the test. This included incorporating a crash link into the steering column and

Featured on Carbodies' stand at the Commercial Motor Show was this FX4 chassis, which was updated to meet European safety regulations.
The steering wheel has an energy-absorbing rubber boss, and the steering column has a crash link. All other modifications to the cab were to the bodywork or interior trim

fitting a new steering wheel with a rubberised centre. Making body modifications was Carbodies' job and they fitted the mandatory burst-proof door locks, finding, after a long search a new type, sourced from Hapitsch in Germany, along with a push button handle to suit. The interior handles were moved to the centre of the door to accommodate the mechanism. In addition, the rear seat cushion was re-profiled and a new instrument panel fitted.

Mann and Overton supplied a modified cab for the Motor Industry Research Association to test. Thanks to the robust chassis it passed, the staff at MIRA saying it was one of the best results they had ever seen. One of the new models marked a milestone in FX4 production. On the 28th March 1974 the 25,000th example rolled off the production line.

The End of the Winchester

A casualty of the European safety regulations was the Winchester, which was withdrawn from sale without being tested. Plainly it wouldn't have passed: the doors would have to be completely redesigned to accommodate more sophisticated door locks and it was not likely that either the

chassis or the fibreglass body would pass the crash test. Only 55 MkIVs are understood to have been sold by the time production ceased in 1972.

FX4 Problems: Resolution and Otherwise

The FX4's habit of rusting to quickly had been tackled by Carbodies with the latest methods available to them, build quality had undoubtedly been improved, especially in regard to paint finish and a lot of the criticisms of the original model had been cured with the 'new shape', but customers were still not satisfied. The cab, they were saying was too old and they wanted a new model. There were other points of dissatisfaction that had arisen with the new 2.52-litre engine, which was now cooled by a pressurised radiator and was prone to overheating and also cylinder head cracking. Because of the way the engine was mounted in the AE250 van, it had its oil filler at the rear of the rocker cover. No attempt was made to make a special rocker cover for the cab, with the oil filler at the front. The result was that topping up the oil was a tricky business. On the other hand, money had been spent

The Lucas electric taxi was developed in the 1970s as a testbed for its vehicle motor. The taxi, designed by Tom Karen of Ogle Design was fully compliant with the Conditions of Fitness but never received type approval. Electric cabs had proved a failure, both in the late 19th century and in the Edwardian era, but would reappear as prototype vehicles in the second decade of the twenty-first century

on fitting a fresh air vent in the first 2.52 litre cabs, which, because was directed at the driver's right knee, proved useless.

Bill Lucas, Carbodies' director and general manager was, for a long time unaware of many of the complaints made by the cab proprietors made to Mann and Overton about the FX4, such its propensity to leak rainwater, its lack of draught proofing and the fact that it rusted so badly, so quickly. Lucas set up a liaison with Jack Everitt, the Chief Inspecting Officer of the PCO to discover for himself what were the FX4's most significant problems. Mann and Overton, in their position as suppliers of the sole vehicle on the London market had little to worry about so far as complaints were concerned. They had a waiting list of two years for the cab and they could ask the top price that the market could stand, and as the warranty was for only six months, rarely saw a cab in their workshops any older than that. Apart from the fact that the myriad of small cab garages could service and repair cabs for less money than Mann and Over-

ton, the dealers required the cab to be in their works all day to do a job, such as the first, 600-mile service that might only take half an hour. This was what happens even today with main dealers servicing private cars, but it was a situation that cab drivers were not prepared to tolerate. They knew that independent cab garages, could, unless spares had to be ordered, do this work, often on demand, on a 'while you wait' basis, reducing downtime to a minimum.

There was another factor in the offing, with regard to how many cabs Carbodies needed to make to ensure the factory's viability. Up until the mid 1970s, it was not their prime concern, so long as their orders were met, but things were changing. Until 1977, the FX3 and FX4 were always just one of their many jobs. Their last private car contract was making the Triumph 2000 Estate, production of which, at its peak was more than twice that of the FX4. When this came to an end, the cab became the only vehicle they produced and this would, in time have profound effect on the future of both the cab and the company.

FX4s in the finishing shop at Carbodies in the mid-1970s. On the far left of the picture, finished bodies are taken to the mounting shop, where they are fitted onto the chassis. The assembled cabs return to the finishing shop, where the final detail parts such as windscreen wipers and bumpers are fitted

The FX5

Tired of having to chase Mann and Overton for money for improvements, and realising that the flow of in the flow of work coming into the company was reducing as other manufacturers took in-house the kind of work that had been subcontracted to Carbodies, Bill Lucas went to Dennis Poore and said he wanted to develop a cab independent of the dealers. It would provide a modern vehicle with, he expected better performance and comfort that would appeal to a wider UK market and place all the decision making about it within Carbodies. Poore's board gave an initial agreement, and Lucas instructed chief engineer Jake Donaldson to design what was to become the FX5. Designing a new vehicle from scratch had become enormously expensive, so it made sense to see if an existing vehicle could be adapted. Donaldson though that the roof panel of a Range Rover would be ideal for a cab and over three years undertook a feasibility study. However, Donaldson's conclusion was that the body shell was too bulky and wrongly proportioned for a taxi, and it was rejected.

Next, Carbodies began work on a completely new body design. Donaldson and his assistant Peter James produced an extruded steel tube chassis, and mounted the McPherson strut front suspension and coil spring rear suspension and the rear axle from the new Rover 3500 the SD1, which had been introduced in 1976. A quarter scale model was made up and shown to Dennis Poore, who immediately gave it the go-ahead.

Cab trade representatives were invited to see a full size mock-up. Mann and Overton were included in the party: Carbodies had no reason to abandon them as dealers, only as major financiers. They liked the new cab, numbered, naturally, FX5. However, where Carbodies once had the skilled men to design their own press tools, many of them had gone as a result the decline of the contract work of the and the job of tool making would have to be put out for tender. Another factor was that one of Manganese Bronze Holdings' other companies, the Triumph motorcycle factory at Meriden, had been the subject of a prolonged and acrimonious industrial dispute. Production there was negligible and therefore income was being lost. Meriden

The Carbodies FX5 would have had the running gear from the Rover SD1 and a Peugeot 2.5 diesel engine. The project got no further than this full size mock-up

139

was draining MBH of funds that might have been reinvested and thus the financial base that might have provided funds for the FX5 was starved of income.

Mann & Overton are Taken Over

The enormous leap in inflation in the 1970s that had pushed cab prices sky-high also increased Mann and Overton's annual profits from a steady £500,000 to £950,000 in 1976. The increase in profits attracted a number of investors, some of whom Mann and Overton were not keen to be involved with. Carbodies MD, Bill Lucas tried to persuade Dennis Poore, the Chairman of Manganese Bronze Holdings, to buy Mann and Overton. Poore, still faced with the problems at Meriden, declined. Mann and Overton were particularly interested to talk to Lloyds and Scottish Plc. A part of Lloyd's Bank, they had been behind Mann and Overton's original finance

Andrew Overton, photographed when appointed managing director of Mann and Overton

house, Mechanical Investments Ltd and were directly financing Austin cabs in Glasgow and Mann and Overton.

In 1977, Lloyds and Scottish took over Mann and Overton, and Andrew Overton was appointed deputy managing director under David Southwell. In 1979 Southwell left and Robert Overton, the long-time chairman retired. Bill Reynoldson, managing director of Lloyds and Scottish industrial and commercial division and Mann and Overton's new chairman, appointed Robert Overton's son, Andrew as managing director.

The FX4 Brake Servo Fiasco

The FX4's drum brakes had remained unchanged since 1958, and needed uprating to match the increase in performance the 2.52 - litre engine gave the cab. Brake fade when trying to stop a loaded cab at speed was happening on the Motorways that had been built since the cab was on the drawing board and the options were to either fit disc brakes or improve the old ones. There were disc brakes made that would fit the suspension uprights, but they would restrict the turning circle and Mann and Overton would not sanction the money available to either have the front suspension re-engineered or new brakes designed.

Carbodies' engineer Peter James produced a design for full servo braking with pendant pedals that would mate to the drum brakes. But Austin could not, and Mann and Overton would not pay for it. There was no change in the law or the Conditions of Fitness that obliged to adapt this system and did not see it as a necessity, so it was shelved. But, bowing to pressure, Mann and Overton decided to compromise and have a servo working on the front brakes only, which was a design that most motor engineers considered unsound. Cabs with the new brakes went on sale in 1976 and performed in a very unpredictable and dangerous fashion. Below 10mph the brakes would grab and the cab would lurch to stop. One must ask why the PCO approved them but with the FX4 the only cab on the market they would be wary of interrupting supply or upsetting Mann and Overton. Front brake drums were wearing out in 5000 miles (8,000km) and front brake linings were lasting a mere 2000 miles. (3,000km) Despite great pressure from the cab trade press, who cited independent reports on the poor safety of the system, Mann and Overton stood firm. They maintained that drivers had to learn to drive the FX4 with the new system. Faced with the inevitability of the situation and no action from the PCO, the trade made the best of a bad job.

A New Engine Trials for the FX4

In 1974, Labour Prime Minister Harold Wilson commissioned the Ryder Report on British Leyland. It called for the resignation of the chairman Donald Stokes and for the entire company and its model range to undergo a thorough shakeup. This plan, if implemented would cost an estimated £1.5 billion, but the alternative, the report claimed would be the end of British Leyland. Wilson resigned in 1975, to be replaced by James Callaghan. He decided not to implement Ryder, but saw an alternative and in 1977 appointed Michael Edwardes as Chairman and Managing Director. Edwardes would go on to cut out waste across the entire organisation and eventually bring it back into profit. One casualty among many would be the closure of the Courthouse Green

For the London cab trade to celebrate HM Queen Elizabeth II's Silver Jubilee in 1977, the London General Cab Company's MD, Geoff Trotter invited HRH the Prince of Wales to their premises in Brixton. The prince responded by saying, "Why don't you come round to my place?"
In accepting, 'The General' turned out their cab museum and also brought along a number of prominent people from the trade and from Austin and Carbodies to a reception at Buckingham Palace. Lined up here in the courtyard of the palace are the General's old Unic 12/16, their Low Loader, DYH 310, (which doubled as 'PEG 1' in the film, 'Carry on Cabby') an FX3 and an FX4, prepared in a special Silver Jubilee livery by Carbodies. The Prince of Wales took a turn around the yard in the FX4

engine plant in Coventry, where the 2.52 litre Austin diesel was made. Unlike the chassis plant, however, Carbodies were not offered the engine, as it would not pass forthcoming emission regulations. Instead, it would be sold to off to India and Austin-Morris did not offer a replacement engine. Fortunately Carbodies were given three years' notice to find one.

The 2.25 litre Land Rover diesel seemed to be an obvious replacement, but Harry Webster, formerly Standard-Triumph's chief engineer but now with the Austin-Morris, advised that its power characteristics were wrong for the cab. The 1.8-litre Perkins 4.108 diesel, which was the standard diesel option in most British 15cwt vans was too small for the FX4 and Perkins could not give Carbodies an assurance that their newly announced 3-litre would last five years. Ford's 2.3-litre diesel was an underpowered unit and the company would only guarantee it for 45,000 miles, the sort of mileage a London cab would do in a year. Through a contact at Rootes, Bill Lucas got in touch with Peugeot, who had a new 2.5 litre diesel under development and were delighted to be involved with the London cab trade. Birmingham fleet operator Horace Faulkner, tested the cab for 22 hours a day, only experiencing a single incident with a damaged cylinder head, which Peugeot's engineers fixed in a one-day flying visit.

A New Managing Director for Carbodies

In 1979, ill-health forced Bill Lucas to take early retirement from Carbodies. His replacement was Grant Lockhart, previously a plant director with BL at Cowley. By now, the FX4 was the only vehicle made by Carbodies. The cab trade in major UK cities such as Manchester, Birmingham and Glasgow were already required to use London-type cabs, so to increase the market, Carbodies' needed to tap both smaller conurbations and the export market. The cab trade in many towns outside London were allowed to operate saloon cars, so make the FX4 more appealing to these markets, Grant Lockhart knew that he had, as best he could, to make improvements to the specification. But he faced strong resistance from Mann and Overton, whose attitude was a total contrast to that which Lockhart had been used when he was at British Leyland, where the customer, not the dealer or the manufacturer, controls the market. They were loath to pay for any improvements that were not demanded by legislation or a change in component availability, and showed no interest in reducing the two-year waiting list for new cabs in London.

However, Lockhart had some luck on his side. Consumer finance regulations had been changed and a new option, lease-purchase, was available to the potential owner-driver. For a down-payment equal to the cost of one month's instalment he (London cab drivers were still almost all male at this time) could have brand new cab. If he could afford the payments and could satisfy the PCO that he was 'a person of substance', i. e. he had sufficient funds in the bank to support the running of a cab, he could be an owner a lot sooner than he might have been before. No more the steady build-up from owning an elderly cab, as he might have had to do up to a year before the change in legislation. The demand this created enabled Lockhart to maintain production levels against the background of the 'Winter of Discontent' of 1978-79 and, despite Mann and Overton's objections, bring down the waiting list. This had an adverse effect on big fleets like the London Cab Company, who found that their drivers no longer rented, but sought finance from Hertz, Taxi Leasing Services or indeed Mann and Overton, to buy a new cab of their own.

There was more: Carbodies and Mann and Overton could make additional profit in the form of 'optional extras'. In theory, a cab or hire car could always have been had in any colour in Austin's range at extra cost, but there were few takers: cab masters preferred a standard colour and mushers preferred the anonymity of black. Alternative colours such as grass green, blackcurrant, tan and aconite (a bright mauve) had been offered in the mid-1970s, but were not popular. Now Carbodies offered a new range of colours, including midnight blue and a tan as well as Carmine red and white. Vinyl roofs were offered as an option, and a sunshine roof that hinged on the leading edge.

The PCO's new Principal, Bryan Philips, was more approachable and forward-looking than his predecessors and, without compromising standards wanted to bring the institution up to date. One option that was finally approved after several years of lobbying was the fitting of a personal radio in a cab. Despite the practice being forbidden by the PCO, who had al-

ways insisted that passengers' privacy and convenience was paramount, some younger cabmen began strapping portable radios to the dashboards of their cabs. The number of complaints received by the PCO was minimal and so personal radios were finally allowed in cabs, provided their volume was kept low and the driver turned the radio off at the passenger's request. Mann and Overton approved of this and of the new colours, sunshine roofs and vinyl roofs: they were making extra profit with little or no capital investment.

The musher, now spending quite a few hours in the driving seat, preferred to choose an automatic gearbox. The Borg Warner 35 gearbox had been available since the early 1960s but it was designed for a smaller engine than the 2.5 Austin diesel and in consequence its life was not as great as it might have been. For 1978, a tougher automatic gearbox, the Model 65 replaced the 35, ensuring the reliability needed by the trade.

Despite holding a monopoly position in the London market, Carbodies were not out of trouble. There would be a new competitor who would challenge both the position in the London market and the much-sought after provincial market as well.

Chapter 11

A Newcomer, and the Formation of London Taxis International

The 1980s, the 'Thatcher Years', were the age of the 'Yuppie', the search for personal wealth, rapidly growing home ownership, union strife and the Poll Tax riots. After horrendous inflation and sky-high interest rates, Britain settled down to enjoy more stable, prosperous times. Carbodies would face big challenges and introduce a new prototype cab. And, at long last the trade would see a viable alternative to the FX4.

The CR6

Manganese Bronze's chairman, Dennis Poore, began to have doubts about whether Carbodies should build the FX5. Carbodies' new managing director, Grant Lockhart had none at all. He scrapped it, and resurrected the plan to build a cab based on the Range Rover body. First, he had to persuade Rover to sell them Range Rover bodies at an economical price, and to set the process in motion, artwork, and a scale model of the proposed cab was presented to Land Rover Ltd's managing director, Mike Hodgkinson. He liked the concept, but more than this, his attention was drawn to the cab's four doors. The Range Rover was then only available with two doors. Rover wanted a four-door model but couldn't afford to tool up for it, so Lockhart offered to design and build the four-door conversion for the Range Rover as part of a deal that included Range Rover supplying body panels to Carbodies for the new cab at a beneficial rate. It was, then, settled on this basis. Carbodies would build a new cab using a modified Range Rover body on the FX5 chassis. And it was given a number: CR6.

Carbodies' scale model of the CR6 that was shown to Rover's board

The first prototype CR6, with front lights borrowed from the Morris Ital to distinguish it from a Range Rover

CR for City (not, initially for 'Carbodies' as is often thought) Rover and 6 simply because it followed the FX5.

Sadly Jake Donaldson, whose health had been failing, died within months of the start of the CR6 project. He had been with Carbodies since the 1940s and had made a major contribution to Carbodies and especially to the FX4.

The FX5 chassis was adapted to take a 2.25 litre Land Rover diesel engine and a three-speed Borg Warner automatic. Fitted too was the running gear from the Rover SD1 with a choice of Borg Warner automatic or Rover five-speed manual gearbox. The front end of the Range Rover was redesigned to take Morris Ital headlight and indicator units to make the cab distinguishable from a Range Rover. A quarter scale model was released in June 1980 to the trade at a dinner in Manchester, where it received a warm reception. Development then began.

Wheelchair Accessibility for the CR6

1981 was declared 'The International Year of the Disabled', and a seminar held by the Department of Transport asked wheelchair-bound delegates how the Department could best alter or introduce legislation to meet their needs. The universal

The second CR6 prototype, finished in pale beige. This vehicle would be displayed at the Department of Transport, fitted with wheelchair accessibility. Pictured at the wheel is Geoff Chater, who had joined Carbodies from British Leyland in 1979

response was, 'Start with taxis. Pavements are so bad that even if we could get on trains and buses, we can't get to the stations and bus stops.'

The organiser of the seminar, the DoT's Ann Frye asked Andrew Overton if a London taxi could accommodate a wheelchair. Carbodies had modified an older FX4 to accept a wheelchair, and this they showed to representatives from the DoT. They were also shown the CR6, and asked for it to be adapted to take a wheelchair and to be presented at their London headquarters by December. A second prototype, painted in beige was built and was fitted with a split partition so that its luggage platform side could slide forward to accommodate the wheelchair-bound passenger. Viewing the CR6 at the presentation, cab trade representatives liked its huge windscreen, its modern looks and up-to-date running gear. Representatives of disabled people's groups were delighted with it.

The Department of Transport provided funds to enable the wheelchair facility of the CR6 to be properly engineered and the Transport Road Research Laboratory at Crowthorne, Berkshire set up a Road Transport Study group at Newcastle University and purchased both prototypes.

Carbodies' new logo, designed when the company became a vehicle manufacturer in its own right

In July 1982 they purchased the prototypes and put on them on test, not as taxis but as a wheelchair-carrying vehicle, one each in Peterborough and Newcastle Under Lyme, out of sight of the curious London trade.

Carbodies Acquire the Intellectual Rights to the FX4

By 1981 Austin-Morris were supplying the engine, the manual gearbox and the Austin name to the FX4. National Type Approval and other regulations emerging from the European Union were looming and with far too many problems of their own they were not prepared to get the FX4 ready to meet them. If nothing were done, the cab would be doomed. To ensure the survival of both the FX4 and themselves, Carbodies acquired the intellectual rights to the vehicle from BL Cars and obtained National Type Approval for it in their own name. Now the cab would be badged as the Carbodies FX4 and for the first time in its history the Coventry company would become a manufacturer in its own right.

The RG7

In September 1982, 'Cab Driver' newspaper carried a story of another proposed new cab. This was the RG7, named after the company that intended to build it, Ross Graham Ltd. They had acquired a premises in South Wales, a part of the UK that the government were keen to see redeveloped after the collapse of the mining industry. The story unfolded in two parts. The first claimed that the cab would resemble the MkIV Winchester, implying that Ross Graham Ltd. had acquired the body moulds from Wincanton Engineering. The second part said that the cab would use either a Ford Transit or Leyland Sherpa chassis. There was no third part to the story: the project disappeared without a trace.

The FX4R

Despite having three years' notice of the impending loss of the Austin engine, finding a replacement was causing Carbodies some serious problems. The 2.5 litre Peugeot engine on test in an FX4 still needed considerable development and the idea of using it had to be abandoned. Of the other options available, the new Perkins 3-litre was considered too big physically and too powerful and Ford would not give a release date for their new 2.5 litre direct injection engine. The Land Rover diesel was the only other option, especially as strong links had been forged with Rover over the CR6 and it was already in use in the prototypes. An example was fitted into an FX4 and in fleet tests with Horace Faulkner in Birmingham, no major faults were found with the installation. This coincided with the CR6's test period at Newcastle-under-Lyme and Peterborough, which would soon end, and

with time running out for the Austin engine, Carbodies gave themselves three months to get the changes ready for production. The new engineering director, Barry Widdowson restructured his team in order to streamline the design process, but three months of thirteen-hour days and seven-day weeks spent on design and development proved insufficient to get the cab right.

Carbodies had plans to sell a greater number of FX4s to provincial operators, who much preferred manual transmissions to the automatic that had become almost universal in London, so the smoother, modern five-speed gearbox from the Rover SD1 was adopted, along with its light diaphragm clutch, which was a great improvement over the industrial-strength clutch of the Austin. The automatic option was the Borg Warner BW66, a slightly different version of the BW65 that had proved reliable for the Austin, with a floor-mounted change replacing the steering column gear selector. Now that Carbodies settled on the Land Rover engine, the new model was named the FX4R, with 'R' standing, naturally for Rover.

Power steering was to be offered as an option, the first for a London cab. Because

An FX4R alongside the first generation of cabs commissioned by Mann and Overton, a restored 'Chinese' Austin 12/4. The FX4R was identified by the badges and the bulges on the front of the bonnet, provided to clear the power steering box. The cab also sits an inch or so lower, because of blocks placed under the front axle beam

they were required to part-fund a modification they thought unnecessary, Mann and Overton were hostile to the idea, but the original steering box would not be in production for very much longer and they had to acquiesce. A smaller steering wheel was fitted to power steering models. The full-servo brakes developed in the mid-1970s were at last to be fitted, moving the master cylinders from under the floor to under the bonnet. Disc brakes had to be ruled out- there was neither the money nor the time to engineer the job, although larger wheel cylinders were fitted. As Land Rover petrol and diesel engines were built on the same cylinder block, a petrol engine could be offered once more with a minimum of additional expenditure.

The FX4R was announced in late 1982, priced between £8,869 for a manual FL without power-assisted steering to £10,071 for an automatic HLS with power-assisted steering. This was noticeably more expensive than the last of the Austin engined cabs, partly because the development costs had to be recouped but also because Austin were no longer partners and there would be no more of their subsidised funding. The FX4R was quiet and smooth, it could top 80mph with ease and the power brakes reduced driver fatigue. Power steering would not be immediately available as early examples of the box could not be prevented from leaking and the PCO would not pass them until the problem was cured. Because of the short development time, an interim version of the meter drive from the manual gearbox had to be engineered until a better version was developed, and early owners had to have the later version retro-fitted. Also, no luggage partition was fitted to manual transmission models. The gear lever of the Rover gearbox was situated much further back than that of the Austin and the original partition would have fouled it. rather than spend time and money, both of which were short, Carbodies decided against designing a new one.

The power steering, when it was finally available and the servo brakes received a qualified welcome: both were very light in operation, but with little feel, but it was not long before major problems started. Carbodies, who were body engineers, not mechanical engineers, had been recommended to use the wrong parts in installing the manual gearbox. The first-motion shaft bearing was of the wrong type and would collapse, putting the gears out of line and wrecking the gearbox. Engine vibration caused the mount of the stamped steel clutch to wear a hole in the actuating arm. The clutch

A left-hand drive export model Carbodies FX4R, destined for Saudi Arabia, alongside the second prototype CR6

pipe, borrowed from a Triumph TR7, had a plastic pipe heat-shrunk over the steel unions. In the cab, the clutch slave cylinder was on the same side as the exhaust pipe and the heat of the exhaust perished the pipe, causing it to blow off under pressure. The radiator was inadequate, causing the cab to overheat in traffic in warm weather. This last matter was a complaint that Mann and Overton claimed could not happen, despite the trade submitting ancillary electric radiator fans for type-approval by the PCO and receiving it.

But the most damning criticism was reserved for the engine. The combustion chambers were of an inefficient design, resulting in excessive black smoke and poor fuel consumption. The engine's maximum torque was lower than the Austin's, so although the cab was fast, it had poor acceleration. The rockers in the valve train were pivoted off-centre, placing a great load on the valve lifters, which wore excessively. The timing chain was weak, and in time it stretched, aggravating the injector timing. The power steering took a high percentage of the engine's power, worsening the cab's already poor performance.

Mann and Overton were swamped by complaints from irate owners, demanding that the engines be properly tuned to give them better fuel consumption and ade-

quate performance. Mann and Overton fitted an automatic cab with a one-gallon fuel tank and on this quantity it ran for 25 miles, giving the same as might be expected from an Austin diesel, but the trade was unimpressed: depending on traffic conditions, fuel consumption could vary tremendously, and the tests were not thought to be varied enough to be accurate. Andrew Overton invited the London Cab Company's engineering director, Roger Ward, to visit the Land Rover factory. What Ward, a former marine engineer specialising in diesels discovered, shocked him. Where one in one hundred Austin engines was tested, every Land Rover engine received a two-hour test and a 120-point computer check. When an engine did not pass the test it was removed and retuned. The engineers at Land Rover were bitterly disappointed at how their engine was behaving. Within a year, cabs were being recalled to have a new governor fitted to the injector pump. The manual transmission models also fitted with a luggage partition, because gear levers were sometimes being broken off by badly loaded or unsecured luggage.

Proprietors would not buy the FX4R in anywhere near the same quantity as it had the Austin, and production dropped by around 25 percent. This had a marked ef-

A picture from the FX4R brochure, with a cab in New York City. The lyrics of the song, 'New York, New York' says, "If I can make it there, I'll make it anywhere." As a vehicle to enable Carbodies to break the world's markets, it not only failed in New York but just about everywhere else

fect on the second-hand price of Austin cabs. During the high inflation of the early 1980s, a 1979 or 1980 Austin changed hands at more than the £7,000 they had cost when new, whilst FX4Rs at £11,000 or more remained in the showroom or sold depreciated badly.

Worst of all, the FX4R gave Carbodies a terrible reputation in the new provincial markets, the very people the company needed top bring on side if it was to expand and prosper as it hoped. Poor after-sales service, which left almost-new cabs sitting idle for days, even weeks at a time hardened the attitudes of provincial operators against the FX4.

Cab drivers and proprietors were justified in aiming criticism at Carbodies, who were after all, the manufacturer, but they were body engineers, not mechanical engineers and had taken outside advice that proved to be wrong. Considering this, and the almost impossible time scale, it is remarkable that the cab materialised at all. Some FX4Rs ran well, others very badly. For Carbodies it was time to undertake a major overhaul of the business, that would include improving build-quality.

CR6: the Problems Mount

The wheelchair trials of the CR6 were a qualified success: they showed that the idea of such a vehicle was feasible, but there were design deficiencies in the vehicle itself as far as it function as a carrier of wheelchair-bound passengers. A 1983 report by Newcastle University recommended a higher roof and wider doors, requirements that would increase the cost of cab by £2m, as well as its size. The Department of Trade and Industry and the Department of Transport would continue to fund the CR6, but there would be a shortfall of £0.7m in the development funds. The Greater London Council's Labour administration was exercising a policy of equal opportunities for disabled people. This would include improving public transport and the GLC were willing to give a grant to make up the shortfall.

One of the CR6 prototypes was modified by fitting a higher roof, making the bulky cab even bigger. But black clouds were on the horizon. Because of the drop in FX4R sales, Carbodies' income was reduced. Mann and Overton had paid nearly £1.93m towards the CR6. They and were due to pay a further £1.92m to a project that was now estimated to cost £4.5m, as well as another £1.4m needed to extend the factory. In January 1984, Carbodies postponed the CR6's release to 1985.

The FX4Q

It may be considered foolhardy at the very least for a company to introduce something that competes directly with its main product, but that is exactly what Carbodies did with the FX4Q. When sales of the FX4R slumped, Grant Lockhart developed the 'Q' in order to try and keep the production lines going. This model was based on an old cab chassis, fitted with the old Austin diesel engine, which was imported from India. This was possible because the chassis was approved for use with this engine prior to the date of the emission regulations that outlawed it. Carbodies fitted the chassis with a completely new body and running gear, FX4R brakes and a Borg Warner automatic gearbox. No manual gearbox option or power steering was offered. However, the Department of Transport demanded that all examples were given the non year-related index number suffix 'Q', rather than the

The FX4Q was all but indistinguishable, visually from the FX4R, except that the number plate carried a 'Q' prefix and the badge on the boot read 'FX4Q'. The roll-down radiator grille blind was a useful accessory, cutting down the draughts that forever blew into the driver's compartment. Very few owner drivers bought them, despite the advantages they brought

registration of the donor vehicle.

Carbodies' subsidiary, Carbodies Sales and Service Ltd. sold the FX4Q through the London dealers Rebuilt Taxis Ltd., a subsidiary of London Fleet proprietor E. A. Crouch in Westgate Street, Hackney. It cost around £1500 less than the FX4R automatic and the whole business greatly upset Mann and Overton. Angry owners who had bought FX4Rs were claiming that the Q was an admission by Carbodies that the R was a failure, and although Carbodies did not admit it, it was a hard accusation to deny. But the Q was far from perfect. There were some warranty problems due to the use of reconditioned components and the poorer build quality of the engine. The Q never posed serious threat to the sales of new cabs.

Another Attempt at an 'FX5'

The FX4R and the protracted development of the CR6, as well as other ill-starred projects had stretched Carbodies' finances to the limit and Mann and Overton feared that the Coventry company

Following the trials in Peterborough and Newcastle-under-Lyme, the second CR6 prototype was fitted with a higher roof panel

might go bankrupt. They still held a 50percent stake in the FX4, which was Carbodies' only product and clearly they had to protect their interests by investigating whether a cab might be made by another maker. With Lloyds and Scottish money, Andrew Overton authorised the design of a new cab, once more tagged FX5. They engaged Robert Jankel, the man behind Panther cars, to design a new chassis. It was built using a 2.3-litre Ford diesel and had disc brakes, but work was halted as some changes in senior management improved the situation at Carbodies. Barry Widdowson replaced Grant Lockhart as Carbodies' managing director and Lockhart was moved to head up Carbodies Sales and Service.

Engine Conversions for the FX4R

Although Carbodies did what they could to improve the FX4R's performance, there were a number of people who were not satisfied and were prepared to spend money on an alternative engine. Taxi Leasing Services (TLS) was a finance company set up in the late 1970s in Southwark, South London by David Day and John Lewis, offering lease purchase finance to cab drivers, following a change in finance law. In 1982 TLS acquired the America Street Garage in Southwark, and began offering Perkins Phaser 3-litre engine conversions for FX4Rs, installed by Motor and Diesel Engineering Ltd. in Cambridgeshire. With power to spare, this engine proved a popular choice for those preparing to spend a further £2,500 or more over the cost of a new cab. Another option was 3.5-litre Mazda engine, which was even more powerful but it is not known if many, if any were fitted. In late

1985 the London Cab Company fitted a Ford FSD 2.5 litre diesel from the new Transit van into an FX4R, mated to the Borg Warner automatic gearbox. Although noisy, it proved reliable and economical, but no more were converted. The London Cab Company also offered a conversion to 2.5 litres for the original 2.2 engine, using a new crankshaft, which gave the engine a longer stroke. A gear drive conversion for the FX4R's camshaft was cheaper and proved both popular and effective in improving performance and fuel economy but by far the most common and most cost-effective remedy was the fitting of a two-row timing chain conversion. All these conversions would be rendered superfluous by Carbodies' next model.

The Formation of London Taxis International

In 1984 Mann and Overton's owners, Lloyds and Scottish Plc were taken over by Lloyds Bowmaker and they decided to sell off Mann and Overton. Grant Lockhart persuaded MBH's chairman, Dennis Poore to buy them. From this purchase, London Taxis International was created, with three divisions: a manufacturer, LTI Carbodies, a dealer, LTI Mann and Overton and a finance house, London Taxi Finance (LTF). Andrew Overton moved to Coventry to become sales and marketing director and Peter Wildgoose was appointed managing director of LTI Mann and Overton.

The FX4S

The FX4R was a commercial flop, right at the time when Carbodies needed a winning product. Its power steering and brakes were welcomed but what was most needed to redeem it, until the CR6 was ready was a more powerful, more reliable engine, coupled to dedicated transmissions. Land Rover had enlarged their diesel engine to 2.5 litres, but there was some doubt at Carbodies about using it for the FX4, as customer confidence in Rover's ability to deliver the goods was very low. In 1984, Barry Widdowson engaged Ricardo Engineering, a long-established engine design and research establishment in Sussex, to find a better engine. They chose the Japanese Nissan diesel, but it had no dedicated automatic gearbox, vital now for the London market and the existing version would soon be obsolete, so it was decided to wait for the replacement. In the mean time, Carbodies decided to fit the 2.5 litre Land Rover engine and in 1984 put five cabs fitted with the 2.5 litre engine, three with automatic transmissions and two with manual transmissions out on trial with some of the most reputable of London's cab fleets, including the London Cab Company and Camberfield Taxis. The 2.5 engine's installation was not straightforward, as the new fuel pump was mounted very low on the front of the block. This necessitated raising the engine at the front and tilting it the left. To do this, new engine mountings were sourced from the range offered by specialist maker Metalastik, as there was neither time or money to develop exclusive ones.

Internal plastic draught excluders were designed for the door sills and insulation was added under the dashboard. Rocker-type switches were fitted on the instrument panel, necessary because Lucas no longer made the old toggle switches. Different too were the stalk-mounted wiper switches, incorporating an electric washer button, standard equipment for private cars, but a first for the FX4. To the chagrin of the trade, the old radiator remained, and with it the inherent overheating problems. There was also a new gearbox. Borg Warner had closed their Letchworth, Hertfordshire, where the gearbox was being built. No more in-line boxes were to be made in Europe, so Carbodies were supplied with the Australian-made BW40 transmission.

The new model, the FX4S was introduced on the 4th November 1985 at Mann and Overton's new premises at Carnwath Road. It was identified by badges carrying

A pre-production FX4S. New rolled steel bumpers were produced when the tools for the original chrome bumper blades wore out and Carbodies were unwilling to pay for new ones when they anticipated the CR6 would soon be in production

the LTI logo -the first cab to do so- and black steel bumpers. It was priced at £11,239 for the basic manual model, which was marginally more expensive than the FX4R. With more torque from the engine, the performance of the 'S' was better than the 'R', although it was a little noisier and it sold in far better numbers than the FX4R. LTI also offered the new engine as a replacement for the FX4R's 2.2 at a cost of £2,400.

The FX4S was not fault-free, despite LTI's new approach to building the cab. The off-the-shelf engine mountings were less than ideal and caused vibration problems at tick-over. There was a short-term, although serious problem was caused by a faulty batch of engine timing belts which, when they broke caused major internal damage. Whereas all previous diesel engines fitted to the FX4 had had a manual fuel stop, the fuel pump on the 2.5 Land Rover had an electrically-operated Micronova system, whereby the fuel supply was turned on and off from the starter switch. All the time it worked, it was fine, but if it failed it would drain the battery in a matter of minutes. Thanks to the retention of the FX4R radiator, the overheating problem persisted, and electric fan makers sold a few more fans to cab proprietors.

The FX4W

Dealing with Ann Frye at the Department of Transport and the subsequent wheelchair trials with the CR6 had given Carbodies an insight into an aspect of transport hitherto neglected, not only by the cab trade but providers in general. The conversion of an FX4 to wheelchair accessibility for a private customer in the 1970s had proved that the cab had the potential to perform this job. The introduction of the London Taxicard scheme, whereby disabled people who were unable to or had difficulty in using buses could have subsidised taxi rides opened up a whole new market. Because no cabs were built to take wheelchairs, the scheme was at first limited to those people who had some mobility or, if they used a wheelchair were able to get out of it and step into a taxi.

But a demand for wheelchair taxis was created by this very lack of supply. Towards the end of 1985 at Carbodies Sales and Service had, under Roger Ponticelli

Coventry cab operator Clive Allen, pictured with one of his regular passengers was an early purchaser of cabs with the FX4W wheelchair conversion. Note how the passenger door folds back against the wing.
Pictured are two Austin FX4s and four FX4Ss

produced a wheelchair accessible version of an FX4Q, with the doors turned around to hinge on the B-posts, against the initial wishes of LTI. Roger Ponticelli made the partition slide back and forth to accommodate the extra room that the bulk of the wheelchair. A second prototype FX4W, as it became known was built, with the doors hinged on the rear pillar. This design was offered as a conversion from April 1986, with the nearside rear door fitted on over-centre hinges that could be clipped back in place on the rear wing. It cost £1,700 plus VAT, and was available for used as well as new cabs. An FX4W was exhibited at the 1987 Mobility Roadshow at the Transport Road Research Laboratory at Crowthorne, Berks and shown by Andrew Overton to HRH the Princess Royal.

Towards the end of 1986, London radio taxi provider Computer Cab, who would eventually become the sole service provider for the Taxicard scheme sought sponsorship from their many corporate account customers to have existing cabs converted to wheelchair accessibility.

The End of the CR6

Changes at Land Rover Ltd. were to threaten the CR6's future. Management at Land Rover's body plant demanded, and got the manufacturing rights for the four-door conversion, although they re-engineered the front doors to accept the two-door model's external hinges. The CR6 doors were now exclusive to the cab, which almost doubled their cost. The roof panel had originally inspired the idea of using a Range Rover body for a cab, but even that had been replaced, so there were no panels common between the CR6 and the Range Rover at all, which was a com-

plete reversal of the original plan. And the image of the Range Rover had moved on. No longer was it a comfortable farmer's utility but a luxurious and desirable vehicle for the 'yuppie' generation. To Rover's new top management the use of the Range Rover as a base for taxi was completely undesirable and they made their opinion known. It seems that in their desire to move into the customer base that bought Mercedes-Benz cars, they forgot that this company provided the most esteemed saloon car-based taxis in the world.

Now, MBH's chairman, Dennis Poore was becoming uncomfortable about the whole project. In January 1986 MBH announced that the CR6 was to be axed. A press release claimed that the traditional appearance of the FX4 was what the market now wanted and it resources would be directed into further development of the existing cab.

Development of the Metrocab

In 1983, the editor of 'Cab Driver' newspaper, Ernie Keats learned from John Paton, the dealer for Austin cabs in Scotland, that Metro-Cammell-Weymann were at long last planning to build a cab. Keats published the details of the new project, called the Metrocab in his December 16 1983 issue. The cab, Paton said was to be built in partnership with Taggarts, the biggest distributors of BL cars in Scotland and the North of England. Like its predecessor, the new Metrocab was to have a GRP shell, but with completely detachable aluminium front wings. The diesel engines that were said to be under consideration were the new 2.5 Land Rover, a General Motors engine or a 2.3 litre Peugeot. It would have a choice of 4-speed manual gearbox or 4-speed ZF au-

This artwork rendition of the Metrocab was first published in 'Cab Driver' newspaper in 1983

tomatic and would come fitted with all the features and accessories found on a modern car.

But the project would materialise in a very different way from what Paton had said, and some time later than projected. MCW already built trains for the London Underground and the Metrobus, and would attempt to take over Leyland Buses, but the chairman, Tony Sansome's plan for MCW was to have a presence in every field of public land transport. This included the London taxi market and he knew where he could find people with experience in building cabs: Carbodies. He first recruited rate

fixer Jan Scott and purchasing manager Derek Cripps, but both had left by 1984 when he recruited Geoff Chater, an ex-Jaguar man who had joined Carbodies in 1979 as a production manager. For the job of chief design engineer he found Bob Parsons, from the Talbot, ex-Rootes plant at Ryton, in Coventry. Although MCW's main drawing office was at Washwood Heath, Chater and Parsons were allocated space for development at MCW's plant at Oldbury, to the west of Birmingham, to keep them away from prying eyes. When Chater asked what his budget was, he was told there was none. When he asked who

The first mock-up of the 1980s Metrocab. Geoff Chater described it as 'looking like Rommel's half-track'

the rest of his team was, he was told, "it's just you two". With these 'resources', plus a sketch on rough piece of paper by Sansome, which was the basis of the artwork that had been published in 'Cab Driver', a directive to produce results in an impossibly short time and their collective skills and knowledge of automotive design and the operations of the PCO, they set to work.

Throughout this story we have seen proof that a small production run does not afford cab makers the luxury of funds to secure exclusive parts. Every available 'parts bin' is likely to be rummaged through for suitable components and the Metrocab would be a classic example of this. The best engine available was the new 2.5 litre Land Rover diesel, mated to the Borg Warner 66 automatic. Parsons designed a box-section chassis, which would be galvanised as proof against rust. To this he bolted the complete front suspension from the FX4. The rights to it belonged to its makers, G KN, not Carbodies so it would not be a problem for MCW to use it, although the Metrocab's slightly longer wheelbase required some minor adjustment to the steering geometry. Parsons fitted a left-hand drive version of the FX4's power steering box, although of course fit-

ted on the right of the vehicle. The rear axle was a proprietary GKN unit that could be adapted to fit either an independent set-up or a rigid axle. A rigid set-up was chosen, hung on semi-elliptical, steel multi-leaf springs. Brakes from the FX4R were fitted: they were readily available and their commonality would be an advantage to the Metrocab's serviceability.

Seeing the bad press that the first FX4S models were receiving, with timing belts breaking, Geoff Chater decided to abandon the Land Rover engine in favour of Ford's new 2.5 litre FSD direct injection diesel, fitted in the new generation of Transit van. It had pushrod operated overhead valves, with the camshaft driven by a toothed belt. Although the engine came with Ford's own 5-speed manual transmission, it had to be matched to the Borg Warner 66 automatic for the Metrocab, as the automatic box was now almost exclusively chosen by the London market.

As they were starting with blank sheet of paper, Chater and Parsons could build a cab with modern styling and set about building a mock-up. On seeing it, Sansome was disgusted. It was hideous and he told its creators to destroy it. Chater and Parsons then produced a much more attractive mock-up. Again, it had modern

Much better is MCW's design engineer Bob Parsons' mock-up

The pre-production Metrocab, very close in appearance to the production version. The grille was actually made of wood

styling, but with much cleaner lines and better proportions. The windscreen was the largest seen on any post-war cab. The passenger doors hinged forward, on the B-post. It would seat five people and, most importantly it would have wheelchair accessibility built in from the start. The wheelchair occupant would travel facing rearwards, on the nearside in a special dogleg in the partition. This was established by experiment as the safest way for a wheelchair occupant to travel by MIRA, the Motor Industry Research Association. Chater's experience at Carbodies with the FX4W and CR6 was proving very useful in many ways.

The body would be of glassfibre, bonded to a steel cage and the job of building it was contracted out to Reliant in Tamworth, Staffordshire that, alongside Lotus probably the greatest experience in using the material for production car bodies. The first prototype, finished in white, was made and road tested. Now came the tricky part- getting it type approved by the PCO. They didn't like the cable-operated handbrake, insisting at first that rods should be used. Bob Parsons persisted, and eventually persuaded the PCO to accept what had been normal industry practice for decades. It was not as though the PCO

had not encountered cable handbrakes - Beardmore fought hard to persuade them to accept the 4-door Mk VII with one, back in the early 1960s! In 1986, a mere year and half after work began, it was given type approval.

Manganese Bronze Holdings was not at all pleased with the announcement of a competitor. Grant Lockhart, by this time the managing director of Carbodies Sales and Service, claimed, "the UK market is not sufficient to support one manufacturer, let alone rivals." Jamie Borwick, who would become MBH's chairman just before the Metrocab's launch, went on record in later years to say that its announcement 'terrified us'. It was plain that Carbodies, although working hard to improve their product were nowhere near ready to meet a competitor.

A London Dealership for Metrocab

Taxi Leasing Services (TLS) which was offering Perkins engine conversions for FX4Rs were advertising their business in the 'Cab Driver' newspaper. Its partners, David Day and John Lewis had established a good relationship with its editor, Ernie

A pre-production Metrocab, pictured in one of London's most famous streets. The meter is mounted on the dashboard, with its 'for hire' light on its front. The PCO would not allow this, insisting that the 'for hire' sign should be mounted on the door pillar. The man on the pavement on the right of the picture is Geoff Chater

Keats, and his assistant, Stephen Tillyer. They all knew that the time was right for a new cab, if one were to come forward and news of the Metrocab spurred them into action.

A partnership was formed between Day, Lewis, Tillyer and Keats with the intention of acquiring the Metrocab distributorship for the south of England. Against competition from the London Cab Company they were awarded it. Premises were found in Southwark Street, close to London Bridge, and the new company, Metro Sales and Services, eagerly awaited the arrival of the Metrocab.

The Launch of the Metrocab

At the Wembley Conference Centre in December 10 1986, amid a cloud of stage smoke and to the sound of 'Fanfare for the Common Man', the Metrocab was launched. MCW's managing director, Peter Steadman told his audience that £5 million had been earmarked for investment in the cab, and not a penny of it was coming from the government. This was a sideswipe at the CR6, which had swallowed a considerable amount of UK taxpayers' and London ratepayers' money in its aborted development. Transport Minister David Mitchell, who was also present, no doubt appreciated this fact. Referring to the wheelchair facility, Mitchell said, "The Metrocab would transform the lives of disabled people."

From the point of view of both driver and passenger, the biggest advantage the Metrocab had over the FX4 was the sheer amount of interior space. The driver at last had a decent-sized windscreen to look through, and plenty of head and legroom. The dashboard carried the modern-style instrument panel from the Austin Montego and the switches were large push-button items, mounted in the centre of the dash. Electric windows were standard on the front doors, which was important, as the wider internal dimensions of the body and the intrusion of the dogleg in the partition meant that the driver would have to struggle to close the platform window if it were the constant-balance type fitted to the FX4. Because of the cab's squarer shape, the Metrocab's interior was more spacious, particularly in the back, giving it a very airy, light feel, despite the black vinyl trim. The windows in the rear doors were of a sliding type, using channels and catches from the BMC Mini.

Peter Steadman believed that the demise of CR6 was his opportunity to present a real alternative to the FX4S. But although the market was ready for the Metrocab, the Metrocab was not ready for the market. Unknown to most, the vehicle on display at Wembley was without engine or gearbox. The prototypes had been fitted with a Borg Warner automatic gearbox, but Borg Warner would not offer MCW the Australian-made Model 40 box that was used by LTI. Ford had a four-speed automatic transmission, but the only diesel engine to which it had been fitted was an airport service vehicle and this adaptation was being readied for the Metrocab. After three months testing in the Birmingham area, it seemed to work. MCW honestly believed they'd got it if not exactly right, then as good as they possibly could. They launched the cab, and it was almost their undoing.

Metro Sales and Service had 200 orders within three months of the launch, but the delay caused by further testing of the gearbox caused many of those customers to cancel. However, delivery began in early May 1987 and soon the Metrocab was selling steadily to a still sceptical cab trade.

Transport minister David Mitchell MP, in the driver's seat of the Metrocab talks to MCW's Peter Steadman at the launch of the Metrocab. Clearly seen is the Metrocab's instrument panel, an up-to-date design and a clear contrast with the FX4's a hangover from the 1950s

The first model was ordered by a suburban cab driver, Mrs. Sheila Anker. Steve Tillyer took the cab to the PCO for passing. As well as being the first new model to be type-approved since the Mk4 Winchester in 1968, it was the first ever five-seater to be presented, so with a great sense of occasion, they found an old plate bearing the number 1. Subsequent plates issued to Metrocabs and all subsequent five-seater cabs carried the prefix 'E'.

There was some hesitancy from the trade about buying an unknown vehicle, even though they had wanted something new for years. The trade had criticised Mann and Overton and latterly LTI over the FX4, but at least they were they devil they knew. MCW, despite their size were unknown to the London cab trade. The other concern was the Metrocab's shape. After the CR6 was scrapped, LTI had begun to convince the trade and the public that the 'traditional' appearance of the FX4 was desirable from the point of view recognition, moving away from what the modern style that been put forward with the FX5 and the CR6 and had been a reality in the Mk4 Winchester. Now, here was a cab that copied the styling of a modern car, the Mk2 Ford Granada Estate. Would the public accept it? There had been ample publicity about it, and the first wet Friday

Amidst a cloud of stage smoke, the Metrocab is launched at the Wembley Conference Centre

night after the cab's introduction convinced many passengers, very quickly!

Mixed Fortunes for Metrocab

The Metrocab gained sales very quickly, and at one point in the summer of 1988 actually outsold the FX4S, but trouble with the Metrocab's gearbox materialised very quickly. On one Monday morning, Metro Sales and Service staff arrived for work to find seven cabs lined up outside, all with wrecked gearboxes. All they could do was replace the faulty box with an identical one, in the knowledge that it was likely to fail as quickly, simply because the problem had yet to be identified, let alone resolved, and to promise that work was going on to correct the faults. Ford finally found the cause when the testing procedures they were using were altered to match the stop-start work of cab, and could see the damaged gearbox parts. The problem lay in the torque converter, which was flexing under load and wearing out the short input shaft to such a degree that it would eventually shear its splines. The metal worn away from the splines was pumped around the gearbox in the fluid, damaging all the in-

ternal parts it came across. The repaired cabs were back on the road within two to three days, but cab drivers are quick to tell their colleagues of their troubles, and word soon got around. The stress that was on Metro Sales and Service was colossal. They sent the Metrocab's designer, Bob Parsons, a list of no less than 91 faults, ranging from broken air cleaner spouts (a problem that was quickly cured by fitting a different air cleaner housing) to faulty brakes. Parsons was keen to rectify what he could, and to his credit made every possible effort to do so, but there was little money from MCW: they were in deep financial trouble and their parent group, Laird, were making moves to sell this division off.

The FX4S-Plus

LTI had to meet forthcoming EEC regulations that would ban the production of passenger vehicles that had doors that hinged on the rear, 'C' pillar. To begin to meet these rules, and to start to address the matter of a new model, LTI began a series of projects, the first being the Alpha Project. In addition to re-hanging the doors, the project included a plan to re-

The first Metrocab passed by the PCO. Posing proudly by the cab's plate No 1 from the left are Metro Sales and Service directors Ernie Keats, David Day, Stephen Tillyer and John Lewis

shape the existing body shell and enlarge the windscreen, but this plan was soon abandoned as a waste of money, because the real demand was one that LTI at the time could not meet, a completely new cab. However, they knew that had to do it and approached the matter in a way described by LTI's new engineering director Ed Osmond as 'bite-sized chunks', a series of step-by-step improvements to the FX4 that would both enhance its potential in wider markets and provide a testbed for the running gear for the next model.

Brought in to work on the Alpha Project was Jevon Thorpe, a young consultant who had spent his educational placement from Coventry University at Reliant under Ed Osmond. In 1986 Osmond had asked Thorpe to redesign the FX4S's interior. Dennis Poore was impressed by Thorpe's design for the new dashboard and smart five-seat grey interior and brought him into the company to bring the new design into production. The new interior would be the major feature of a revised model, the FX4S-Plus. It was announced at the 1987 London Taxi Driver of the Year Show, held in Battersea Park every September. The dashboard was a modern design, of moulded grey plastic, featuring push-button switches mounted centrally, full heater controls, fresh air vents and modern instruments from the BL Mini Metro. The seats were offered with a vinyl or velour trim option, and optional electric front windows were offered. The Plus's mechanical specification was carried over almost unchanged, with the exception of telescopic shock absorbers on the rear and GKN's new 'Literide' laminated plastic rear springs, which were claimed never to sag or break. There was a larger radiator, installed to accommodate the gearbox oil cooler rather than to cure the overheating problems that had occurred on the FX4R and FX4S, which LTI never accepted had existed. Still there were no disc brakes. There were two trim options; Fleetline and HLS with prices ranging from £12,210 for the Fleetline manual to £13,678.45 for the HLS automatic. As well as black, the range of colours on offer were Midnight Blue, Rattan Beige, Royal Burgundy, Ermine White, Carmine Red and City Grey. The vinyl roof and sunroof options were carried over and the personal radio was moved to the dashboard instead of its add-on position in a roof binnacle. There was criticism in the trade press that there was no facility for a built-in two-way radio.

Apart from an extra badge on the grille that said "Plus', the FX4S-Plus was externally indistinguishable from the FX4S. All the changes made were mechanical or to the interior

Each of the three main London radio circuits had to bolt its set to the partition between the driving seat and the luggage platform. The S-Plus had a moulded centre console, which prohibited this. Surely, the press said, the dashboard could have been design to incorporate a two-way radio? LTI's answer was that they had considered it, but if they also included the variety of radio sets available to the provincial trade, there were simply too many for it to be practical. The S-Plus did not have built in wheelchair accessibility, but an improved version of the original conversion, with a fixed partition and a nearside rear door that opened through 180 degrees could be fitted for a further £998, a significant reduction on the original conversion price of £1700. As LTI had intended, the Plus soon outsold the Metrocab.

A New Owner for Metrocab

In October, the Financial Times carried an article saying that the Laird Group were to sell off MCW without first finding a buyer. The January 12 1989 edition of 'Taxi', the largest London cab trade journal, picked up the story, saying:

"Long-mounting losses on bus operations, coupled with a failed bid to take over Leyland Buses, has persuaded the Chairman of Laird to sell off the MCW bus, train and taxi manufacturing subsidiary... The taxi manufacturing section, which is profitable, with over 1,200 units worth £18 million already sold, may be sold separately. Although the decision to sell was made in July, Laird waited until December (1988) to make the announcement."

Then, MCW's board sacked Peter Steadman and shortly after him, three other directors. Rumours ran like a virus

through the cab trade. Metrocab, the troublemakers said, was dead. In an interview published in the January 26 edition of 'Taxi', Ernie Keats of Metro Sales and Service stated, 'Metrocab production and sales are still continuing'. Two weeks previously, Keats had written to all Metrocab owners, telling them that some twelve major companies had approached Laird with a view to purchase the transport interest. He wrote:

"The rumours, clearly designed to cause as much damage as possible, originate from sections of the trade who want to return to a monopoly to improve their own financial gains which have obviously suffered from Metrocab innovation and competition. In other words a return to their 'good old days'."

Although Keats was careful not to name any names, he had, as editor of 'Cab Driver,' recently lost advertising support from LTI.

Jevon Thorpe, designer of the FX4S-Plus's interior, would go on to design the TX1 and in 1997 become managing director of LTI Carbodies

Chris Johnson, left, Reliant's Group's executive deputy chairman, and Carl Turpin, the Group's chief executive, with the product of their new acquisition. The rectangular badge on the grille, covering the original Ford oval, carries Reliant's eagle logo

By mid June 1989 Metrocab's new owner was revealed. It was the Reliant Group, whose car division had been building GRP bodied family cars since 1956 and were producing a range of composite plastic products as varied as high roofs for Ford Transits and spark-proof floors for oil platforms. They were also making the Metrocab's body for MCW. The Reliant Group's owners, Chris Johnson and Carl Turpin had profited during the property boom of the 1980s and, knowing how that business can fluctuate, were looking for a stable industrial concern in which to place their money. They chose the Reliant Group.

They refurbished 24,000 square feet of the Reliant factory at Kettlebrook, Tamworth, Staffordshire for use as a finishing shop and Metrocab production was moved there from Washwood Heath. Many of the staff moved to Tamworth as well. The next year, Reliant brought Geoff Chater, who had lost his position with MCW into the company. The fall of MCW dealt a bitter blow to Metro Sales and Service. They were involved in litigation with MCW over warranty claims and believed they had an understanding with Reliant that they would continue as London dealers. But it was not to be. Reliant awarded the dealership to Nelson Crouch in East London and Exclusive in West London.

Now, the purpose-built cab was beginning to be a more attractive proposition to the markets where its use was not mandatory and sales of both models would improve, but it would not be all plain sailing.

Chapter 12

Towards Wider Markets

The cost of developing a motor vehicle of any sort had grown exponentially since the end of the Second World War. Crucial for motor vehicle makers is to sell it to as large a market as possible, increasing the volume of sales and enabling the development and production costs to be spread over as many units as possible, so as to reduce the purchase price. Despite the steady increase in the number of cab drivers in London - 21,584 at the end of 1995, compared to 13,291 at the end of 1970 - the London market was still relatively small, as was that of Birmingham, Coventry, Manchester and other English cities. The Scottish markets of Edinburgh and Glasgow, though important were tiny by comparison. LTI needed to expand, and to do that they needed a more modern vehicle.

The Fairway

LTI's next version of the FX4, the Fairway was seen by the trade as an answer to the Metrocab, which indeed it turned out to be but it was part of their pre-determined strategy to develop a new model regardless of any competitor. Code-named the 'Beta' project, it was already under way it was and would incorporate a better powertrain and wheelchair accessibility. The latter, necessary to meet legislation due to come into force in February 1 1989

was developed from the aftermarket conversion already offered on the S-Plus but would be fixed, with a dog-leg, similar to that on the Metrocab. New swan-neck hinges were fitted to both rear doors, enabling them to be held open in a 90-degree position, although a wheelchair could only be loaded from the nearside, because of the shape of the partition. The rear seat cushion could be folded up to allow the wheelchair to be turned to place the passenger in a rearwards-facing position.

At last the new Nissan engine was available, and of the 2.3, 2.5 and 2.7-litre versions, LTI chose the 2.7 litre, along with its dedicated five-speed manual and new four-speed automatic transmission. In its original form, it was fitted with a turbocharger, but this would not be fitted to the engines supplied to LTI, as it was felt to be powerful enough without one. Excellent as the engine was, it troubled LTI to install a Japanese engine in such a thoroughly British vehicle. And for LTI it was expensive to buy in, but time would prove that it was the right choice.

The new model was released in February 1989. For the first time in the FX4's history, it was given a name: Fairway. It was offered with three trim options; Bronze, a basic model, Silver, with a vinyl roof, a sunroof, carpeting all around and Gold, with wood finish door cappings, headrests and heavy-duty carpet in the

The Fairway was the first FX4 to have a name. It was an appropriate choice, for two reasons. One, it had been a name used on two previous models of private car made by Carbodies in the 1930s, and two, many London cabmen love their golf! All-over advertising, known as a livery, had recently been approved by the PCO, as seen by this smart Guinness livery

passenger compartment. A 40,000-mile/12 month warranty was offered. The Plus's colour range was carried over, and added to, it were Sherwood Green, Champagne Beige and Royal Burgundy. Prices ranged from £14,273.80 for the Bronze manual to £16,749.75 for the Gold automatic. A few residual FX4 S-Plus manual cabs, without wheelchair accessibility were offered, at £13,726.40. The Fairway was hailed as the best FX4 ever, and sales reflected the trade's opinion of it.

Changes in LTI Dealerships

Mann and Overton had held he exclusive rights to sell Austin, and later Carbodies and LTI cabs in London since 1929, but their dominance had provoked a lot of criticism from the trade, who said they did not give the kind of service that could be expected from a private car garage. Any prospective new customer asking for a test drive, for instance, would be dismissed by a polite but quite firm refusal and a patro-

The Fairway was the first version of the FX4 to have wheelchair accessibility. The back seat folded up to allow the wheelchair to be turned to face rearwards

The Fairway windscreen featured a slightly larger glass area

nising smile that soon put him in his place. Things certainly changed when Andrew Overton took over and the firm moved to Carnwath Road, but even so, MBH felt that there should be second dealership in London.

In 1989, they chose KPM-UK Plc, a conglomerate of two long standing companies, KPM and UK Taxi Services, who were situated in Brady Street, Bethnal Green, in London's East End. KPM was started in 1975 by Keith Marder, Peter Da Costa and Michael Troullis. Da Costa was a London cab driver and Marder and Troullis were trained and qualified motor engineers and their aim was to run the best cab garage in London. UK Taxi Services, formed in 1978 provided finance for cab drivers who wanted to buy their own vehicles. In 1988, the two companies merged to form KPM-UK PLC. The company's location, at the other side of London from Mann and Overton plus their track record and quality of service and also their meter fitting and body shop facilities - Mann and Overton did not provide these last two, even at Carnwath Road - made them the ideal choice, and in October 1989, KPM-UK was appointed as a second LTI dealer

in London.

With KPM-UK taking a substantial share of sales and service, Mann and Overton found Carnwath Road too large for their needs and relocated to Holloway Road, a move that was criticised by cabmen and women living in the south and south-west, for whom access to Mann and Overton's had been fairly simple. Nevertheless, they made the move.

Hooper Buy Metrocab

Reliant's tenure of Metrocab had all too short a date. In the recession of the early 1990s the property market collapsed, bringing down with it the fortunes of the property side of the Reliant Group. Fortunately, Geoff Chater had managed to turn the substantial losses of the vehicle and plastics side of the business into a healthy profit, ensuring that it and the cab making business was a viable concern. On December 27 1990, Official Receivers KPMG Peat Marwick handed over the assets of Reliant to Hooper and Company (Coachbuilders) Ltd. Hooper was the most famous name in coachbuilding, but the company that

Two new Hooper Metrocabs pictured on London's Lambeth Bridge, prior to delivery. Redesigned wheel trims and black bumpers mark them out. These examples have the original drum brakes

bought Metrocab was owned by US lawyer John Dick, who had bought the name but had no direct connections with the old company that ended its days as part of the mighty BSA empire. With a small force of twenty people, the Tamworth factory began work once again on January 7 1991.

During 1991, Metrocab (UK) Ltd. worked on improving the cab. The confidence that the name of Hooper created in the brand was reflected by £700,000 worth of home orders and a remarkable £800,000 worth of export sales, taken at the Taxi Driver of the Year Show in early September 1992. At a press day in late September, Paul Crowder, by now Hooper's Chairman launched the latest version. It had disc brakes, the first to be fitted as standard on a London cab. This project had started at Reliant, when Bob Parsons approached Girling and asked them to find the most suitable type of calliper to fit the old BMC steering upright. They produced a solid disc that stood out further from the upright than the drum brakes, so Parsons selected a deep dish, six-stud wheel to accommodate it. New rear brakes, of a type similar to those fitted to the Ford Transit had 25 percent more drum area, and were self-adjusting. A new range of

colours was available, including a choice of metallic paint. Leather trim was an extra-cost option. However, Crowder's big surprise was that, metallic paint and leather options aside, there would be no price increase.

At the beginning of 1992, Metrocab announced the fitting of a new, 'greener' version of the Ford engine, incorporating a new Bosch fuel injection system, which would give better fuel consumption, lower emissions and better acceleration. The shape of the new curved four-branch inlet manifold would earn it the nickname of the 'banana' engine. The cab's initial acceleration was further enhanced by the fitting of a new lower ratio differential and the latest Cosworth torque converter. The driver's compartment featured an improved dashboard, better storage space, a better quality carpet and an uprated heating and ventilation system.

The Fairway Driver

The Nissan engine had brought the FX4's performance up to that of modern traffic, but its front suspension was the same as the 1958 model, and the brakes

The Fairway Driver could be distinguished from its predecessor by its domed silver wheel trims and extruded mesh radiator grille

were only enhanced by a servo and marginally larger wheel cylinders. LTI's engineering director, Ed Osmond addressed these matters in the next stage of the cab's development, code named the Gamma project. Component manufacturer GKN were engaged to design a new front suspension system with new wishbones with ball joints and coil springs with concentric telescopic dampers. The old back axle was replaced by a new GKN light commercial unit, hung, initially on GKN's 'Literide' plastic leaf springs, but soon after on new steel leaf springs, as GKN had discontinued the plastic springs due to a lack of take-up by the motor industry. The development of the suspension took two years, and prototype vehicles underwent strenuous testing at MIRA, including punishing work on their rough pavé surface.

The new front suspension allowed for the installation of the long overdue disc

brakes. While the Fairway Driver was under development, LTI had heard that Metrocab were about to introduce front discs. They didn't want to be at a disadvantage, so adopted as a dealer installation by Mann and Overton an aftermarket disc brake conversion for the Fairway and FX4S-Plus that Putney Bridge Engineering had developed. LTI arranged for this conversion to be available on new or older Fairways and FX4R, S and S-Plus models. Thus both companies could claim 'firsts' - LTI for being the first to introduce a London taxi with disc brakes, and Hooper for being the first to fit them as standard!

For the brakes, manufacturers AP Lockheed worked in conjunction with GKN to produce a twin pot calliper system with vented discs. Along with these, the wider rear drums and six-stud wheels similar to those introduced on the Metrocab were fitted. An electronic diagnostic

As standard equipment, the Fairway Driver was fitted with a swivel seat and a separate low step to make access easier for disabled people

The Fairway Driver was fitted with this new front suspension system, developed by GKN, and ventilated disc brakes by AP Lockheed

system was installed, enabling main dealers to trouble-shoot rapidly. A new 'Five Star' paint process was used too, beginning with an electrophoretic process, during which the entire body was immersed in an electrically charged paint bath, enabling paint to enter places inaccessible by spray gun. Stone chip-resistant pant was also applied to the front of the body panels. New silver-painted plastic wheel trims covered the deep-dish wheels and a new extruded mesh grille was fitted. A new KAB seat was supplied as standard, giving extra comfort for the driver. Besides the mechanical and paintwork improvements, the nearside tip-up seat could be swung out which, in conjunction with a detachable low step enabled the infirm to get into the cab more easily.

The new model was named the Fairway Driver, and it was released in February 1992. A manual transmission model cost £19,912 and the automatic, £21,312. Initially the cab was prone to steering shimmy, where the front wheels would vibrate dramatically at any speed from 30mph upwards. After a short period of denial by Mann and Overton that it happened at all, it was cured by the fitting of a steering damper, both to new models and retrospectively to existing cabs.

Driver Plus and Driver 95

Further detail modifications were made in 1993, on the 'Driver Plus', including a hatch to allow the passenger to pay the driver before leaving the cab. This last item was unpopular, as it created a draught around the driver's neck. The problem with the hatch was remedied with the next special edition model, the Driver 95, introduced in the spring of 1995. Sliding glass, similar to the original Fairway's

but lockable from the driver's side and located on the nearside of the partition, replaced the hatch. Other new, standard features were electric front windows and a detachable radio/cassette player. The chrome rubbing strip for the front wings and doors was no longer available as standard and the old model range of Bronze, Silver and Gold was dropped. The 95 would be the only model available, although extra equipment such as a vinyl roof and a sunroof could be ordered at extra cost.

One point of contention was the fitting on all new Fairways of a Cygnus LTI300 taximeter as standard. Buyers had no choice in the matter, regardless of whether they had a preferred make, or even if their annual meter contract had not expired by the time they bought the cab. (Almost all taximeters in London, were, and still are rented rather than purchased.)

For the first time, LTI (or Mann and Overton for that matter) conceded openly that cabs sold outside of London were of a slightly different specification from those sold within the capital. However, the price differential was beginning to narrow with the Driver 95, the prices of which had been raised. A manual 95 was £20,210 in London, compared to £20,440 outside and automatic model, £21,618 in London and £21,849 outside.

The Asquith

At their factory in Banbury, Oxfordshire, the Asquith Motor Carriage Company Ltd's business was building 1930s-style vans and minibuses on modern running gear. Owners of these vehicles could have all the visual appeal of a vintage commercial with modern-day running costs, performance and reliability.

Around 1990, a cab driver that was visiting the factory saw Asquith's 'Highland' van and commented to Asquith's Marketing Director, Crispin Reed that all it needed was windows and it would be a vintage-style cab. Reed had read a 1924 treatise called 'Motor Bodywork - the Design and Construction of Private, Commercial and Passenger types' by Herbert J. Butler, which contained details of motor cab bodies. The cab driver's suggestion was all the impetus Reed to make the decision to build a retro-style cab. He also had an eye on the export market, and knew that if the cab complied with the Conditions of Fitness, then it, as a type approved London taxi would have far greater sales potential.

The company built a mock-up and exhibited it at the London Motor Fair in 1991, then set to work building the first prototype. The body was of GRP around a steel frame, with four full doors, five-seat capacity and wheelchair accessibility. Underneath was a separate chassis. When the first prototype was presented to PCO, they dismissed it out of hand, saying that the quality of the cab was totally unacceptable. Reed obviously had a lot to learn about the PCO and indeed the London cab trade.

After much work, a better prototype was built and tested in late 1992. The cab would have the option of a Ford Transit diesel, similar to that in the Metrocab but with a higher compression ratio, or Ford petrol engine coupled to an automatic transmission. The axles and steering were sourced from General Motors: the coil spring front suspension was from the Vauxhall Midi van and the rear axle was from the Vauxhall Frontera, hung on Dunlop air suspension. Disc brakes were fitted all round, another first for a London cab.

The cab was introduced by Transport Minister Stephen Norris at Marylebone Station in April 1994. Reed anticipated selling 20 cabs per year in the UK, with greater emphasis on the export market. The base price was £29,950, with a £500 deposit but high-specification interiors and air conditioning could be ordered at extra cost. Although the cab's buyers loved the concept and were pleased with the reactions of their passengers, they were less than pleased with the problems that arose, particularly with the back axle, and the way that Asquith dealt with them. Sadly, Asquith had failed to understand the need for an immediate supply of spare parts

Asquith's Sales and Marketing Director, Crispin Reed, with the Asquith retro-look taxi. The company also would produce a private hire version with a landaulette body, a body style that would not be approved by the PCO as it had been banned since the 1950s

The Series II Metrocab received a front and rear re-style, with a more upright grille, new light clusters and moulded bumpers.
The extra-deep wheel trims accommodated the deep wheels necessitated by the disc brakes

and the highly efficient warranty service that was vital for the cab trade. They did not appoint a London dealer or service agent, but instead sent parts down to London, to whomever the owners could find to work on the cab. And very few cab garages would: there were many that would not work on Metrocabs for fear of finding problems that they could not fix in the short time demanded by the trade, or did not want to stock spare parts for several types of vehicles. Their fears for the Asquith were much magnified, and as it was soon proved, with justification.

Metrocab: a Six- And Seven-Seater Version and a Series II

On April 1994 Metrocab (UK) Ltd announced a new 6-seater version of the Metrocab. Instead of a dogleg partition, a straight one was fitted, and a third tip-up seat accommodated the sixth passenger. A new, 60-40 split rear seat could be lifted to allow a wheelchair to be manoeuvred into place. A 7-seater version with a seat beside the driver was also available for the provincial market. The 6- and 7-seater models were sold alongside the original 5-seater

and within six months accounted for 30 percent of all Metrocab sales.

The most significant of Hooper's changes to the Metrocab to date were seen in late 1995, with the introduction of the Series II. It incorporated the more powerful and more economical 76PS version of the Ford engine, which had been installed at the beginning of the year. The Series II had a redesigned front end with new colour-coded grille and profiled bumpers, a much improved paint finish, new light clusters, reshaped side glass and a redesigned interior. Wheelchair ramps were stowed in the floor instead of in the boot. The cab was a considerable improvement upon the original model, but it is significant that the basic chassis, engine and bodyshell remained the same, showing the soundness of the original design.

CETA - Metrocab's Global Taxi

The Disability Discrimination Act of 1995 (DDA) would demand that all purpose-built taxis had to be wheelchair accessible by 2000. Diptac (Disabled Persons Transport Advisory Committee [UK Dept. of Environment, Transport and The Re-

Asquith's modern-style vehicle was to be built on the retro-vehicle's chassis. It was designed by Dale Harrow, who taught Transport Design at the Royal College of Art

gions]) regulations were to specify dimensions for wheelchair accessible cabs, but by the mid-1990s these still had not been written. Both LTI and Metrocab had to guess what the regulations might be. An alternative to producing a new cab was to modify the Series II by making the roof much higher, which was considered by Bob Parsons and Geoff Chater to be impossible to engineer successfully. The best alternative at the time was to build a new model and in 1998, John Dick gave approval for its development. Code-named CETA, it was styled by Roy Axe, former head of Design at Chrysler UK and later

Austin-Rover, and was noticeably larger than the current model. The Ford FSD diesel would not meet the forthcoming Euro 3 exhaust regulations, so a new engine had to be found. Ford offered the new DuraTorq 2.4 turbo diesel but it would not fit into the CETA, or for that matter the existing model. The project began to use a great deal of development money and at the same time there was no sign of the Diptac regulations. Metrocab's board took the decision to scrap CETA and in early 2003 it was transported to John Dick's private auto museum in Germany.

Metrocab (UK) Ltd's Global taxi, the CETA project, could carry two wheelchair passengers side-by-side

A New Asquith

News of an Asquith with a modern body reached the trade press in 1996, when a mock-up was displayed at the London Motor Fair. A new company, the New Asquith Motor Company was formed to make it, in Sri Lanka, to fulfil the company's intention to sell the cab for about £1000 less than a Fairway or Metrocab. The cab was to be fitted with the same air suspension system as used on the retro-style model, but in this case allowing the back to be lowered to enable disabled passengers to enter more easily. Production was planned for late 1997, but nothing more was heard of it, as the company was in financial trouble, mainly due to the cancellation of large order from Japan. This forced the company into liquidation in 1997. The company was bought from the liquidators and continues to make retro-style light commercial vehicles, but no more taxis were built after the collapse of the company in 1997.

The TX1

However good the Fairway Driver was, it was still a derivative of a vehicle that had been around since 1958 and, as the cab trade had been pointing out since the beginning of the 1970s was long overdue for replacement. As part of their strategy to design and build a new cab, LTI examined the idea of adapting other makers' vehicles to meet the Conditions of Fitness, and studied, amongst others the Renault Espace MPV. It was indeed possible to convert some other makers' vehicles into vehicles that complied with the Conditions of Fitness, but considerations other that the turning circle, such as floor height re-

duced the options available. But the lesson of the CR6 was still remembered; do not depend on another manufacturer's donor vehicle, as they might pull the plug at any point, or change the specification to one that prohibited any possible modifications. For this reason, LTI decided to stay with their own design of purpose-built vehicles. A crucial factor in the design of a new cab was the Disability Discrimination Act, (DDA) which would demand that purpose-built taxis in the UK had to be wheelchair accessible by 2000 and the only way they could be sure of having a vehicle that would comply with rules that demanded such things as specific door opening sizes was to be in total control of the design.

After carefully considering a redesign of the FX4, LTI opted to build a complete new cab. This was originally code-named Delta so as to be sequential with the previous models, but it was renamed 'Eta' to avoid any obvious association with the Automotive Engineering Centre's hybrid power cab that had been displayed in 1995.

Overseas customers, whom LTI had finally begun to foster, demanded that the new vehicle should have to have a 'retro' look, because their passengers expected to

'Delta' the Automotive Engineering centre's cab, designed by Roy Axe of Design Research Ltd and Jim Randle, the director of the Automotive Engineering at Birmingham University as part of the Hermes project, investigating hybrid gas turbine power

see a taxi that was instantly recognisable as a taxi, not a van look-alike. Forthcoming M1 European passenger vehicle regulations demanded that all doors should hinge forward, the DDA regulations demanded that those doors should have a minimum height of 1350mm. (The FX4's were just under 1200mm high) When the FX4 was designed, the Conditions of Fitness required that inspection panels be built into the floor of a cab so that the top of the chassis could be examined for rust. This regulation had been scrapped some time before, although the Fairway Driver still retained the FX4's removable plywood floor panels. Now LTI could incorporate a welded floor in the new cab, increasing the bodyshell's rigidity. The wheelbase of the Fairway Driver chassis was lengthened by 75mm, the track widened by 60mm and the ball joints on the front suspension and the steering box were uprated. The Nissan engine, with a slightly modified injector pump, and its transmission options were carried over.

The new cab took just twenty-eight months to design and put into production. It was launched at the London Motor Show in October 1997 by Minister of Transport for London, Gle nda Jackson

MP, and at the launch, LTI Carbodies' managing director, Jevon Thorpe, said, 'we have brought saloon car standards of comfort, safety and refinement to the driver's working environment. And despite the large number of changes and improvements, the end result is still recognisable as a London taxi.'

The TX1 went into production at the end of the year, although it would not be until the early spring of 1998 that delivery could be made in significant numbers. But once steady deliveries of the cab began, it was very well received by the trade. In March 1998 LTI recorded the highest ever sales for any cab breaking all records, including substantial sales in Scotland and more than 500 were on order. What the trade welcomed was all the established features that the London taxi is famous for, in a draught-free, comfortable, modern vehicle that felt solid to drive. Its vastly improved visibility and headroom was welcomed too, although it did not have quite the same leg room as the FX4, as the driving position was slightly further forward and the transmission tunnel reduced the space available for the pedals.

What was definitely not liked was the fact that rainwater would run off the roof

The last of the old and the first of the new: the last Fairway was built on November 7 1997, just one year short of the FX4's 40th birthday and was presented to the National Motor Museum, with the registration number R1 PFX (RIP FX)

175

The LTI TX1. MBH's chairman Jamie Borwick wanted to call it the Fairmile, but failed to get support for the idea. At a brainstorming meeting, he wrote the word 'taxi' in capital letters on a flipchart, then crossed out the 'A', to form 'TXI (TX1). The numbering continues Austin's heritage, going back to the HL of 1929

onto the driver when he opened the huge door to get out: FX4 owners had had enough of getting wet, and they didn't appreciate getting the same treatment with the TX1! Build quality was further improved over the Fairway, with new paint and body protection and checks made throughout the entire manufacturing process. A new three-year/100,000 mile warranty helped boost proprietors' confidence. A real accolade was the presenting of a Millennium Products Award, in recognition of its design and accessibility features.

Wheelchair Conversions for Older Cabs

The Disability Discrimination Act demanded that all purpose-built taxis should be wheelchair-accessible by December 31 1998. Already, new vehicles had to have been built with a wheelchair facility since 2000, and if proprietors wanted to keep older vehicles, particularly the FX4S and S-Plus on the road from 1999 onwards, they would have to have them converted.

One of the companies set up in late 1995 to convert older cabs to wheelchair

The TX1's interior initially featured patterned upholstery with cartoon taxis and a pull-down child seat in the centre. Door handles and seat edges are yellow to aid the partially-sighted

accessibility was Taxi Access of Maida Vale. Taxi Access was run by Steve Hawes, a long time member of the Licensed Taxi Drivers Association. The conversion included hinges that allowed the nearside rear door to open through 90 degrees, a stepped partition and a set of ramps. At £1500, its cost enabled owners of good condition older cabs to continue to run them for at least two more years. Other conversions were offered by Pool Motors, Rainham Radio Cabs and Crayford Garage.

Metrocab Series III

The Metrocab Series III, unveiled in November 1997 at the RAF Museum, Hendon, was Metrocab (UK) Ltd's answer to the TXI. MD Mike Thurlow hoped that the new cab would increase Metrocab's share of the UK taxi market to over its existing 25 percent. (In some parts of the West Midlands, the market share was as high as 40 percent.) The Series III featured no less than 61 detailed improvements. Amongst them was a more environmentally efficient Ford engine, quieter manual

The standard interior trim of the Series III Metrocab was velour. The extending stay for the lifting rear seat cushion can be seen below the seat. The new passenger door windows are electrically operated

The dashboard and driver's compartment of the Series III Metrocab was as comprehensively equipped as most contemporary cars

Metrocab UK's Sales Director Steven Ferris presents HRH The Duke of Edinburgh with his new private Series III Metrocab. This green example was powered by a Ford petrol engine converted to LPG and replaced a red Series II that the Duke previously owned

gearbox, an uprated starter motor and alternator and an improved silencer system. On the body, many of the parts were resin-injected to produce a better finish, and electric windows were fitted in the rear doors. For the passenger compartment, there were optional radio speakers and a new partition with greater visibility. The driver's compartment had a new dashboard, an intercom as standard and a new heating and ventilating system. However, Geoff Chater was convinced that the timing of its introduction was not wise. He

tried to convince Metrocab's board to hold back its introduction until some time after the TX1's introduction. His argument was that it would take LTI several months to get TXI production up to speed. If they, Metrocab had continued to offer the Series II, they would have had the market to themselves. Instead, they encountered their own production difficulties with the Series III and were unable to meet the demand caused by LTI's teething troubles, so accurately predicted by Chater.

Chapter 13

The New Millennium

As the new millennium began, both LTI and Hooper were cautiously optimistic about the future. The latest Metrocab was selling well and they had made plans for the next few years ahead. LTI too had plans, but in the light of new emission regulations, perceived problems with driver licensing and challenges to the Conditions of Fitness, the next decade would pan out very differently from what either company could have anticipated.

Metrocab TTT

Euro 3 exhaust emission regulations were due to come into force in January 2001 and Metrocab's Ford FSD engine would not comply with them. The new Ford DuraTorq turbo diesel, which was designed for the next generation of the Transit van and for medium sized passenger cars, seemed a logical choice. However, according to Metrocab's chief engineer, Bob Parsons it would not fit in the Metrocab's engine bay without major work to its ancillaries, which would affect its reliability and performance and increase development costs. Parsons and Geoff Chater instead spoke to Japanese manufacturer Toyota, and chose their 2.4 turbo diesel and its dedicated 4-speed automatic and five-speed manual transmissions. The new cab, named the TTT ('Triple-T') was announced in March 2000, almost a year before the Euro 3 deadline. The front suspension and ventilated front disc brakes developed for LTI for use on the

Toyota were delighted to provide the engine for a London taxi. Pictured with the Metrocab TTT are, from the left, Yoshihiro Kumagai of Mitsui & Co UK Plc, Adrian Harrison, managing director of the Hooper Group, Mike Thurlow, executive director of the Hooper Group and Osamu Arakawa of the Toyota Motor Corporation

Fairway and carried over to the TXI were at last available to outside users and they were fitted, along with a new rear axle. Other changes included a 'for hire' light with an LED display for greater visibility in daylight, an optional factory-fitted 'Lux Pack' which included amongst other features, chrome effect wheel trims, rear carpet, rich velour trim, flat bed wheelchair ramp, step facility, and lap seat belts for the rear facing seats. A wide range of solid and metallic colours was also available. The Triple-T was met with much praise. The new engine was significantly quieter than the old Ford, and cab trade journalists and prominent trade personalities compared its performance and comfort to that of a private car.

TX1 Improvements

The introduction of wheelchair accessibility to London taxis in the late 1980s gradually brought an increase in work for the trade, aided by the Taxicard scheme. This gave people with disabilities of all types a number of rides per year, for which they paid a modest sum, initially 80p but rising in 2011 to £2.50. The Fairway, having been adapted to take wheelchairs rather than being purpose-built restricted larger wheelchairs, but the TX1, with its larger doors allowed bigger wheelchairs.

A further hindrance, especially in busy streets is that ramps used to aid loading of wheelchairs were stowed in the Fairway's boot and took time to unload and reload. The ramps on first TX1s were the same , but later TX1s were fitted with a fold-out ramp, which speeded up the process considerably.

The LTI TXII

LTI's hopes for the TX1 had been exceeded by its reception by the trade and sales continued to hold up, but they faced the same problem as Metrocab, because the TX1's Nissan TD27 engine would not meet the new Euro 3 exhaust emission standards. It was LTI's understanding that Nissan had no plans to modify it to comply, so a new engine had to be sought. In 1997, Jevon Thorpe was appointed managing director at LTI, replacing Barry Widdowson, who moved to head up MBH's Vehicle Division. Thorpe had begun negotiations with General Motors for their light truck diesel, but in early 2001 he moved out of this position and

A wheelchair ramp that folded out of the floor of a TX1 speeded up the loading of wheelchairs in busy streets. It also helped passengers who are unable to climb up even the low step of a cab.
An additional section serves as both an extension for where there is no kerb and as a slide-in low step

The picture says it all- the first TXII off LTI's production lines

into one of research and development. Barry Widdowson and Ed Osmond left LTI in January 2001 and Peter Shillcock, who had come from the BMW plant at Cowley, was appointed to replace Thorpe. With no sign of the General Motors engine being anywhere near ready for installing in a cab, let alone be ready for prolonged development, Shillcock brought in a new engineering director, Paul Woolley and with just a year to go, Woolley and Shillcock spoke to several manufacturers, including Volkswagen and Peugeot to try and find a new engine.

Although they all thought that the idea of having their engine in a London taxi was very attractive, all except one turned the invitation down, citing the unfeasibly short development time as the only reason. Only Ford said yes, announcing that they were particularly pleased to be associated with the London cab trade. Their new DuraTorq turbocharged diesel seemed a good choice, and despite having a smaller displacement that the Nissan, it produced 9 percent more brake horsepower and greater torque.

The Ford engine was developed for a transverse layout and needed to be adapted to a fore-and aft one to fit the TX

chassis layout, with the necessary relocation of the ancillaries and the addition of an air conditioning pump. Nor did it come with an automatic transmission. The nearest option was Ford's ASM, or automatic shift manual transmission, an American

A left-hand drive TX1 in New York City. This effort to tempt the 'Big Apple' to take to London cabs was as unsuccessful as every other since 1950

181

LTI's promotional picture of the TXII. External differences between it and the TX1 are the passenger doors windows, which are one-piece and the taillights. The black grille signifies a lower specification model. Gold models came with chrome grilles

transmission which provides auto-clutch and 'Shift-By-Wire' electronic control system technology. This was tested in the cab and performed well, but LTI knew that the London market demanded a full automatic transmission. The gearbox for the Nissan TD27 engine was developed by Jatco in Japan, which was, fortunately for LTI now run by people that Shillcock knew from when he was with Rover. According to Shillcock, the engineers rose to the challenge of adapting the Jatco transmission to the Ford engine 'brilliantly'.

Very much the industry standard, the Ford Duratorq engine is a far more complex piece of engineering than the Nissan TD27

The job involved flying cabs out to Japan for the work to be done, but the gearbox programme was brought to production in around 10 months.

Introduced in January 2002, the new model, called the TXII featured additional improvements that included a passive anti-theft system, which was fully integrated into the engine management system. Externally, the TXII was almost identical to the TXI, with the exception of new badges and, not long after production began, full width glass in the rear doors, which had restricted opening to reduce the possibility of bilkers escaping through the window. The cab was offered with the same three trim options as its predecessors; Bronze, Silver and Gold. Dealer-fitted options included CCTV for added driver security, an electrically powered swivel seat and a plug-in occasional front seat.

As 2002 drew to a close, the results of the TXII's too-brief testing programme began to show, in the form of a very noticeable vibration in the propshaft and a noise from the timing chain. The timing chain also gave problems in the Transit which, it has been alleged was something Ford dealers would not acknowledge. As the miles built up, engine life suffered in the stop-start of London traffic, as sludge build-up increased wear and tear. Occasionally too, a faulty water pump pulley caused the water pump to fall off, shedding the drive belt and leaving the cab with no power assistance to the steering or brakes. It was an indication of how badly the relationship between LTI and Ford had deteriorated that, rather than Ford agreeing to design, make and pay for a special one for the TXII, they insisted that LTI paid to have a new design made for every single DuraTorq engine.

The many problems encountered with the early TXIIs, all, seemingly at once gave the TXII a poor reputation that, more than eight years after its introduction it still had not shaken off, despite LTI's assurances that later examples were much better, more reliable cabs. LTI put in place improved build quality standards and backed this up with a three-year/100,000 mile warranty, but the TXII's reputation as a poor cab, like that of the FX4R, stuck with it.

A Challenge to The Conditions of Fitness

When LTI sought to increase their market by persuading provincial licensing authorities to adopt London-type cabs, they not only made some allies but found some detractors too. LTI's case was based on two main points. One was wheelchair accessibility. LTI maintained that local authorities ought to provide transport for wheelchair users, as prescribed by the Department of Transport and the Fairway was fully wheelchair-accessible. The other point was one of driver safety, as drivers of saloon car taxis had suffered an increase in robberies, serious assaults and even murders in the previous few years. A separate partition, whilst not totally obviat-

ing the risk had been shown to deter the opportunist from committing an offence. The provincial operators' argument was that they were not willing to find the extra cash to buy a much more expensive purpose-built cab to carry out a very limited amount of wheelchair work which, in most cases was not subsidised as it was in London with the Taxicard scheme. For years, provincial operators had bought saloon cars, either new or comparatively new, for much less than the cost of an FX4 of a similar age but ran them for a shorter time. Some opponents also fitted swivel seats to the front of their cabs to demonstrate that it was possible to transfer most wheelchair-bound passengers to it. The point about driver safety was countered by suggesting the fitting of partitions in saloon cars. LTI demonstrated the wheelchair access successfully, continued to provide statistics about the safety of a solid partition and countered the cost argument by saying that the cost of a purpose-built cab was equivalent to that of two saloon cars run consecutively. The local authorities that adopted London-type cabs stuck to their guns, but as the antagonists were not about to lie down and give up and buy London-type cabs, the market became ripe for a competitor to produce a modern, cheaper alternative to London-type cabs.

The Jubilee Automotive Group of Wednesbury, Staffordshire, produced a taxi conversion based on a Fiat Scudo van that complied with the Conditions of Fitness in every respect but one: the turning circle. More than that, the vehicle, named the Eurocab carried a base price of around £18,000 in comparison to the Fairway's £23,000-plus. JAG's Mike Holland managed to persuade an increasing number of licensing authorities to adopt this type of vehicle as well as a conversion of the Mercedes-Benz Viano MPV, both of which were the very latest of their type, not a re-vamp of a thirty-year-old design.

Holland and his associates then decided to try and tackle the London market. The people associated with him were dedicated to licensed taxi trade and the principle of the purpose-built taxi market. They included Geoff Chater, who had left Metrocab in January 1999, John Paton, who had sold Austin cabs in Glasgow since 1957 and former Scottish Metrocab dealer Gerry Facenna. Although the Eurocab had to meet European Whole Vehicle Type Approval (EWVTA) Class M1 as a passenger car, as had the Fairway, TXI and Metrocab, the PCO, which since 2000 had been under the jurisdiction of Transport for London (TfL) would duty-bound to reject it if it was presented for type approval, as its turning circle was too large. Thus the cab was not presented, and the next step was to mount a challenge the turning circle rule in the Conditions of Fitness.

On being presented with the challenge, Mayor of London Ken Livingstone, as PCO supremo, commissioned the Transport Research Laboratory to conduct a consultation exercise. A small number of Eurocabs were tested around London to see if they could cope with the tight turns required to access some ranks and railway stations. The vehicles were found to be at a disadvantage, struggling to manoeuvre around such places as Euston Station and the entrance to the Savoy Hotel.

In June 4 2003 the PCO released Notice 10/03, which announced TfL's decision to retain the turning circle. The Notice said:

"About half of London's annual 90 million taxi trips are hailed on the street, and this is where the turning circle is useful for both drivers and passengers.

"Outside London, taxi pickups are predominantly from taxi ranks. Without the turning circle, many of London's ranks would have to be relocated or redesigned, as they would not be practical or safe if taxis had to do three point turns. Such vehicles (e. g. the Eurocab) would have difficulty accessing places such as Euston Station, East Croydon Station, Clapham Junction Station and the Savoy Hotel.

"The major risk of abolishing the turning circle requirement was that there would be a rapid reduction in vehicles with the facility in favour of those with cheaper upfront costs but without the manoeuvrability.

The Peugeot E7 taxi, based on the Expert van provided a viable alternative to the Fairway, TX1 and Metrocab in the provinces, but had a turning circle greater than 7.6m.
The original E7 and Fiat Scudo taxis were built on almost identical base vehicles

"Over time it is very likely that there would be no vehicles with the tight turning circle with the consequential loss of customer benefits noted above. The greater choice sought by drivers would be short-lived with there ultimately being no more choice than now."

However, TfL did not give the existing manufacturers carte blanche. The Notice went on to say:

"Retaining the turning circle has the effect of limiting the number of suppliers of London taxis in the short term (until other manufacturers produce vehicles which comply) to two, with one very dominant. It is proposed to exercise stronger oversight of these suppliers to ensure that their vehicles comply meet the needs of both passengers and drivers. It is also proposed to encourage the two manufacturers to work closely with driver and passenger representatives to improve comfort and ergonomics, and to remedy the shortcomings of existing designs. If they are deemed to be abusing their duopoly position, this will result in a further review of the Conditions of Fitness to confirm that the best interests of London are being served."

To the Notice, Ken Livingstone added: "I am already looking forward to the next generation of taxis which I expect to build on the current features to provide better comfort for both drivers and passengers including better suspension, better accessibility for wheelchair users and people who are disabled, and improve environmental performance."

The Notice ended by stating, "It is now intended that another review of the Conditions of Fitness will be conducted not later than 2013."

Other changes to the Conditions of Fitness were; a requirement for cabs to have a one-piece rear window and, if sliding doors are fitted, that they are power-assisted. This would mean additional cost for the builders of the Peugeot/Fiat vehicle, as its sliding passenger doors were not power assisted and had two side-hinged rear doors.

A Judicial Review

On September 12 2003, Allied Vehicles Ltd., producers of the Peugeot E7 taxi, a similar vehicle to the Eurocab, instigated a Judicial Review in the High Court against TfL, claiming that the PCO's decision was unlawful "as a result of the inclusion of the turning circle requirement and the sliding doors and 'one piece whole rear window' requirement". On 29 September 2003 the PCO announced its decision to reconsider the three Conditions. A major point of the challenge was that under European law, the Conditions of Fitness prevent major European manufacturers from selling vehicles in London, contrary to European law on free movement of goods between EU member states. Allied also claimed that the existing rules, in barring the kind of vehicles they made, kept prices higher than otherwise they might be, which resulted in:

'fewer taxis, higher fares, less suitable taxis for the needs of the disabled and the unavailability of safer and more comfortable taxis to the disadvantage in general of passengers and drivers alike.'

Allied Vehicles found support from the Licensed Taxi Drivers' Association, who campaigned hard for the Conditions of Fitness to be amended to allow a greater choice of vehicle for London. They did not wish to see the end of LTI, but to for London's cab drivers to be offered the choice of a more expensive vehicle with a tight turning circle or a slightly cheaper vehicle with a wider turning circle. This was to reduce the chance of any company in a monopoly situation from abusing their position.

However, for LTI to be financially viable they have to sell in other markets besides London, and in the majority of these markets there are already different types of vehicle, some of which are very different from anything that would be type-approved in London. Thus, LTI were already competing in a market that that was far more mixed than the one the LTDA envisaged should exist in London.

In Notice 19/04, the PCO announced that they were reconsidering three elements of the Conditions of Fitness review outlined in the Judicial Review; the turning circle, 'whether (it) offers tangible, significant benefits to the travelling public and, if so, whether the disadvantages or risks associated with retaining the requirement outweigh any such benefits'; the power-assisted doors and the one-piece rear window. These terms of reference were agreed to, and accepted by Allied Vehicles Ltd. PCO Principal, Roy Ellis was charged by Mayor Ken Livingstone with making the final decision and initially the results were promised for early 2005, but the task proved extremely complex, as a wide range of input came from all interested parties, including Allied, who provided a great deal of information, all of which, according to the PCO was well-informed and 'very welcome'. Advice was also sought from disinterested parties such as Human Engineering Ltd., one of the world's leading human factors and ergonomics consultancies. This wealth of complex information obliged Ellis to prolong the study in order to make sure that enough time was given to all parties to put their case and for him, so that he could make the best decision he could. He also pledged that TfL would ' keep an entirely

open mind as to whether the three requirements should be retained, modified or scrapped.'

In the end, Ellis came down in favour of the status quo with regard to all three points. The turning circle was deemed to be essential for the manoeuvrability of taxis in London's narrow and crowded streets and passengers would have to pay an unnecessarily higher fare and might be delayed unduly if a taxi had to 'go around the block' instead of performing a U-turn. The idea that alternative vehicles without the tight turning circle would sell at a lower price and thus bring competition was dismissed: it was thought that a manufacturer who invested in a vehicle with the required turning circle might be priced out of the market and the taxi proprietor, who wanted such a vehicle would be offered less choice, not more. The requirement for power doors was retained, in view of the considerable number of disabled and infirm people carried by taxis in London, many of whom might not be capable of opening an unassisted door. The split rear window was rejected on the grounds of public safety: in a complete turnaround of the old principle that taxi passengers should have privacy, the need for people to see into a cab as well as the occupants to see out was made a priority. The safety of one occupant with regard to his or her companion was held to be potentially at risk if they were not on view, as was the likelihood of dangerous or improper behaviour in what is effectively a public place.

Metrocab Fall

In December 2003, Metrocab went into administration, with the loss of 100 jobs. Production had halved to ten per week.

The trade press partly blamed this slump, which also affected LTI on the rumour that the PCO's planned to introduce a 'quickie' Knowledge test. This would, the trade's opponents said increase the number of cab drivers in a very short space of time and seriously affect cab drivers' earning ability. The PCO had no intention of reducing the standard of the test, but rather they wanted to cut administration time by increased use of computerisation. However, cab drivers who remembered the slump of the early 1990s decided to hang on to their existing cabs, rather than risk buying a new model that they might not be able to pay for. Metrocab had spent a substantial sum on the CETA project and could not afford to sustain the losses they were incurring. They had no option but to put the company into administration.

After six months of negotiation, Metrocab (UK) was bought by KamKorp Europe Ltd., a division of Kamkorp, a high-tech development specialist based in Singapore. In September 2004, the acting managing director of Metrocab (UK) Ltd., Mark Morris, announced that the company would begin trading again. He expected that new Metrocab TTTs would come off the production line by the end of the month, and that they would have a clearer idea of when they could reach full production. He promised a to supply existing Triple-T owners with spare parts, and announced a totally revised model for 2005. In April 2005 Metrocab announced that they had just begun delivery of new cabs. Production would be slow at first, with just one manual model per week, building up gradually and introducing automatic models within ten weeks.

In April 2005 Metrocab delivered one new cab, a manual model for the dealer Birmingham Taxi Warehouse, which was only a new vehicle inasmuch as it had not

been previously registered, but had actually put together out of parts sitting in the factory. Metrocab announced that they intended to bring production up to between 4 and 5 a week in the immediate future, but since that time, not one single new Metrocab has been sold anywhere.

Improvements to the TXII

Largely as a result of driver feedback the TXII received a number of important changes for 2004, including a one-piece centre division, increased luggage room and better visibility.

London LTI dealers KPM-UK Plc took the challenge of improving the Ford engine by commissioning the development of a new timing chain, which lasted far longer than the original and prevented the onset of the excessive rattling noise.

But there were, as ever changes on the horizon, not only from external, politically motivated sources but from within the trade.

Clean Air for London

The air in London had become progressively cleaner since the Clean Air Act of 1956 and ever tougher Clean Air Acts, plus EC legislation to control exhaust emission made the air cleaner still. Some London boroughs and their subcontractors began running electric or LPG fuelled vehicles, including buses and refuse vehicles, but the Greater London Authority had it in mind to clean up the capital's air even further.

There had never been any specific legislation to control the exhaust emissions of London cabs outside those laws that applied nationally, but in seeking to bring the levels of diesel emissions in the capital down gradually, Mayor Ken Livingstone targeted taxis. At first he put forward a plan to gradually take cabs over twelve years old, which had worse exhaust emissions, off the road by 2007, but this was bitterly opposed by all trade bodies on the grounds that this would remove a substantial number of perfectly serviceable older cabs and force their erstwhile owners to buy either a new or secondhand example of the unloved and unreliable TXII. Next, in 2003 he brought out proposals that would demand the fitting of a form of exhaust fitting that would cut the particulate content of cabs' exhaust to levels permitted by Euro 3. The trade press were alarmed to learn that one type of apparatus under design would achieve it s by injecting ammonia into the exhaust, although this was soon abandoned. Cabs built before September 1998 would have to be suitably modified when presented for licensing after January 1 2006. These included Fairways, the later Ford-engined Metrocabs and Asquiths.

The trade, spearheaded by the LTDA, fought his vehemently. They were not opposed to the idea of their members working in a clean environment; far from it. They welcomed the principle, but strongly objected to the fact that cab proprietors would have to pay around £2,000 for the equipment, that the equipment was unproven and that there was only one type available. Above all, the LTDA considered the statistics, which cited older cabs as being significant contributors to the pollution in London's air to be highly suspect. In March 2005, in the face of this opposition, and on the advice of Roy Ellis, who wanted to ensure that there was more than one make of equipment available, and that they were properly tested, Livingstone pushed the deadlines back. The new deadlines would be July 1 2006 for LTI cabs registered before September 16 1998 and Metrocabs registered before December 4 1997.

This deadline was met for LTI cabs, and two types of equipment were offered. One was by Van Aaken Developments Ltd., a recirculating device, which cleaned up the exhaust by recirculating it through the engine and then through a catalytic converter. This, for the Fairway and TX1 cost just under £2,000. The other was the STT MTech turbocharger conversion from Motor and Diesel Engineering (Anglia) Ltd., the company who had installed 3-litre Perkins diesels in FX4Rs in the 1980s. This was, in the opinion of some,

STT EmTech turbocharger is a tight fit in the already crowded engine compartment of a TX1

better for the TX1's Nissan TD27 engine, as the TX1 was heavier than the Fairway and as they were newer, the engines would have done a lower mileage and would be less likely to suffer from the extra stress caused by the turbocharger.

Although a lot of older Fairways were taken out of service, some were converted, which would give the oldest ones a working life of over twenty years. By far the most common FX4 model converted was the Fairway Driver. One reason for these owners choosing to spend the money was that the only secondhand models they could buy were the Metrocab, which was on the brink of extinction and the TXII, was earning a reputation for unreliability.

The deadline for Metrocabs was delayed, as the equipment took longer to deliver: manufacturers considered that because the market was much smaller, it was not worth their while developing specialist equipment. In the event, the STT

MTech turbo was offered.

A full engine swap for the Metrocab, consisting of a 2.3 litre Ford petrol engine converted to run on LPG was offered by the London Central Cab Company, run by David Day, formerly of TLS and Metro Sales and Service. As it involved a complete engine swap, its price of over £12,000 meant that only a small proportion of Metro owners took it up, but it worked successfully. Such cabs were easily recognisable; the gas tank was mounted in the boot and the spare wheel had mounted on an external bracket over the boot lid. For older cabs, the PCO ruled that if there were no equipment available for certain engines, and if these vehicles were only a small minority then they would be allowed to continue in service unconverted. In the event, a single FX4S was kept working until the late 2000s, which might, in some eyes be symbolic of the trade as a whole, for very major changes were in the offing.

Chapter 14

Today and Tomorrow

For more than a century, the London cab trade and the dedicated vehicle manufacturers have faced many and varied challenges, ranging from warfare, economic downturn and industrial disputes, through the ever-increasing costs of design and manufacture of the vehicles and the cost of fuel to the threat to their very existence from minicab operator Michael Gotla and his ilk.

The challenges continue: issues about construction and outward appearance are already being addressed, whilst the biggest, the long-term one of what will power cabs in the future, is the subject of debate by governments, environmentalists and transport operators alike and incurring costly and protracted and costly development by all major manufacturers.

The LTI TX4

The move to continue improving the air quality in European cities led the EU to introduce the Euro 4 standard for exhaust emissions, which were scheduled to come into force in early 2007. The TXII complied only with Euro 3, so LTI had to find a new engine for the TX-series. This time they made sure they had sufficient time. Determined not to continue their troublesome relationship with Ford, they decided on VM Motori Spa of Italy, who had been

supplying diesel engines to, amongst other customers the Chrysler Corporation, for the Jeep range of vehicles. The 'north-south' alignment of the engine of the Jeep Grand Cherokee ensured that dedicated inline manual and automatic transmissions would be available for the engine.

VM worked very closely with LTI to make sure the engine was absolutely right for the cab. Bosch, makers of the electronic fuel injection system insist on their own timescale for testing, to ensure the installation was right for the application, as different installations of an engine can compromise its efficiency and thus the quality of the exhaust. The engine chosen was a VM Motori R 425 4-cylinder, DOHC 2.4-litre turbodiesel, a slightly smaller capacity version of the engine supplied to the Jeep Grand Cherokee. LTI were pleased to put a 'Powered by VM' badge on the back of the new model, named the TX4, where they weren't prepared to put a Ford badge on the back of the TXII. Incidentally, the TX4 number was chosen because the cab complied with Euro 4, not because there was an interim 'TX3' that never made it into production.

The transmissions offered were an Eaton five-speed manual gearbox or a Chrysler five-speed automatic. The five speed manual box, made in Brazil was specially adapted for the cab, with the latest composite construction gearchange tech-

The TX4 is easily identified by its full-height radiator grille. LTI's global aspirations are reflected in the backdrop of this shot of a liveried TX4

nology. The automatic box was electronically linked to the engine management system.

The mechanical improvements also included ABS brakes all round, which was a new requirement specified in the Conditions of Fitness and coil spring rear suspension with anti-roll control. For the passenger, there were three head restraints for the back seat and two against the partition, and restyled interior trim. The driver gained a new headrest and an improved in-car entertainment system with MP3 facility. For both driver and passenger there was improved air conditioning, a one-piece partition glass with integral chip and pin payment facility and a new, and more powerful intercom system.

The TX-series body was restyled, with a full-height grille and new taillights and number plate housing. The interior was revised to make it brighter and there was a new air conditioning system, controlled by front air-blend and rear water valve systems. Four models were offered: the entry-level Driver, plus Bronze, Silver and Gold with increasing levels of equipment and trim on each. Standard on all were a redesigned driver and passenger intercom with improved microphone and the

The interior of the TX4, with passenger headrests built in to the partition glass. The wood-grained dashboard was a feature of the Gold model

speaker located in the headlining of the passenger compartment. There were head restraints for all five passengers and a one piece moulded centre division with integral payment/chip and PIN slot. Crucial to the cab's specifications was the equipment for disabled passengers, with an induction hearing loop, a swivel seat on the nearside, an additional removable step for the left hand rear door and a wheelchair ramp that pulls out of the floor.

The TX4 was launched in October 2006 and its reception was exceptional: better, possibly that that given to the Fairway back in 1989. Sales went through the roof, and by July 2007, 1,000 cabs had been sold in London alone, which was a record for any purpose-built London cab in any era. However, there is no pleasing some people, and when those people are London cab drivers, they will make their opinions known. When LTI launched TX4, there were TXII drivers telling them 'I can't believe you've stopped making this, the TXII was the best thing you've ever made!' But this simply goes to illustrate that when it comes to the London cab trade, neither LTI, nor any other manufacturer can ever please everyone!

TX4 Engine Fires

In 2008, around 15 engine fires occurred in early TX4s over a period of three months. All the vehicles were on a '56' plate and were recalled for remedial work by LTI. By November, all the affected cabs were understood to have been modified, but the whole episode was a blow to customer confidence in LTI, who were said by some members of the trade to have denied there was anything wrong with the design of the vehicle.

The Mercedes–Benz Vito

The demise of the Metrocab had left LTI once more with a monopoly position. Unlike the early 1970s, there were now others with the intention of providing a remedy for that situation. The 'alternative' vehicle makers, including the Allied group had already made moves to enter the London market, but had been thwarted by the final ruling over the Conditions of Fitness. However, a successful new arrival was championed by none other than Jevon Thorpe and Jamie Borwick, no longer in-

The Mercedes-Benz Vito London taxi. The 'taxi' legends, applied on both sides and the rear were optional, but considered necessary in the cab's early days

volved with LTI but now making Modec electric commercial vehicles in Coventry. In late 2006, Thorpe approached Peter Da Costa, managing director of London taxi dealership KPM-UK Plc to see if he was interested in being a partner in a new project to build a taxi based on the Mercedes-Benz Vito Traveliner MPV. The Traveliner had proven itself in cab work in the provinces, and indeed worldwide and Mercedes-Benz was and still is the benchmark for durability and reliability in the taxi trade globally. However, the Vito's turning circle disqualified it from being type-approved for London. Da Costa accepted the invitation, knowing Thorpe and Borwick's track record in the London taxi manufacturing business and the unrivalled pedigree of the Mercedes-Benz marque which, Da Costa believed would be the only one the London cab trade would accept without reservation as an alternative to LTI.

He also knew that the Vito would not be a cheap cab, but went ahead on the principle that there would be buyers who would be willing to pay a premium for a prestige vehicle. Some London private hire companies had, since private hire had been licensed in London in 2000 raised their profile and garnered high-quality work from major corporate clients that had been enjoyed for some time by the London radio taxi circuits, Computer Cab, Radio Taxis Ltd., Dial-a-Cab and Xeta. The Vito, Da Costa believed would enable the taxi trade to win back this work. The private hire companies might offer more luxurious vehicles than the TX series, or the remaining Fairways and Metrocabs, but they could not guarantee that their drivers had gone through the Knowledge of London or could meet the standards provided by the best taxi trade in the world and the Vito, Da Costa believed would give the taxi trade an unbeatable package.

Daimler AG, owners of the Mercedes-Benz name were interested in the project and representatives from the UK arm, Mercedes-Benz UK Ltd. in Milton Keynes met Da Costa, and gave their ultimate approval of the vehicle, a Letter of No Objection. Consulted too, in secrecy was the Public Carriage Office. It was proposed that the problem of meeting the 7.6m turning circle could be solved by fitting part-time rear wheel steering, which would come into use, selectively at speeds below 5mph. (8kph) This was a point that the PCO needed to be consulted on. There is no specific rule that bars rear wheel steering and no rule that specifies that the 7.6m turning circle should be achievable at any speed: it is of course highly dangerous to use such a tight lock at any speed much above walking pace! The PCO were satisfied with this solution and the project went ahead. The steering was engineered by a Coventry company, one80 Ltd., as was the additional equipment, such as the electrically-operated retractable low steps and the power-assisted doors. The latter item complied with the new Conditions of Fitness rule, as did the one-piece lift-up tailgate with its single window.

The Vito Taxi was type approved by the Public Carriage Office on June 26 2008 and launched immediately after. The base model, which is the short-wheelbase, shorter length model is made in Spain and converted to taxi specification in Coventry. It is powered by a 2.15 litre four-cylinder turbocharged diesel engine, coupled to a full automatic transmission with Tiptronic control. It has independent suspension and disc brakes all round with ABS and power-assisted steering. It is a full six-seater with mandatory wheelchair accessibility and separate air-conditioning systems for the driver and passenger compartment. The passenger seats are available with optional leather facings. A choice of six colours was offered: obsidian black, brilliant silver, amber red metallic, Atlantis blue, andradite green metallic and arctic white. But according to the dealers, KPM-UK the most popular choice is, not surprisingly black.

According to drivers of the early examples, the public were unsure about whether the Vito was a genuine London taxi, and let some go by on the street rather than hail one. However, news got around that these were indeed the real thing and very comfortable vehicles and stories were told of how some passengers were selecting a Vito in preference to an LTI cab, either on the street or on a rank. Owners found they were being booked for lucrative private work, especially long-distance runs and radio circuits found account customers specifying Vito cabs for prestige work. Peter Da Costa's venture has, so far paid dividends for his company and for the Vito's owners, even in the toughest economic climate the country has seen for two decades.

Due out in the spring of 2011 was the Euro 5 version of the Vito, with a cleaner, more powerful engine. New lights and bumpers identified this vehicle at a glance.

LTI in China

The age of the Coventry factory had been of concern to LTI for some time. It had been built up, piecemeal since Carbodies moved there in 1928, and very few, if any of the major buildings had been renewed since the 1980s. The new managing director, Peter Shillcock had come from the new BMW Mini factory in Cowley and was well aware of the improved efficiency, and the likely reduction in build cost that would result from a modern,

state-of-the art plant. LTI wanted to acquire a new factory in Coventry in order to retain the skilled workforce, and looked at the plant at Walsgrave that Alvis had vacated when the moved to Telford. In order to achieve this, they needed to sell the old Holyhead Road factory, but their plans ran into implacable opposition from a local preservation group, the Spon End Red Brick Residents' Association. A site opposite Carbodies, once occupied by Alvis had been converted into a retail park and this was already causing traffic congestion. The DIY giant, B&Q was one of the front runners to acquire the site and it was a certainty that siting such a store in what was the narrowest part of Holyhead Road would add to the traffic problems.

LTI's main reason for wanting to reduce the cost of production, and thus the cost of the vehicle was that they, London Taxis International wanted to remain just that: a player in the international taxi market, and to build on it. They had exported Fairways, TX-series cabs all over the world, but they had not established their vehicles as the prominent cab in any city outside of the UK. To do that, they needed to have a vehicle that was cheaper to buy and an effective way of achieving this was to move to a country with lower labour costs. After an unsuccessful attempt at establishing a factory in Mexico, MBH looked to the burgeoning Chinese economy and spoke to several Chinese vehicle manufacturers, with a view to setting up a factory in China. In September 2006, it was announced that a deal had been agreed with Geely Automotive of Shanghai, to build cabs for the Chinese and other overseas markets and to make components for cabs built in Coventry.

At the 2010 Beijing Motor Show, LTI and Geely displayed their TXN Concept Vehicle, a taxi designed to showcase LTI's

Geely's chairman, Mr Li Shufu with Manganese Bronze Holdings' CEO, John Russell at the 2007 Shanghai Motor Show

experience in designing taxis, but not intended to replace the TX4. In a statement, Peter Shillcock, Managing Director of LTI said;

"The TXN is a concept car which is intended for international markets ... our relationship with Geely allows us to explore other vehicle designs and the TXN is the first example of this."

In late 2010 the first version of a Coventry-built TX4 with Chinese made components was announced. There were were two trim options, the Style and the Elegance model. Prices for the Style begin at £28,403 for a manual model, up to

£32,324 for a top of the range Elegance automatic. Overseas markets, including those in eastern Europe and the Middle East are being now supplied direct from the Shanghai factory and new markets are being penetrated.

In November 2010, the Mann and Overton name was dropped by Manganese Bronze holdings Plc and Andrew Overton, who had served what was his family firm for forty-one years, retired. All dealership franchises were withdrawn and LTI now sell taxis directly through their own dealerships under the name of The London Taxi Company.

A TX4 Style passes one of London's most distinctive sights, Michelin's 'Bibendum' building in the Fulham Road

The London Taxi of the Future

The future of the London taxi is largely dependent on the answer to three main questions: to what extent will the rest of the UK and the world adopt it, what will it look like and what will power it? The first two points are intertwined, because the cost of developing new models has grown to astronomical proportions, endangering so many independent vehicle makers who may not be able to source adequate resources. LTI on its own was at a disadvantage compared with big manufacturers, but with Geely, they have the muscle of a big organisation behind them, thus giving some guarantee to the survival of the marque, if not necessarily the traditional appearance of the London taxi.

With Geely's low labour costs, The London Taxi Company has already been able to reduce the price of cabs assembled in Coventry, and Shanghai-built cabs have sold into markets the management never dreamed of in the 1980s, when Grant Lockhart realised that the future of Carbodies depended on widening the market for the FX4R and its intended successor, the CR6. Increased production and far lower labour costs will keep prices competitive, which is vital to the survival of a niche product and enabled eastern European markets and even Asian ones like Azerbaijan to be tackled. The cost of developing cleaner engines is also a huge, but vital part of the price of a purpose-built taxi, and Geely's resources may, in the immediate future be of benefit to the TX-series and its successors in producing cleaner engines.

The consortium behind the Vito taxi has already begun exporting the vehicle, including to Middle Eastern markets. It has to be said that earlier sales of the TX-series has been to specialist operators, such as wedding vehicle providers in Malaysia, whereas the Mercedes-Benz Vito in its standard production form has been used as a taxi around the world for some years. The interior configuration of the London cab is a novel variation on a vehicle that has a proven track record and has Mercedes' own, well established service network in place, thus there is a sound foundation on which to build export sales.

The very look of the London taxi may depend on development costs. The TX1 was developed, admittedly on existing running gear for around £24m. Daimler AG spent over £3bn developing the Vito alone. These included the cost of ensuring the Mercedes engine meets the required European emission standards. Although it might be presumed that an engine, once developed will meet these whatever vehicle it is installed in, the different load and work-cycle demands mean that it may perform differently, and often in a very 'dirty' way in some, so that the engine has to be retuned for each installation. If that engine has already been set up for a taxi or minibus version of the donor vehicle, then that is one expensive job already done. If EWVTA, European Whole Vehicle Type Approval has already been met, in, say a minibus version, then that is yet another task already signed off.

For certain, the traditional, 'iconic' look of the London taxi, championed for two decades by LTI has been given notice by the Vito. The London cab trade's reputation has been built, since the late nineteenth century at least on two pillars: the Knowledge of London, which ensures that London cab drivers enjoy a reputation as the finest in the world, and the integrity of the vehicles, underpinned by the Conditions of Fitness and the PCO's strict regime of vehicle inspection. Passenger safety has been the PCO's most important priority since its inception, and to promote passenger safety, cab trade bodies have always urged people to take licensed taxis and not climb into rogue, un-booked minicabs. For decades, London's taxis have always been distinguishable from private cars and light vans and the recognisability of the vehicle was one of its unique selling points, both to the trade nationally and to the travelling public. If it is a genuine licensed London taxi, the proponents maintained, it would be driven by a safe, licensed London cab driver. 'You know,' they say, 'what a genuine London taxi looks like.' It was that traditional appearance that has been sold to the public and after scrapping the CR6, LTI made a virtue of it, especially when selling it to their new overseas markets. And it was these overseas customers that insisted that the new model, the TX1 should have this retro look and this was a major factor in its design.

The Conditions of Fitness demand a certain configuration: a partition between driver and passengers, specific minimum interior and door dimensions and floor height, as well as the turning circle. Not one of the rules demand a body style reminiscent of days gone by. Until LTI's announcement following the scrapping of the CR6, it had been expected that any new model of London cab would have a more modern appearance than its predecessor, and this was borne out over the decades, from the Birch prototypes through to the production Metrocab. In the provincial market, the builders of the so-called 'alternative' taxis that have proved so popular with operators had little of this heritage to compete with. Provincial customers outside of the big cities were used to riding in saloon cars and, on occasions van-based minibuses. What mattered to all concerned was that

the vehicles did the job they were meant to do, and in the case of the 'alternatives', carried able-bodied and wheelchair-bound passengers alike and give protection to the driver. Although there is anecdotal evidence that a potential passenger anywhere in the UK will hail a London taxi on the street but let a saloon car taxi go by, similar evidence indicates that the same people will recognise and hail an 'alternative' purpose-built taxi too. If it's big and (often) black, with a yellow light on the roof, what else could it be but a taxi?

When the Mercedes-Benz Vito was introduced into London, its appearance met with a mixed reception. Would it, the pundits said be overlooked by cab passengers, as the original Metrocab prototype and the Birch had been, decades ago? Although it took a short while for the public in London to realise that this new vehicle was indeed a taxi and not an MPV, a van or a private hire vehicle, its quick acceptance has already proved that recognisability of the vehicle by virtue of an outdated style rather than by a 'taxi' sign on the roof was little more than a myth. Metrocab owners would say they could have told you that, years ago.

So has the mould been broken? Parent company Daimler AG are committed to the Vito London taxi, so Jamie Borwick, Jevon Thorpe and Peter Da Costa's hopes for the future are as secure as they can reasonably believe. Will other minibuses and MPVs be converted? Peugeot have long been associated with the taxi trade, especially in France. The latest Peugeot E7, developed from the Expert Window Van could be fitted with rear wheel steering to comply, so would Peugeot be willing to give similar support to Allied that Daimler-Benz have given to the builders of Vito London taxi?

And how might this affect the TX-series replacement? At some point in time it will become obsolete. For one thing, it is a heavy vehicle and weight adds to fuel costs. If LTI were put under pressure to produce a lighter vehicle, a simple way would be to develop a taxi based on a unit-construction platform shared with a light van. Geely have a large MPV, the GV5 in their line-up, but it is not known if the floorpan of could be used as the base of a cab that would comply with the Conditions of Fitness. It is feasible, though that a new generation MPV or minibus could be developed to comply, so the very company that has bought into the iconic design of the London taxi could engineer the demise of the icon. Indeed the release of the TXN Concept Vehicle at the 2010 Beijing Motor Show makes it plain that the London Taxi Company is keen to explore al possible alternatives. This of course is pure speculation, but at this point in time, it is impossible to say what will happen five years from now. The London Taxi Company's chief executive, Peter Shillcock has gone on record as saying they plan to stick with a purpose-built vehicle of their own design, because they have complete control over that vehicle's design. Taxis based on mass-production commercial vehicles have a greater commercial appeal to taxi operators world-wide, so market forces may, it might be said see the end of the traditional appearance of the purpose-built taxi.

The Fuel Debate

The power source for the immediate future, for UK and European markets at least will be cleaner diesel, because it is simpler, cheaper and more practical to clean up the existing engines, which depend on existing fuel supply infrastructure than try and introduce newer technology to a very conservative market. Whilst petrol engines produce noticeable levels of hydrocarbons and carbon monoxide, the levels of these compounds are negligible in a diesel engine. For some time it was considered that diesel engines were therefore more acceptable than petrol engines until nitrous oxide and the level of carbon particulates that are present in diesel exhaust were discovered to be harmful. At first, combustion chamber and injector design was thought to be an effective method of reducing both types of emissions. However, these would be more effective on direct injection engines, such as the Ford FSD, rather than in an indirect injection engine like the Nissan TD series.

Previous Attempts with Alternative Fuels

Gas, either liquefied petroleum gas (LPG) or liquefied natural gas (LNG) seemed at one time a clean, practical alternative to diesel. LPG in Britain has historically carried very little fuel duty, (price per litre in early 2011 was around 75p against diesel at 132p). During the first decade of the twentieth century, the number of LPG outlets grew in London, so a lack of availability would not have been a handicap. However, successive tests have proved, if not a failure then insufficiently conclusive to warrant putting gas cabs into production.

W. H. Cook's attempt to use LPG in the late 1960s foundered over the increase in fuel cost. In late 1989, Compucab UK Ltd., a subsidiary of East London proprietors BJ Caledonian began discussions with British Gas about the possibilities of a dual-fuel cab, using natural gas. These discussions came to nothing, but British

Gas ran a mixed experimental fleet to assess its potential as a viable fuel for road use. One of the vehicles was a Carbodies FL2, which was subsequently bought privately, converted to a taxi and was licensed in London for several years.

LTI had three Fairways fitted with Iveco spark ignition engines that were converted to gas operation in late 1997, two bi-fuel LPG and one bi-fuel compressed natural gas (CNG) and these were put on test. Later, LTI commissioned Perry Engineering of Benfleet in Essex to fit four TXls with 2.0 litre Ford bi-fuel engines converted by to run on liquid petroleum gas (LPG). None of these experiments established liquefied gas as a viable fuel for London taxis.

A gas conversion for the Fairway from the Ecological Engine Company was offered by LTI dealers KPM (UK) Plc in the late 1990s. Called the Ecocab, it consisted of the Eco 120 1.8 litre four-cylinder spark-ignition engine, sourced from the MG TF and converted by Janspeed to run on LPG. An Energy Savings Trust grant was available to buyers, which brought the price of the conversion down to £2,950. With LPG at 38p a litre, it appeared an economical option, but the engine was un-derpowered and owners reported serious overheating problems. On the other hand, the London Central Cab Company offered the fitting of the 2.3 Ford DOHC petrol engine, adapted to run on gas in both LTI cabs and in particular the Metrocab, for just over £12,000. This engine has run without any reported trouble, although the withdrawal of Metrocab from the taxi trade and the resultant drop in confidence of the resale value of the model must have restricted the number of owners of these cabs willing to lay out a large sum of money to have their cabs converted.

As the new century dawned, LTI investigated LPG power once more and in February 2000, placed a TX1 on trial in Bristol, two in London and fourth in Scotland, for a period of six months. However, the trials did not prove conclusive. The engines were heavier on fuel, but the cost of gas per litre was considerably less, resulting in only a marginal improvement in fuel costs. Nor were emissions significantly cleaner. The project was abandoned.

In addition to the lack of advantage in fuel costs, a petrol engine returns perhaps less than half service life of a diesel, necessitating, in a vehicle designed to last ten years, a replacement engine halfway

A Fairway Driver, converted to LPG power by Janspeed, using the 1.8 litre engine from an MGTF

through its life. This would have an adverse effect on the whole-life cost of the cab, something that both LTI and Metrocab have always put as a significant sales point when trying to persuade provincial cab operators to switch to London-type cabs. Thus, whilst the cost of the fuel, as well as its comparative cleanliness was very attractive, engine life was much shorter than a diesel's, rendering the whole life cost similar or even less than that of a diesel cab.

The Greater London Authority's Air Quality Strategy

Vehicle manufacturers and owners alike have to face the reality that fossil fuels will become more and more expensive before they finally run out. What will power the cars and commercial vehicles of the future is as uncertain as it was over a century ago, but makers are making serious investments in time and money to discover what will be the most economical and practical source of power. With Euro 5 imminent, the whole matter of air cleanliness is being tackled in the short term by improving existing technology, but the UK Government has pledged to cut greenhouse gas emissions by 80 percent by 2050, which is a target that will not be met by the use of diesel or petrol engines.

Vehicles used in cities are targeted particularly, as they can spend a lot of time stationary in traffic, or moving slowly and thus creating a higher proportion of pollutants than vehicles moving at a steady speed on a highway. Boris Johnson, elected as Mayor of London in 2008 was given legal responsibility under the government's Air Quality Strategy to establish and review an air quality strategy for the Capital.

Besides complying with UK government's demands, he also had to conform to the broader European Union Air Quality Directive, which set standards for a variety of pollutants that are considered harmful to human health and the environment. In 'Delivering London's Energy Future', a document published in October 2010, Johnson went further and declared that it was his vision for London 'to be the greenest big city in the world, with a thriving low carbon economy. By 2025 it will have left behind its reliance on polluting fossil fuels. Instead it will have highly energy efficient buildings, generate its own low and zero carbon energy, and provide attractive options for low carbon living.'

The Fifteen-year Rule

Johnson acted swiftly to impose restrictions on taxis. Under new rules, no vehicle over fifteen years old will be licensed after January 2012. After a hiatus of almost three decades, London's taxis will have a limited life. This rule will remove all remaining Fairways and almost all Fairway Drivers and Metrocabs. Only those newly registered after January 1 1997 will be exempt when the law comes into force, but will subsequently be removed as they reach the age limit. Next, all cabs presented for their first licence would have to comply with Euro 5 exhaust emission standards.

To help with compliance with this rule, The Mayor pledged to work with the taxi manufacturing industry to 'identify tyres and brake pads which reduce PM10 emissions. The new components will be mandated for all London taxis and will significantly assist in reducing the 35% of PM10 emissions which it is estimated results from road transport tyre and brake pad wear in Central London.' He also pledged to help the industry develop affordable zero-emission taxis.

The document also recognised that proper driving and waste mileage are factors as important in reducing pollution as technology, and to help this, all new taxi drivers entering the trade would be required to undertake a mandatory Eco Driving course. In addition, existing drivers would also be encouraged to undertake these courses. Additional ranks would help reduce cruising cabs, and the Mayor would also 'support the development of new technologies which will encourage taxi sharing and enable electronic hailing.'

Power Sources for Future London Taxis

It will have to be a new power source, or sources that will deliver the required low or zero emissions. The three types currently under investigation are hybrid power, hydrogen fuel cells and electricity. All systems use electric traction motors, The difference is in the way the electricity is delivered, but each type is at a different stage of development and at present, only hybrid power is widely available in vehicles produced in quantity.

Hybrid Power

Hybrid Power is the most common alternative power source in use today, with Japanese makers Toyota and Honda offering hybrid cars for sale worldwide. Hybrid electric vehicles (HEVs) use petrol or diesel engines to drive a generator. The electricity produced is stored and used to run an electric propulsion motor and for much of the time that the vehicle is running, it generates no exhaust gas. Typically, HEVs are about one-eighth as polluting as a similar sized petrol powered vehicle. Also the fuel (petrol of diesel) consumption is significantly better. Unlike a battery electric vehicle, the range of an HEV is not limited by battery capacity, only by its fuel tank size. However, it is more complex than a straightforward internal combustion engine and thus its maintenance would be a challenge to some of the smaller cab garages that rent and service older cabs, which are the backbone of the trade. Hybrid powerplants are, at present expensive to produce and those cars sold with them are subsidised, so at present, although it is proven technology, and much cleaner than an internal combustion engine on its own, its complexity and cost act against it for such commercial applications as purpose-built taxis at the present time.

In April 2003, Manganese Bronze Holdings Plc signed an agreement with Azure Dynamics of Canada to develop a hybrid electric motive power system for use in a cab. Azure took delivery of a TXII in June 2003 and fitted it their second generation with the G2r powertrain, designed for vehicles between 5,000 and 8,500lbs GVW. This project too was abandoned. Frazer-Nash, once a famous British sports car company but now a subsidiary of KamKorp fitted a hybrid powerplant into a restyled Metrocab in early 2008, but nothing more was heard of it.

Hydrogen Fuel Cells

Hydrogen fuel cells produce electricity that powers the vehicle, but its technology is quite advanced and is not likely to be seen in production cars for some time. Its complexity and cost does not work in favour of the London taxi, but in June

2010 LTI launched a demonstration hydrogen fuel cell taxi at London's City Hall, presented by Deputy Mayor Kit Malthouse and John Russell, CEO of Manganese Bronze Holdings. The vehicle was part of a consortium project, led by Intelligent Energy in conjunction with Lotus Engineering and TRW Conekt, some of the leading UK engineering companies in the field. The project is part sponsored by the Government, through the Technology Strategy Board, and part by the consortium It was planned, with further funding to develop a small fleet of fuel cell taxis for the 2012 Olympics, but it was understood at the outset that "it would be some time in the future before the technology became viable for general use on British streets in terms of the cost of manufacture and the availability of hydrogen re-fuelling stations."

Battery Power

Battery power is the simplest and oldest of the alternative power sources, and if battery technology can be improved to give a longer range, and charging stations or battery exchange facilities are set up around the capital and elsewhere, for instance in motorway service stations, it may prove viable. LTI's parent company Manganese Bronze Holdings Plc signed a development agreement in early 2008 with commercial electric vehicle manufacturer The Tanfield Group to develop an all-electric TX4, the TX4E. The agreement was for LTI to ship a basic TX4 to Tanfield's factory in Tyne and Wear for fitting of a Smith's advanced electric drive train and Lithium-Ion Iron Phosphate battery pack. Top speed was estimated to be 50mph and the range to being excess of 100 miles on one battery. The cab was planned for use in congested urban areas and is estimated to cost less than 4p per mile to run, based on current electricity prices, but the initial cost of the TX4E would be higher than the diesel TX4. However, the proposed launch date of mid-2009 came and went with no sign of the cab going on sale.

A Mercedes-Benz Vito taxi, converted to electric power by Zytech Automotive Ltd. took part in the first RAC Future Car Challenge in November 2010. The Future Car Challenge was set up to try and bring focus to the technology being developed to produce low and zero emission vehicles and took the form of a Brighton-to-

The Lotus-TRW Conekt TX4 on a demonstration run at the 2010 Goodwood Festival of Speed

London run, the day before, and in the reverse direction of the annual Veteran Car Run. Prizes were awarded for the most fuel-efficient entry in each class.

Zytech Automotive Ltd is a Staffordshire company that has worked on electric powertrains for several years. Zytech's customers include Modec, an electric truck maker owned by former LTI chairman Jamie Borwick. Unlike the diesel cab it has front-wheel drive, the removal of the propshaft providing room for the under-floor batteries. The range was 120km ((75 miles) which is nowhere adequate for a working taxi, but according to Zytech's MD, Neil Heslington, it was purely a development vehicle, produced to investigate what is needed for such an application and, indeed to see if electric taxis themselves are viable. The Vito actually won its class, arriving at the RAC headquarters in Pall Mall with plenty of battery capacity to spare, despite the last fifteen or so miles being run in Greater London's Saturday morning shopping traffic.

In late May 2011, a fleet of twenty battery powered TX4s went on trial in Amsterdam. These yellow, left-hand drive cabs were supplied by the London Taxi Company and converted by All Green Vehicles of Ousterhout, for the Amsterdam based Holland4Electric organisation. They are said to be capable of covering 250km on a single charge, and recharging is understood to take around four hours. Credit for this much-extended range is in part down to the TX4's construction, enabling it to accommodate a larger battery pack. Obviously it is too early to say whether these vehicles will be successful or not, but certainly the increase in range and the reduction in charging time bodes well for battery electric vehicles.

Conclusions

Battery power may be the best form of clean energy or taxis in the future, provided of course that the mains electricity that is supplied to the batteries comes from renewable sources. The technology is by far the simplest, with just one motor and transfer box and an engine management system that is, given the much smaller number of tasks it has to accommodate probably less complicated than that of a modern petrol car.

The other problem is range. The Amsterdam vehicles indicate that much

Pictured at the halfway stop in Crawley, Sussex, the electric Mercedes Vito cab taking part in the RAC Future Car Challenge

progress is being made in this field, but battery technology needs to improve to provide at least double the seventy miles of current vehicles to make it viable and there are charging stations built to provide a short 'top-up' charge, or to swap exhausted batteries for cabs that are needed for long runs towards the end of a shift. Although battery cost is, and will no doubt remain high, and thus add a substantial premium on top of the cost of new and secondhand cabs, the additional purchase price will be offset by the driver or proprietor will not having to pay out every day at the pumps.

The cost of manufacture of hybrid systems and hydrogen fuel cells, and the maintenance my work against them for taxis in the future. What has underpinned the high initial cost of taxis in the past is the high resale value and long service; the whole life cost. If the running costs of a five-year-old cab become prohibitive, then the secondhand value will suffer, forcing proprietors to buy new, which will most likely create a demand for higher fares and even in the end price the purpose-built cab out of the market. But this is a long way off, as the fuel of the future for the London, and indeed the world cab trade is, as yet undecided.

Other Challenges

There is another threat to the very existence of the London taxi as we know it, previously mentioned, that of whether the licensing authority will still maintain the Conditions of Fitness and the Knowledge of London in the immediate and near future. The private hire trade, now licensed in London and promoting that status to its customers (even if a small but high-profile proportion of its number still continue to flout the laws regarding plying for hire) now have modern, smart MPVs and limousines. Representatives of the private hire trade have gained the concession from Transport for London to be exempt from the Congestion Charge. They are now campaigning for the right to use bus lanes, a privilege granted to taxis. This attempt is being opposed fiercely by the taxi trade and TfL have given no indication that they intend to change the status quo. Sections of the private hire trade would love to have the right to ply for hire and become taxis by default. This is also, not surprisingly opposed vehemently by the taxi trade. Quite naturally, they state that the controls in place over the taxi trade - the Knowledge of London and the Conditions of Fitness – have proved their worth over the

The current Peugeot E7 is less van-like in its appearance than its predecessor. An electric version was released in 2010.
Vehicles of this shape may be the London taxis of the future

years and are still valid, so why scrap what works and is acclaimed as the best in the world? But if it were to happen it would consign the purpose-built taxi, and its world-renowned driver to the same fate as the horse cab, a century before. The TX-series has proven itself, with some exceptions to be a worthy vehicle for London and a premium vehicle like the Vito will ensure that the taxi trade, with drivers who have passed The Knowledge of London ensure that the a distinct difference between it and private hire is maintained.

What is recognised is that a strong licensing authority and the belief by the trade in what it stands for has made the London taxi trade a benchmark for others to follow and a symbol of the capital that is recognised throughout the world. Between the integrity of the drivers and the shape and configuration of the vehicles,

the integrity of the drivers is without doubt the more important of the two; it is a human being that either behaves properly or improperly, as shown historically by the criminal activities of a section of the minicab trade. The fact that the appearance of the vehicles has changed over the decades without compromising the practical nature of any of them shows that the configuration is more important than the outward appearance. The adoption of all-black MPVs by one major London private hire company (one might say a plagiaristic step) pays a back-handed compliment to the iconic value of the London taxi, without having to comply with all that is deemed necessary by the licensing authority. For how long the status quo will remain, only time will tell, but London will be the poorer if either driver licensing or vehicle requirements are lost.

Appendix 1: The Public Carriage Office

London's cabs and cab drivers have been regulated by the Public Carriage Office, a division of the Metropolitan Police since 1843. The primary duty of the PCO is to safeguard the travelling public, by ensuring that all drivers are properly licensed, and that cabs are properly maintained and built to meet a standard that ensures safety and convenience for the passengers.

Apart from at a single building at Scotland Yard, adjacent to the Metropolitan Police's HQ in London's Westminster horse cabs were inspected locally, occasionally in public view, but when the motor cab first appeared in 1903, the huge variety of vehicles that appeared, and the increased knowledge required to inspect and license them created many logistical difficulties for the PCO. In 1927, to cope with this change the PCO moved to new a Metropolitan Police building in Lambeth Road, where facilities for inspecting cabs were provided.

Originally, the PCO divided London into ten administrative Districts, but following the move to Lambeth, these were reduced to four, each with several Passing Stations. By the 1950s, there was just one Passing Station in each district. With the exception of Lambeth Road, the Passing Stations had only basic equipment, which made inspecting the underside of any cab difficult. The arrival of the FX4, with its lower ground clearance made this job even harder.

As the Lambeth Road premises had been designed to accommodate several other of the Police's administrative departments, it was becoming overcrowded, so it was decided to move some departments, including the PCO into homes of their own, and to erect a new building on the Lambeth site. The PCO was to be accommodated in one single building, dealing with The Knowledge, proprietor, driver and vehicle licensing and lost property.

A suitable site was found in Penton Street, Islington and a new, purpose-built building was opened in 1965. It remained the home of the PCO until 2010. Here cabs were presented for 'passing', i. e. the inspection and granting of a licence to work, which would last a calendar year. For years, there was no fee for this service but in the **1980s**,

Inside the Public Carriage Office in Penton Street, where cabs are passed.
The parallel lines resembling a badminton court are for testing the turning circle

a fee was introduced and has been in place ever since. This and the fee for issuing driver licences every three years, are the only charges the PCO makes on the cab trade and must operate on this income alone.

Unlike provincial taxi plates, London taxi plates have no commercial value. They remain the property of the PCO and cannot be bought or sold and can be revoked at a moment's notice. Also, the PCO's Inspecting Officers have the power to inspect any cab at any time and place an unfit notice, known colloquially as a 'stop note' on the vehicle, demanding that the proprietor remove the cab from service, put right what was found to be wrong and present it for inspection as promptly as possible at Penton Street. The strictness of this regime has ensured that proprietors keep their vehicles in very good order.

When a cab is presented for passing, the inspecting officers expect to find it clean and in good mechanical repair. Every year, as soon as, and occasionally before the licence expires, a proprietor will have the cab thoroughly overhauled, with all mechanical components made good, all bodywork repaired, the interior sound and the cab thoroughly cleaned, including steam cleaning the chassis and engine. If a cab passes, a licence is issued and two plates, one for the interior of the cab and one for the back are issued, which must be fixed before the cab is allowed to be worked. If the cab fails, the proprietor has to correct all the faults listed and re-present the cab before it is allowed to return to work.

Besides the annual inspection, the PCO has the authority to make inspections on the road and to remove any unfit cabs. These must have their faults remedied and be presented before the cab is allowed to return to work. If the PCO has no record of inspecting a cab on the streets between overhauls they may issue a quarterly notice against it, demanding that the cab is presented for inspection.

In 2000, control of the Metropolitan Police passed to the newly formed Greater London Authority and along with it went the PCO, which was placed into a new body, Transport for London (TfL) along with London Regional Transport. The trebling of the numbers of cabs on the road from around 7000 in 1958 to over 20,000 by 2007 meant that to ease the workload, the inspection of vehicles was subcontracted in that year to a private company.

In 2000 the PCO also assumed responsibility for licensing London's private hire trade. In 2010, the PCO was moved to new headquarters in Southwark, and renamed Taxis and Private Hire (TPH).

Steam cleaning the 'unders' of a cab has been a vital part of the overhaul process for London's taxis. Here two FX3s of the London General's fleet are put through the process

Appendix 2: Taximeters and Fares

Taximeters were made compulsory on London's cabs in 1907, the very same year that a New York City cab operator, Harry N. Allen installed meters on his own fleet of cabs and coined the phrase 'taxi-cab'.

Although the origins of the taximeter, or 'Taxameter' as it was first called, and its name have been the subject of much debate and research, meters first came into general use in Germany in the late 19th century, built by the Bruhn company. The first attempts to try them in London, in 1847 met with failure, as they were either damaged or ignored by cabmen as was a subsequent attempt by the Taxameter Syndicate Ltd in 1898. Nevertheless, as we have seen in chapter 2, some fleet proprietors persevered; in the case of the General Cab Company to try and gain extra revenue by running a non-approved tariff. This resulted in the imposition of taximeters by the PCO and a new tariff, specially formulated to accommodate the waiting time registered by the meter, so as not to make motor cabs more expensive than horse cabs. This had a hiring charge (known almost immediately as the 'flagfall') of 8d (3.3p) instead of the one shilling (5p) of the horse cab tariff, and incremental rises of 2d (0.8p) every quarter-mile instead of 6d every half-mile. The difference was, one must surmise because when stopped in traffic, a meter would continue to register a fare, and thus register a final fare higher than that likely to be charged by a cabman driving a cab with no meter. Extra charges were also applicable, for extra passenger over two persons, and for luggage and for dogs. These, as we have seen in chapter 3 became a source of dispute, where fleet proprietors expected them to be handed over as part of the percentage of the meter the cabman paid for hiring the cab, whereas the cabman expected to keep them for himself, as he had done with horse cabs.

Nor were cabmen innocent of any misdemeanour. In his book, 'W. O., An Autobiography', (Hutchinson, 1958) W . O. Bentley, founder of the Bentley car company tells of

KOSMOS TAXAMETERS

Specially adapted for OWNER DRIVERS, and for such is undoubtedly the best Taxameter on the Market.

LARGELY USED IN LONDON AND ALL PROVINCIAL TOWNS.

Special terms to OWNER DRIVERS.

Apply to .

The Premier Taxameter Co., Ltd.,

106, ALBANY STREET, LONDON, N.W.

This advertisement for Kosmos Taxameters was published as late as 1912, in Mann and Overton's Road Atlas

an episode where he worked as a fleet manager for the National Cab Company. He found that the takings from some drivers, calculated from the figures recorded on the meters did not tally with the miles the cabs were doing. scrupulous testing of the drive mechanism found no faults, until he discovered that some cabmen had drilled very fine holes on the glass covering the mechanism that recorded the meter readings and were inserting needle through the hole and turning the figures back!

For over half a century, taximeters were complex mechanical devices, with the intricacy of a well-made clock, but set in a solid cast casing that would withstand the rigours of the job, including every type of weather. The meter runs on a combination of time and distance: when the cab is moving, the fare is registered as a component of the distance travelled, and when the cab is stationary, the clock part takes over. The part that records the distance is driven off the drive train, originally from a kind of screw device on the front wheel but later from a take-off at the rear of the gearbox. The time component on the original meters was driven by clockwork, and the mechanism had to wound by hand every day.

From the late 1950s, electromechanical meters were introduced, with the clock controlled electrically. These were replaced from the latter half of the 1970s by electronic meters, which are still in use today.

When a tariff increase was awarded, the mechanical and the electromechanical meters had to be rebuilt and it took almost a year for all of the meters on London's fleet of cabs to be changed when this happened.

Those cabs that had not had updated meters carried conversion charts on the partition, which showed the old and new fares, and these were a constant source of arguments between driver and passenger.

The rampant inflation of the 1970s created a hiatus in the updating of the electromechanical meters, with two tariff increases but only one meter upgrade. The greatest advantage of the electronic meter is that the tariff can be changed in a matter of seconds, simply by downloading a software update. This facilitates application for, and to date the granting of an annual tariff increase, which has enabled the trade bodies to try and keep fares in line with the cost of living.

Each meter in use in London has two seals, which used to be made of lead, but now are made of plastic. One is put in by the

Left: a Metropolitan meter from before the Great War, and right, a fare table showing the tariff on which it ran

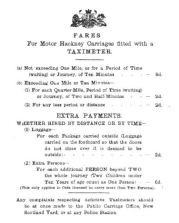

National Physical Laboratory, the other is issued by the Public Carriage Office and installed every time the meter is changed. The PCO seals cover the screws that secure the meter in place, to ensure that it has not been removed or tampered with.

Almost all taximeters in London are rented out, and are changed immediately prior to re-licensing, or if they malfunction. Until very recently, the PCO seals were put in by the inspecting officers, but now they are put in place by the companies that rent them to proprietors, or the agents of those companies.

Front and rear views of an Argo meter from the 1930s. The meter is set at an angle so that both driver and passenger can see the fare. The Conditions of Fitness demanded that the figures be illuminated, and early meters had no internal lighting, a small lamp was fitted. The large four-pointed 'key' on the front winds up the clock mechanism and the small figures on the left of the front show the number of trips, units, miles and extras registered.
When the cab is for hire, the flag is in the up position. When it is hired, the cab driver swings the flag forward to the the horizontal, 'hired' position. When the job is complete, the flag is swung down to stop the meter, and then swung back up again when the fare has been paid

 *Left and right: two post-war mechanical taximeters. On the left is a Swedish-made Halda and on the right an Argo.*
The bell on the Halda rings when the meter is set to 'hired'. The glass in the flag on the Argo is blue and is illuminated. The cables running from the side of the Argo connect to the 'for hire' light. Note the lead seals on the front faces of both meters

Electromechanical meters were in use in London for around twenty years and were fitted to all FX4s, later FX3s, MkVII Beardmores and Winchesters. This is one two types supplied by Argo under the Geecen name, one of only two available in that time. The other make available was Halda
The meter is set in motion by pressing a button on the lower left hand side of the rear of the meter. This button visible on the right hand picture. The small button on the right records the extras and the large screws on the ends hold the internal lamps

One of the last examples of the much-reviled but necessary conversion tables, fixed to the partition glass when a tariff increase had been granted, before the meter had been upgraded. The difference between the two tariffs is marginal: by this time the trade had been able to secure annual increases and because the loss of earnings was minimal and the changeover time for electronic meters was so quick, the trade opted to abandon these charts, called 'Bingo Cards' completely

Two types of electronic taximeter. Above left is one of the first Halda electronic meters and is very similar to the British-made Cavalier meter, which was the first available in London. Being of a similar size to the electromechanical meters, it is located on a similar bracket in the same position. Later versions from Halda and Lucas were more compact. They were fitted on brackets in FX4s but on the dashboard of Metrocabs.
On the right is a Lucas Kienzle meter, made in Germany. This meter was fitted on top of the dashboard of later cabs like the FX4S-Plus and the Metrocab. Later meters would be fitted in roof binnacles in Fairways and TX-Series cabs

Appendix 3: Licence Plates and Stencils

London's taxis, like horse cabs before them carry a white plate at the rear showing a licence number in black figures. The plate is surrendered on expiry every year. The original style of plates, known retrospectively as 'Lion and Unicorn' plates were made of enamelled steel and showed the royal coat of arms and a number. Along with these, a mark was made on the rear of the cab with a stencil showing the month and year in which the cab was licensed, the initial of the Commissioner of Police and the number of passengers it was licensed to carry. These changed in design every year. The original style of plates was gradually replaced around the time of the Second World War with a new design of plate carrying the licence number, the number of passengers the cab was licensed to carry and the legend 'Licensed by the Metropolitan Police'.

Around 1960, the stencils were phased out and the month the plate was issued was discerned by the first one or two figures of the licence number. A plate issued in January would have a three- or four- figure number, beginning with '1' to signify the first month of the year, whilst a plate issued in November would have a five figure number, beginning with '11'. However, because of the great increase in the number of cabs during the 1970s, more plates were made, shoeing five figures, but the first two figures would be between 13 and 24. Thus if a cab had been passed in February of one year, it would have plate with the number beginning with '2', but if it was licensed again in the following February, its new plate would begin with '14'.

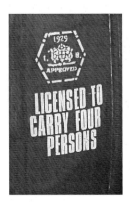  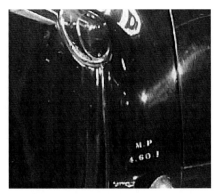

Three types of stencil, applied to the nearside rear of a cab's bodywork. The design was changed every year to make each one easily identifiable.
Left, from 1929. shows the initials are JB, Julian, Viscount Byng of Vimy.
Centre, from 1957 shows (or should show!) JNB, for Sir John Nott-Bower
Right, the 1st type used, from 1961, with just the date and the imitials 'MP'. The number of passengers for which the cab was licensed to carry was shown on the plate

When the five-seat Metrocab, and later the FX4S-Plus were licensed, plates with an 'E' prefix, being the fifth letter of the alphabet so as to denote five passengers were issued to show at a glance that these cabs were licensed to carry five passengers. A 'D' prefix plate was later issued to six-seat Metrocabs. 'F' was not chosen as it might have been confused with an 'E' at a distance.

In 1998, the metal plates were replaced by digitally printed polycarbonate ones, bearing the licence number, the vehicle index mark, the date the licence was issued and a hologram to prevent fraudulent copying. These plates are not reused like the old steel ones, but are destroyed when they expire.

The 'Lion and Unicorn' plate was the first type to be used on motor cabs, and was in use until just before the Second World War. Showing just a number in addition to the royal coat of arms, all other information the Metropolitan Police required was shown on the stencil

The next design used was this one, which could show up any number of figures between three and five. It was initially used in conjunction with stencils, but when these were discontinued, the first digit of a three- or four-figure number, or the first two digits of a five-figure number would indicate the month the plate was issued

The current type of plate in use displays a far greater amount of information than previous designs. Each one is specially printed out when a cab is licensed and destroyed when the licence expires. Note the 'Transport for London' Taxis logo at the top of the plate. The first of these plates, issued when the PCO was part of the Metropolitan Police, carried the Metropolitan Police's 'portcullis' coat of arms

Appendix 4: Technical Specifications

Renault AG, 1905

Engine
Type: 2-cylinder sidevalve
Capacity: 1260cc
Bore & stroke: 81mm x 120mm

Transmission
3-speed, quadrant change

Brakes
Handbrake on rear wheels, footbrake on transmission

Dimensions
Wheelbase: 8ft 4in
Length: 11ft 6 $^1/_2$in

Unic 10/12hp, 1906

Engine
Type: 2-cylinder sidevalve
Capacity: 1750cc
Bore & stroke: 102mm x 110mm

Transmission
3-speed, quadrant change

Brakes
Handbrake and footbrake on rear wheels

Dimensions
Wheelbase: 8ft 4$^1/_4$ in
Length: 11ft 9in

Unic 12/16hp, 1908

Engine
Type: 4-cylinder sidevalve
Capacity: 1994cc
Bore & stroke: 75mm x 110mm

Transmission
3-speed, gate change

Brakes
Handbrake and footbrake on rear wheels,

Dimensions
Wheelbase: 8ft 4 $^1/_4$in
Length: 11ft 9in

Napier 15hp, 1908

Engine
Type: 4-cylinder sidevalve
Capacity: 2748cc
Bore & stroke: 82.5mm x 127mm

Transmission
3-speed, quadrant change

Suspension
Semi elliptical on front, three-quarter elliptical on rear

Dimensions
Wheelbase: 8ft 0 in
Length: 11ft 0in

Unic 12/16hp, 1922

Engine
Type: 4-cylinder sidevalve
Capacity: 1994cc
Bore & stroke: 75mm x 110mm

Transmission
3-speed, gate change

Brakes
Handbrake and footbrake on rear wheels,

Dimensions
Wheelbase: 8ft 4$^1/_4$in
Length: 11ft 9in

Beardmore Mk1, 1919

Engine
Type: 4-cylinder sidevalve
Capacity: 2287cc
Bore & stroke: 79mm x 120mm

Transmission
4-speed, right hand gate change

Brakes
Handbrake on rear wheels, footbrake on transmission

Suspension
Semi elliptical on front, three-quarter elliptical on rear

Dimensions
Wheelbase: 8ft 4in
Track: 4ft 6in
Length: 11ft 9in

Body type: Landaulette or three-quarter landaulette

Citroën 11.4hp, 1923

Engine
Type: 4-cylinder sidevalve
Capacity: 1453cc
Bore & stroke: 68mm x100mm

Transmission
3-speed, centre change

Brakes
Handbrake on transmission, footbrake on rear wheels

Suspension
Pair leading quarter-elliptical on front, Two pairs trailing quarter elliptical on rear

Dimensions
Wheelbase: 8ft 7 $^1/_8$in
Track: 4ft 6in
Length: 11ft 6in

Beardmore Mk2, 1924

Engine
Type: 4-cylinder sidevalve
Capacity: 2388cc
Bore & stroke: 79mm x 120mm (approx)

Transmission
4-speed, right hand gate change

Brakes
Footbrake and handbrake on rear wheels

Suspension
Semi elliptical all round

Dimensions
Wheelbase: 9ft 0in
Track: 4ft 7in
Length: 11ft 9in

Body type: landaulette or three-quarter landaulette

Hayes, 1924

Engine
Type: 4-cylinder sidevalve
Capacity: 2413cc
Bore & stroke: 80mm x 120mm

Transmission
3-speed

Dimensions
Wheelbase: 8ft 5 $^1/_2$in
Length: 11ft 9in

Yellow Cab, 1924

Engine
Type: Continental 4 cylinder sidevalve
Capacity: 3050cc
Bore & stroke: 86mm x 127mm

Transmission
3-speed, centre change

Dimensions
Wheelbase: 8ft 3in
Length: 11ft 8in

Morris-Commercial International G-Type, 1928

Engine
Type: 4-cylinder sidevalve
Capacity: 2513cc
Bore & stroke: 80mm x 125mm

Transmission
4-speed, centre change

Brakes
Footbrake and handbrake on rear wheels

Rear axle
Overhead worm drive

Suspension
Semi elliptical all round

Dimensions
Wheelbase: 9ft 0in
Track: 4ft 8in
Length: 12ft 8in

Beardmore Mk3 'Hyper', 1928

Engine
Type: 4-cylinder sidevalve
Capacity: 1954cc
Bore & stroke: 72mm x 120mm

Transmission
4-speed, centre change

Brakes
Footbrake on all four wheels, handbrake on rear wheels

Rear axle
Fully floating, spiral bevel drive

Suspension
Semi elliptical all round

Dimensions
Wheelbase: 9ft 0in
Track: 4ft 7in
Length: 12ft 9in

Austin 12/4 HL, 1930 & TT, 1932

Engine
Type: 4-cylinder sidevalve
Capacity: 1861cc
Bore & stroke: 72mm x 114.5mm
Power: 27bhp @ 2000rpm

Transmission
4-speed, centre change (synchromesh on 3rd & 4th gears on TT)

Brakes
Mechanical, footbrake on all four wheels, handbrake on rear wheels

Rear Axle
Crown wheel and pinion

Dimensions
Wheelbase: 9ft 4in
Track: 4ft 8in
Length: 13ft 6in

Unic KF1, 1930

Engine
Type: 4-cylinder sidevalve
Capacity: 1998cc
Bore & stroke: 72.8mm x 120mm

Dimensions
Wheelbase: 9ft 6in
Length: 13ft 7in

Beardmore MkIV 'Paramount', 1934

Engine
Type: Commer 4-cylinder sidevalve
Capacity: 1994cc
Bore & stroke: 75mm x 110mm
Power: 51bhp @ 3600rpm

Transmission
4-speed, centre change

Brakes
Footbrake on all four wheels, handbrake on rear wheels

Rear axle
Fully floating, spiral bevel drive

Suspension
Semi elliptical all round

Dimensions
Wheelbase: 9ft 0in
Track: 4ft 7in

Morris-Commercial International G2 'Junior' 1932

Engine
Type: 4-cylinder sidevalve
Capacity: 1802cc
Bore & stroke: 75mm x 102mm

Transmission
4-speed, centre change

Brakes
Footbrake on all four wheels, handbrake on rear wheels

Suspension
Semi elliptical all round

Rear Axle
Overhead worm drive

Dimensions
Wheelbase: 9ft 0in
Track: 4ft 7in
Length: 13ft 10in

Austin 12/4 LL, 1934 & FL, 1938

Engine
Type: 4-cylinder sidevalve
Capacity: 1861cc
Bore & stroke:72mm x 114.5mm
Power: 27bhp @ 2000rpm

Transmission
4-speed, centre change, synchromesh on 2nd, 3rd & 4th gears

Brakes
Footbrake on all four wheels, handbrake on rear wheels

Rear Axle
Underslung worm drive

Dimensions
Wheelbase: 9ft 4in
Track: 4ft 8in
Length: 13ft 10in

Morris-Commercial G2S 'Junior Six', 1934 G2SW 'Senior Six', 1938

Engine - G2S
Type: 6-cylinder sidevalve
Capacity: 1938cc
Bore & stroke: 63.5mm x 102mm

Engine - G2SW
Type: 6-cylinder overhead valve, water cooled
Capacity: 1818cc
Bore & stroke: 61.5mm x 102mm

Transmission
4-speed, centre change

Brakes
Footbrake on all four wheels, handbrake on rear wheels

Suspension
Semi elliptical all round

Rear Axle
Hypoid

Dimensions
Wheelbase: 9ft 0in
Track: 4ft 7in
Length: 13ft 10in

Beardmore MkV 'Paramount Ace', 1935 & Ace, 1938

Engine
Type: Commer 4-cylinder sidevalve
Capacity: 1994cc
Bore & stroke: 75mm x 110mm
Power: 51bhp @ 3600rpm

Transmission
4-speed, centre change, Synchromesh on 3rd & 4th (MkV), synchromesh on all gears (MkVI)

Brakes
Footbrake on all four wheels, handbrake on rear wheels

Rear axle
fully floating, spiral bevel drive

Suspension
Semi elliptical all round

Dimensions
Wheelbase: 9ft 6in
Track: 4ft 8in

Nuffield Oxford, 1947

Engine
Type: 4-cylinder overhead valve
Capacity: 1802.5cc
Bore & stroke: 75mm x 102mm

Transmission
4-speed, centre change, synchromesh on 2nd, 3rd & 4th

Brakes
Footbrake on all four wheels, handbrake on rear wheels

Suspension
Semi elliptical all round

Rear Axle
Worm drive

Dimensions
Wheelbase: 8ft 11 1/2in
Length: 13ft 11 1/2in
Width   5ft 6in
Track, front: 4ft 8 5/16in
Track, rear: 4ft 8in
Ground clearance, laden: 6in

Austin FX3, 1948

Engine, petrol
4-cylinder overhead valve
Capacity: 2199cc
Bore & stroke: 79.4mm x 111.1mm
Power: 52bhp @ 3800rpm

Engine, diesel
4-cylinder overhead valve
Capacity: 2178cc
Bore & stroke: 82.6mm x 101.6mm
Power: 55bhp @ 3500rpm

Transmission
4-speed, centre change, synchromesh on 2nd,
3rd & 4th

Brakes
Mechanical, footbrake and handbrake on all
four wheels

Rear axle:
Pre-1955, underslung worm drive
Post 1955-1958, hypoid

Suspension
Semi elliptical all round

Dimensions
Wheelbase: 9ft 2 $^5/8$ in
Height: 5ft 10 $^3/4$ in
Length: 14ft 5 $^1/4$ in
Width   5ft 7 $^1/2$ in
Track: 4 ft 8 in

Beardmore MkVII 'Paramount', 1954

Engine, petrol, 1954-1958
Type: Ford Consul 4 cylinder overhead valve
Capacity: 1508cc
Bore & stroke: 79.37mm x 76.2mm
Power: 47bhp @ 4400rpm

Engine, diesel, 1955 - 1958
Type: Perkins 4.99 4 cylinder overhead valve
Capacity: 1628cc
Bore & stroke: 79.37mm x 76.2mm
Power: 48bhp @ 4000 rpm

Engine, petrol, 1958-1962
Type: Ford Consul 4 cylinder overhead valve
Capacity: 1703cc
Bore & stroke: 82.55mm x 79.5mm
Power: 59bhp @ 4200rpm

Engine, petrol, 1962-1966
Type: Ford Zephyr 4 cylinder overhead valve
Capacity: 1703cc
Bore & stroke: 82.55mm x 79.5mm
Power: 63bhp @ 4800rpm

Engine, diesel, 1962 - 1966
Type: Perkins 4.108 4 cylinder overhead valve
Capacity: 1760cc
Bore & stroke: 79.5.mm x 88.9mm
Power: 52bhp @ 4000rpm

Transmission, 1954 - 1966
3-speed, column change, synchromesh on 2nd
& 3rd

Transmission, 1966
4-speed, column change, synchromesh on all
forward gears

Brakes
Dual circuit hydraulic

Rear axle
Hypoid

Suspension
Semi elliptical all round, telescopic shock
absorbers

Dimensions
Wheelbase: 8ft 8in
Height: 6ft
Length: 13ft 10 $^1/2$in

Birch Prototype, 1956

Engine
Type, Standard 4-cylinder diesel, ohv
Capacity: 2092cc
Bore & stroke: 80.96mm x 101.6mm
Power: 45bhp @ 3000rpm

Transmission
3-speed, column change, synchromesh on 2nd
& 3rd

Brakes
Dual circuit hydraulic

Suspension
Front: independent with coil springs
Rear: semi elliptical

Dimensions
Wheelbase: 8ft 5in

Austin FX4, 1958

Engine, diesel
Type: 4-cylinder, overhead valve
Capacity 2178cc
Bore & stroke: 82.55mm x 101.6mm
Power: 55bhp @3,500rpm
Torque: 89lb/ft @ 2,800rpm
Compression ratio 20:1

Engine, petrol
Type 4-cylinder, ohv
Capacity: 2199cc
Bore & stroke: 79.44mm x 111mm
Power: 55.9bhp @3,750rpm
Torque: 112lb/ft @ 2,000rpm
Compression ratio 7.5:1

Transmission
Automatic: Borg Warner DG150 three-speed
with torque converter, later Borg Warner BW35
three-speed with torque converter
Manual: (from 1961) 4-speed & reverse,
synchromesh on 1st, 2nd and top gears

Rear Axle
Type: hypoid, 4.8:1 final drive

Brakes
Foot: four-wheel hydraulic, two leading shoe
on front. Dual circuit with separate master
cylinders. 11in drums all round
Hand: mechanical on rear wheels

Suspension
Front Independent with coil springs and lever
arm shock absorbers
Rear Semi-elliptical leaf springs with lever arm
shock absorbers

Electrical
Type 12v positive earth

Dimensions
Length 14ft 11 $^{7}/_{16}$in
Height 5ft 8 $^{11}/_{16}$in
Width 5ft 8 $^{5}/_{8}$in
Wheelbase 9ft 2 $^{5}/_{8}$in
Track, front and rear: 4ft 8in

Winchester Mk1, 1962

Engine:
Type: Perkins 4.99 4 cylinder diesel
Capacity: 1628cc
Bore & stroke: 79.37mm x 76.2mm
Power: 48bhp @ 4000 rpm

Transmission
4-speed synchromesh, centre change

Brakes
Dual circuit hydraulic

Suspension
Semi elliptical all round

Dimensions
Wheelbase: 8ft 10in

Winchester Mk2, 1966

Engine, petrol:
Type: Ford Cortina 4 cylinder ohv
Capacity: 1499cc
Bore & stroke: 80.97mm x 72.82mm
Power: 65bhp @ 4800 rpm

Engine, diesel:
Type: Perkins 4.108 4 cylinder
Capacity: 1760cc
Bore & stroke: 79.5.mm x 88.9mm
Power: 52bhp @ 4000rpm

Transmission
4-speed synchromesh, centre change

Brakes
Dual circuit hydraulic

Suspension
Semi elliptical all round

Dimensions
Wheelbase: 8ft 10in

Winchester Mk3, 1966

Engine, petrol:
Type: Ford V4-cylinder overhead valve
Capacity: 1663cc
Bore & stroke: 93.66mm x 60.35mm
Power: 73bhp @ 4750 rpm

Engine, diesel:
Type: Perkins 4.108 4 cylinder
Capacity: 1760cc
Bore & stroke: 79.5.mm x 88.9mm
Power: 52bhp @ 4000rpm

Transmission
4-speed synchromesh, centre change

Brakes
Dual circuit hydraulic

Suspension
Semi elliptical all round

Dimensions
Wheelbase: 8ft 10in

Winchester Mk4, 1968

Engine, petrol:
Type: Ford Cortina 4 cylinder ohv
Capacity: 1599cc
Bore & stroke: 80.98mm x 70.62mm
Power: 71bhp @ 5000 rpm

Engine, diesel:
Type: Perkins 4.108 4 cylinder
Capacity: 1760cc
Bore & stroke: 79.5.mm x 88.9mm
Power: 52bhp @ 4000rpm

Transmission
4-speed synchromesh, centre change

Brakes
Dual circuit hydraulic

Suspension
Semi elliptical all round

Dimensions
Wheelbase: 8ft 10in

Metrocab Prototype, 1968

Engine:
Type: Perkins 4.108 4 cylinder diesel
Capacity: 1760cc
Bore & stroke: 79.5.mm x 88.9mm
Power: 52bhp @ 4000rpm

Transmission
4-speed synchromesh, centre change

Brakes
Dual circuit hydraulic

Axles
Beam front, live rear

Suspension
Semi elliptical all round, telescopic shock absorbers

Austin FX4D, 1971, Carbodies FX4D, 1982

Engine
Type: Austin 4-cylinder diesel
Cubic capacity: 2520cc
Bore & stroke: 88.9mm x 101.6mm
Power: 63bhp @ 3500rpm
Torque: 109lb/ft @ 2,000rpm
Compression ratio: 20.5:1

Transmission
Automatic: Borg Warner BW35 3-speed. (Borg Warner BW365 from 1978)
Manual: as per 1961

Rear axle
Hypoid, 3.909:1 final drive

Brakes
Foot four-wheel hydraulic, two leading shoe on front. Dual circuit with separate master cylinders. 11in drums all round
Hand: mechanical on rear wheels

Suspension
Front: independent with coil springs and lever arm shock absorbers
Rear: semi-elliptical leaf springs with lever arm shock absorbers

Electrical
Type 12v negative earth

Dimensions
Length 14ft 11 ^{7}/16in
Height 5ft 8 ^{11}/16in
Width 5ft 8 ^{5}/8in
Wheelbase 9ft 2 ^{5}/8in
Track, front and rear: 4ft 8in
Overall length: 15ft ^{1}/2in from 1977

Carbodies FX4R, 1982 & Austin FX4Q, 1983

FX4R engine, diesel
Type: Land Rover , 4-cylinder
Cubic capacity: 2286cc
Bore & stroke: 90.47mm x 88.9mm
Power: 62bhp @ 4,000rpm
Torque: 103lb/ft @ 1,800rpm
Compression ratio: 23:1

FX4R engine, petrol
Land Rover petrol, 4-cylinder ohv
Cubic capacity: 2286cc
Bore & stroke: 90.47mm x 88.9mm
Power: 77bhp @ 4250rpm
Torque: 124lb/ft @ 2500rpm
Compression ratio: 7:1

FX4Q engine
Kalaskai diesel, 4-cylinder, ohv
Cubic capacity: 2520cc
Bore & stroke: 88.9mm x 101.6mm
Power: 63bhp @ 3500rpm
Torque: 109lb/ft @ 2,000rpm
Compression ratio: 20.5:1

Transmission, FX4R:
Automatic: Borg Warner BW66 3-speed
Manual: Rover 5-speed synchromesh

Transmission, FX4Q:
Borg Warner BW65 3-speed

Rear axle
Hypoid, 3.909:1 final drive

Brakes
Dual circuit, four-wheel hydraulic, full servo-assistance. 11in drums all round, twin leading shoe on front. Mechanical handbrake on rear wheels

Suspension
As per FX4

Electrical
Type 12v negative earth

Dimensions
As per FX4 from 1978

Carbodies FX4S, 1985 & Carbodies FX4S-Plus, 1987

Engine
Type: Land Rover 4-cylinder diesel
Cubic capacity 2495cc
Bore & stroke: 90.47mm x 97mm
Power: 69.6bhp @ 4000rpm
Torque: 115lb/ft @ 1800rpm
Compression ratio 21:1

Transmission:
FX4S: Automatic: Borg Warner BW65 3-speed
with torque converter
Manual: 5-speed & reverse, synchromesh on all
forward gears
FX4S-Plus: Automatic: Borg Warner BW40 3-
speed with torque converter
Manual: 5-speed & reverse, synchromesh on all
forward gears

Rear axle
Hypoid, 3.909:1 final drive

Brakes
Dual circuit, four-wheel hydraulic, full servo-
assistance. 11in drums all round, twin leading
shoe on front. Mechanical handbrake on rear
wheels

Suspension
FX4S: front, independent with coil springs and
lever arm shock absorbers; rear, semi-elliptical
leaf springs with lever arm shock absorbers
FX4S-Plus: front, independent with coil springs
and lever arm shock absorbers; rear, semi-
elliptical glass fibre leaf springs with
telescopic shock absorbers

Electrical
Type 12v negative earth

Dimensions
Length 15ft ^{1}/2in
Height 5ft 9 ^{1}/2in
Width 5ft 8 ^{7}/8in
Wheelbase 9ft 2 ^{5}/8in
Track, front 4ft 8in
Track, rear 4ft 8in

Metrocab Series 1, 1987, Series 2, 1995 & Series 3, 1998

Engine
Type: Ford FSD 4-cylinder diesel
Cubic capacity 2496cc
Bore & stroke: 93.7mm x 90.5mm
Power: 75bhp @ 4000rpm
Torque: 123lb/ft @ 2500rpm
Compression ratio 20:6

Transmission:
Automatic: Ford A4LD 4-speed with torque
converter
Manual: Ford MT75 5-speed & reverse,
synchromesh on all forward gears

Brakes
Dual circuit, four-wheel hydraulic, full servo-
assistance. 11in drums all round. Mechanical
handbrake on rear wheels
Series 1 from 1992; Series 2 & 3:
Front: discs with four-pot callipers
Rear: 10in drums

Suspension
Front: independent with coil springs and lever
arm shock absorbers
Rear: semi-elliptical leaf springs with
telescopic shock absorbers on rear

Electrical
Type 12v negative earth

Dimensions
Overall length 14ft 9in
Wheelbase 9ft 5in

Carbodies Fairway, 1989 & Fairway Driver, 1992

Engine
Type: Nissan TD27 4-cylinder diesel
Cubic capacity: 2663cc
Bore & stroke: 96mm x 92mm
Power: 63.5kw @ 4,300rpm
Torque: 175 Nm @ 2,200rpm
Compression ratio: 21.8:1

Transmission
Automatic: Nissan 4-speed with torque converter
Manual: Nissan 5-speed

Rear axle
Hypoid, 3.909:1 final drive

Brakes
Fairway: Four-wheel hydraulic, two leading shoe on front. Dual circuit with tandem master cylinder. 11in drums all round, full servo-assistance. Mechanical handbrake on rear wheels
Fairway Driver: Four-wheel hydraulic. Dual circuit with tandem master cylinder. Ventilated discs with 4-pot callipers on front, 10in drums on rear. Mechanical handbrake on rear wheels

Suspension
Fairway
Front and rear as per FX4S-Plus
Fairway Driver
Front: Independent with coil springs and telescopic shock absorbers.
Rear, as per FX4S-Plus, replaced with steel twin leaf semi-elliptical parabolic springs plus helper springs

Electrical
Type 12v negative earth

Dimensions
Length: 15ft ^{1}/2in
Height: 5ft 9 ^{1}/2in
Width: 5ft 8 ^{7}/8in
Wheelbase: 9ft 2 ^{5}/8in
Front track: 4ft 8in
Rear track: 4ft 8in

Asquith, 1994

Engine, diesel
Type: Ford FGR 4-cylinder
Cubic capacity: 2496cc
Bore & stroke: 93.7mm x 90.5mm
Power: 80bhp at 4300rpm
Torque: 168Nm @ 2500rpm

Engine, petrol
Type: Ford 4 cylinder dohc.
Cubic capacity: 1998cc
Bore x stroke: 86mm x 86mm
Power: 120bhp at 5500rpm
Torque: 171Nm at 2500rpm

Transmission
Automatic: Ford 4-speed with electronic overdrive
Manual: Ford 5-speed synchromesh

Brakes
Discs on all four wheels, dual circuit hydraulic, servo assisted. Pull up handbrake on rear wheels.

Suspension
Front: independent with double wishbones with coil springs and telescopic shock absorbers
Rear: Dunlop air suspension

Rear axle
Hypoid semi-floating

Dimensions
Height: 6ft 6in
Length: 14ft 1in
Width: 5ft 9in

Metrocab TTT, 2000

Engine
Type: Toyota 2LT 4 cylinder ohc turbo diesel
Cubic capacity: 2446cc
Bore & stroke: 92mm x 92mm
Compression ratio: 22.2:1
Power: 66kw at 3500rpm
Torque: 218Nm @ 2250rpm

Transmission:
Automatic: Toyota 4-speed
Manual: Toyota 5-speed synchromesh

Rear axle:
Hypoid bevel drive

Suspension
Front: independent with coil springs and telescopic shock absorbers: Rear: semi-elliptical leaf springs with telescopic shock absorbers

Brakes
Discs with four-pot callipers on front, 10in drums on rear

Electrical
Type 12v negative earth

Dimensions
Overall length 14ft 9in
Wheelbase 9ft 5in

LTI TX1, 1997

Engine
Type: Nissan TD27 4-cylinder diesel
Cubic capacity: 2663cc
Bore & stroke: 96mm x 92mm
Power: 63.5kw @ 4,300rpm
Torque: 175 Nm @ 2,200rpm
Compression ratio: 21.8:1

Transmission
Automatic: Nissan 4-speed with torque converter
Manual: Nissan 5-speed

Brakes
Front: ventilated discs, rear, 10inch drums

Rear axle
Hypoid, 3.909:1 final drive

Suspension
Front: Independent with coil springs and telescopic shock absorbers
Rear: two-leaf parabolic springs with telescopic shock absorbers

Dimensions
Length: 180in
Width: 80.2in
Height: 72.3in
Wheelbase: 113.7in

LTI TXII, 2002

Engine
Type: Ford DuraTorq 4-cylinder dohc turbodiesel
Cubic capacity: 2402cc
Bore & stroke: 92mm x 92mm
Power: 60.3kw @ 4,300rpm
Torque: 165Nm @ 2400rpm
Compression ratio: 21.8:1

Transmission
Automatic: Nissan 4-speed with torque converter.
Manual: Ford 5-speed

Brakes
Front: ventilated discs, rear, 10inch drums

Suspension
Front: Independent with coil springs
Rear: two-leaf parabolic springs

Dimensions
Length: 180in
Width: 80.2in
Height: 72.3in
Wheelbase: 113.7in

LTI TX4, 2007

Engine
Type: VM Motori R425 dohc four cylinder, 16
valve, direct injection turbodiesel with
intercooler
Cubic capacity: 2499cc
Bore & stroke: 92mm x 94mm
Compression ratio: 17.5:1
Power: 75kw @ 4000rpm
Torque: 240Nm @ 1800rpm

Transmission
Automatic: Chrysler 5-speed
Manual: Eaton FSO 24055-speed

Brakes
Front: ventilated discs with four-pot callipers,
rear, 10inch drums. electronically controlled
Anti-lock Braking System (ABS)

Rear axle
Hypoid semi-floating, 4.4:1 final drive

Suspension
Front: Independent with coil springs and
telescopic shock absorbers.
Rear:coil rear springs with trailing arms and
Panhard rod

Dimensions
Length: 4580mm (180in)
Width: 2036mm (80.2 in)
Height: 1834mm (72.3in)
Wheelbase: 2886mm (113.7 in)
Front track: 1422mm (56.0in)
Rear track: 1482mm (58.4in)

Mercedes-Benz Vito, 2009

Engine
Type: Mercedes-Benz 4-cylinder ohc turbo-
charged & intercooled diesel
Cubic capacity: 2148cc
Bore & stroke: n/a
Power: 109bhp @ 3800rpm
Torque: 290Nm @ 1600 - 2400rpm

Transmission
Automatic: 5-speed
Manual: 6-speed

Brakes
Front and rear: floating calliper discs,
internally ventilated (front) with ABS & ESP.
Automatic pad wear indicator

Suspension
Front: independent McPherson struts with coil
springs, shock absorbers & stabiliser
Rear:semi-trailing-arm axle with coil springs &
shock absorbers

Steering
Front: power-assisted rack and pinion
Rear: Active RWS

Dimensions
Length: 4748mm
Width: 1901mm
Height: 1875mm
Wheelbase: 3200mm

Appendix 5: Production Figures

Production Figures

The availability of production figures for London taxis varies greatly. We are lucky that, for instance Beardmore's sales ledger for the MkVII survives, but figures for any other Beardmore model either cannot be verified, if ever traced. What is listed here has been derived from various sources. The Metrocab figures have come from the Society of Manufacturers and Traders, and therefore can be considered as accurate as they are ever likely to be. Likewise the TX4 figures, which come directly from LTI and the SMM & T. Austin FX3 and FX4 figures include the hire car versions.

Morris-Commercial G-Type International

1928-1932	1700

Austin Heavy 12/4 all models (estimated)

1930	271
1931	400
1932	309
1933	834
1934	1111
1935	1178
1936	875
1937	659
1938	445
1939	445
(includes March - July 1939)	124
and Aug '39 - July '40	201
Total	**6572**

Nuffield Oxford

Ward End	
1946-47	362
1947-48	331
1948-49	234
Adderley Park	
1948-49	184
1949-50	323
1950-5	382
1951-52	44
1952-53	66
Total	**1925**

FX3/FL1

1948/49	745
1949/50	1681
1950/51	2191
1951/52	1473
1952/53	335
1953/54	1285
1954/55	2134
1955/56	1118
1956/57	1426
1957/58	1347
Total	

Beardmore MkVII

1955-1966	656

Austin / Carbodies FX4/FL2

1958/59	216
1959/60	1480
Total:	1,696
1960/61	1365
1961/62	738
1962/63	1309
1963/64	1282
1964/65	1530
1965/66	1423
1966/67	1158
1967/68	1943
1968/69	1468
1969/70	2272
1970/71	1591
Sub total:	16,079

(Chassis production moved to Carbodies in 1971)

Austin / Carbodies FX4/FL2 *continued*

1971	1100
1971/72	2833
1972/73	2397
1973/74	2312
1974/75	2082
1975/76	3122

(15 months' production to Dec 31 1976)

1977	2687
1978	2422
1979	2439
1980	2007
1981	2049
Sub total	25,450
1982	1864

(FX4, FX4R & FL2)

1983	2171
1984	1612
1985	1813

(FX4R & FL2)

1986	2231
1987	2128

(FX4S & S-Plus)

1988	2332

(FX4S-Plus)

1989	2737
1990	3070
1991	1846

(Fairway)

1992	1674
1993	1530
1994	1761
1995	2339
1996	2558
1997	2166

(Fairway Driver)

Sub total	33,832
Total	**77,057**

Production Figures *(continued)*

Metrocab		1991	371
		1992	428
1987	302	1993	312
1988	909	1994	404
1989	259	1995	539
1990	Zero	1996	761

Appendix 6: Motor Cabs Licensed, 1903 - 1991

These figures are derived from Metropolitan Police Commissioners' reports which do vary in their content, hence the absence of figures for certain years

Year	Cabs	Year	Cabs	Year	Cabs
1903	1	1934	8181	1964	7669
1904	2	1935	8180	1965	7390
1905	19	1936	8078	1966	N/A
1906	96	1937	8044	1967	7832
1907	723	1938	7893	1968	N/A
1908	2805	1939	6683	1969	8412
1909	3956	1940 - 1942	N/A	1970	8652
1910	6397	1943	5604	1971	9586
1911	7626	1944	7768	1972	10145
1912	7969	1946	5855	1973	10406
1913	8397	1947	6079	1974	11021
1914	7260	1948	6149	1975	11260
1915 - 1917	N/A	1949	6965	1976	11838
1918	5451	1950	7129	1977	12452
1919 - 1921	N/A	1951	6194	1978	12453
1922	7191	1952	5437	1979	12267
1923	8021	1953	5609	1980	12385
1924	N/A	1954	5553	1981	12560
1925	N/A	1955	5897	1982	12809
1926	8478	1956	5898	1983	13127
1927	7997	1957	6118	1984	13574
1928	N/A	1958	6157	1985	13775
1929	N/A	1959	N/A	1986	14676
1930	N/A	1960	6651	1987	14792
1931	8152	1961	6776	1988	N/A
1932	8074	1962	7008	1989	15622
1933	7995	1963	7372	1990	16190
				1991	16529

Further Reading

Armstrong, Anthony: "Taxi". Hodder & Stoughton, 1930

A much-quoted, definitive work on the subject. Long out of print. H/b

Bobbitt, Malcolm: "Taxi! The Story if the London Taxicab". Veloce, 2002

The history of the London cab, in concise form, for the general enthusiast. P/b, b/w & colour

Garner, Simon, and Stokoe, Giles: "Taxi!" Frances Lincoln, 2000

A description of the London cab trade, its cabs and drivers; an ideal book for the general reader. H/b, b/w

Georgano, G. N.: "A History of the London Taxicab". David & Charles, 1972

The first modern generation book on the subject. Long out of print. H/b, b/w

Georgano, G. N., and Munro, Bill: "The London Taxi". Shire Books, 2009

A pocket history of the subject. P/b, full colour

May, Trevor: "Gondolas and Growlers: The History of the London Horse Cab". Alan Sutton, 1995

An in-depth academic study, but very readable. Now out of print. H/b, black & white

May, Trevor: "Victorian and Edwardian Horse Cabs". Shire Books, 1999

A pocket version of the above. P/b, b/w

Merkel, Ben, and Monier, Chris: "The American Taxi: A Century of Service". Iconografix, 2006

A broad history of a very large subject. P/b, b/w with some colour

Moore, H. C.: "Omnibuses and Cabs". Chapman and Hall, 1902, reprinted by Adam Gordon, 2001

The first, seminal work on the subject, well reproduced in a 500-copy limited edition. H/b, b/w plates

Munro, Bill: "Carbodies, the Complete Story". Crowood, 1998

Story of the company that became London Taxis International. H/b, b/w colour centre. Out of print

Munro, Bill: A" Century of London Taxis". Crowood, 2005

In-depth history of the subject. H/b, b/w with colour centre. Out of print

Munro, Bill: "Taxi Jubilee - Fifty Years of the Austin FX4 London Taxi". Earlswood Press 2009

The definitive story of this iconic vehicle. P/b, full colour

Mustapha, Mus: "In a Year of a London Cabbie". Orion, 2003

A collection of interviews, photographs, discussions with passengers and other stories. H/b, b/w

Ward, Rod: "Taxi - Purpose-built Cabs in Britain". Malvern House Publications, 2008

Pictures of cabs of all ages from all around the UK. P/b, b/w with some colour

Warren, Philip, and Linskey, Malcolm: "Taxicabs -A Photographic History". Almark, 1976

Very wide range of photographs, up to the early 1970s. H/b, b/w. Long out of Print.

Warren, Philip: "The History of the London Cab Trade". Taxi Trade Promotions, 1995

The definitive history of the subject. H/b & p/b, b/w

Warren, Philip: "The History of the Knowledge of London". London Publishing Company, 2003

The last book by this author. Contains data relating to Knowledge candidates and cab licensing

Index